Madame Scotia, Madam Scrap

The Story of Héloïse Russell-Fergusson
1896–1970

Hélène Witcher

The Islands Book Trust

Published in 2017 by the Islands Book Trust

www.islandsbooktrust.org

ISBN: 978-1-907443-78-7

Islands Book Trust, Laxay Hall, Laxay, Isle of Lewis, HS2 9PJ.
Tel: 01851 830316

Typeset by Erica Schwarz (www.schwarz-editorial.co.uk)
Cover design by Raspberry Creative Type, Edinburgh
Printed and bound by Martins the Printers, Berwick upon Tweed, UK

To my family: past, present and future

Contents

ABOUT THE AUTHOR

HÉLÈNE WITCHER enjoyed a 1950s rural childhood by the pebbled shores of Loch Lomond and studied at the University of Stirling. She worked for many years with Scottish schools and colleges, supporting marginalised groups and promoting equality. *Madame Scotia, Madam Scrap* is her first book.

Do not let your heart become proud because of what you know;
Learn from the ignorant as well as from the learned man;
There are no limits that have been decreed for art,
There is no artist who attains entire excellence.

Ptahhotep, 5th century Egyptian vizier

CHAPTER ONE

THE TAPES

S he parked the car, I imagine, at Ganavan Sands where the beach was deserted and resounded only with the mesmerising rhythm of the far Atlantic waves rolling in from the west. Blustery rain flecked across the windscreen and for a little while she remained motionless, adjusting to the silence and absorbing the familiar scene into herself, the misty horizon where heavy grey clouds became the sea, the incoming waves perpetually redrawing the shoreline on each rhythmic beat. The last pansies of summer straggled from the tiny pots set along the dashboard of the car, offering a consoling splash of green and violet.

Satisfied that she was entirely alone, she turned at last to the two reel to reel tape recorders that lay beside her. On one, she had already captured herself singing and playing the clarsach, a small Celtic harp. Now she wanted to add an accompaniment. She pressed the play button on the first tape recorder that sat on the passenger seat beside her and listened intently as she moved the flower pots aside and placed the other recorder on the dashboard. Emitting an unconscious grunt of approval at what she heard, she rewound the tape and, struggling a little with discomfort, reached over her shoulder to find the chanter[1] that lay amongst the sheaves of music, the books and the everyday clutter

---

1   The chanter is used to practise the melody of the bagpipes. It looks rather like a recorder.

strewn across the back seat. Then, consciously straightening herself, she switched on both tape recorders and silently counted in a few bars of the music before taking a breath, raising the chanter to her lips and beginning to play.

She had recorded before in studios in Edinburgh and London, traditional Gaelic songs mostly, some unaccompanied, others with the clarsach, sometimes with an accompanying cello. Much later, she startled the small conventional clarsach playing world by recording four EPs of soaring, intermittent, wordless singing and accompanying her clarsach with an African mbira or the beat of a tom-tom. By the September of 1969, when she parked at Ganavan Sands, driving to a recording studio would have been beyond her and besides, her car was notoriously unreliable. But she had recorded music in the car before, sometimes ambushing a local person known to have a good voice and encouraging them to break into song while she watched the tape spinning. She knew what she was doing.

When she was satisfied with the recordings, she drove back to the Alexandra Hotel which overlooked the esplanade in Oban and went up to her room. She may have glanced at the wallpaper secured neatly in place with drawing pins, thinking perhaps she should roll it up for the last time and put it in the car. But she concentrated on the job in hand, labelled and parcelled the tapes into four small grey envelopes and walked to the post office from where she sent them to Mr C.W. Black, the City Librarian at the Mitchell Library in Glasgow.

Her relationship with the library was longstanding. Over a period of ten years, while she had marshalled her research into the worldwide history and distribution of harps, Mr Black had organised the binding of each of the resulting nineteen volumes as the instalments were delivered into his hands. Previously too, he had received a parcel containing boards of narrative to accompany these anticipated tapes, so he opened this new package and read the covering letter expectantly. She had explained:

We have today posted to you this series of 23 items on tape, and I owe their finish and recording to my very good friends, Mr and Mrs J.H.B. Duncan of Ardencaple, Balvicar, by Oban. As you know, I worked out this series with two small battery tape recorders, and much of the work was done in my car as I have no facilities in an hotel. I haven't delegated any of the original songs to another singer, but sing them in the character which Kenneth MacLeod noted. The chanter playing is mine …

The 4 tapes in small grey envelopes are the Original series. I expect you may want to reserve them, as future copies can always be made … and would-be enthusiasts could so easily press the wrong button and erase the lot! I did, frequently, as had no experience of tapes before this effort. We have given you 2 sets at 2 different speeds, viz 1 7/8ips, and 3 3/4ips – as the Duncans (experts) advise me that these are now the usual speeds used on most recorders.

I am very glad to present these to the Mitchell Library and wonder if I could suggest that the items if borrowed for public use – be kept in their own completeness – and not have narrative divorced from them, etc …
All best wishes to you, Yours sincerely, Russell Fergusson

Three months before she dispatched the tapes, I met her for the first time. Standing in warm June sunshine outside the Crianlarich Hotel, about forty miles from Oban where my mother, my sister Ruth and I had joined her for lunch, I couldn't take my eyes away from the plant pots set along the dashboard and in the ashtray well of her old car. 'I've never really had a house or a garden,' she explained with a gentle laugh, 'this has to do'. It was 1969, I was eighteen and she was my aunt, Héloïse Russell-Fergusson. Six months later, aged seventy-three, she died.

———————

Héloïse was my father's sister and the eldest of four children. I don't recall her ever visiting our house or meeting her before that single encounter at Crianlarich. Perhaps she and my father were at odds.

I have a vague memory of him rolling his eyes whenever her music was mentioned although apart from the Scottish Country Dance programme on the radio, I don't remember him showing a particular interest in music at all. His party piece, played with panache at the upright piano in the sitting room, was called 'The Steamboat Leaving the Pier' and if we children were in luck, he would follow it with 'The Steamboat Returns to the Pier', which he claimed persuasively was the same piece played backwards.

When pushed, my mother would sit at the piano, play Christian Sinding's 'Rustle of Spring' and then rise, smiling, looking a little awkward. I loved it when she played. The rippling notes, her deft fingers, her dreamy expression. I didn't know when she had learned it or from whom; or whether she knew any other pieces. A small pile of 78s, dance tunes from the 1930s and 1940s, lay beside the wind-up gramophone on the broad window sill but mostly, it remained silent.

There were few visitors when I was growing up. We lived in an old schoolhouse on the east side of Loch Lomond, not far from where the road peters out at the foot of Ben Lomond. Electricity came from an unreliable generator, running water was piped in from the burn that ran down the hillside by the house and perishable food was kept outside in a grille fronted meat-safe. When I turned five, Ruth went to boarding school, so for term time at least, I was an only child. We were late children; Ruth born when our mother was around forty and then five years later, as our father neared fifty, I arrived.

I enjoyed meeting Héloïse. Her remark about the plants was funny and sensible at the same time. With white hair coiled in a plait around her head, she wore tan shoes and a blouse tucked neatly into a skirt that reached just below the knee. Her posture was erect and inquisitive as she looked around the hotel, scanned the menu and then turned to us with genuine curiosity. It was reciprocated. Before I was born, she had insisted that friends and family call her Jane and that we children were not to call her aunt; not that we ever saw her. I had been told only that she was a musician, she travelled a lot, didn't have a home but stayed mostly in hotels and that she was rather fey.

That day in 1969, our first and only meeting, I found her warm and easy to talk to, and when I wrote to her after we met, she had replied quickly, 'Yes, it was great fun meeting … things seemed to work out most naturally and interestingly. I feel you and I could yatter long enough about all sorts of things.'

The previous year, just as I turned seventeen and before my exams, my father had declared that now Ruth and I were grown up, he was leaving home and divorcing our mother. About a year later, and before the divorce was settled, he had a heart attack and died. I don't remember whether Héloïse was at the funeral. My memory of the crematorium is darkened by grief, confusion and anxiety that somewhere in the back row, was Mrs Sherower, my father's American lover, whom he'd said he would marry after the divorce. Was there a tea afterwards? I don't recall.

It was the following month that we met Héloïse at the Crianlarich Hotel. Later she wrote to my mother enclosing £250 that she had received from my father's estate, saying that she had never really known him and that Mum should have the money. Then, a few months later, not long after making the tapes in her car, Héloïse too was dead.

By default, I became custodian of her legacy; a box of memorabilia that included personal letters, papers, newspaper cuttings, photographs and some curiosities. Moving through adult life and as family members passed on other items and information, it piled up untidily. The box contained a few greasy shellac discs although I had nothing on which to play them. Sometimes, when there was an unexpected lull in life, I would read some of the cuttings and scrutinise the photographs and occasionally, researchers or musicologists contacted me with questions about her. Although I shared what little I knew, I failed each time to ask them questions, to take the opportunity to learn something about her from them.

In the mid-1990s, around twenty-five years after Héloïse's death, I heard Alison Kinnaird, a Scottish harpist, being interviewed on the radio. It was *Woman's Hour*, a weekday programme, so I must have been on holiday. She sounded such a vibrant young woman that I stopped what I was doing to listen, her enthusiasm prompting a sudden and overwhelming burst of curiosity about Héloïse. That day, I found Alison's phone number and called her, burbling about the memorabilia, seeking her advice, even inviting myself to visit. The following week with the box of disorganised papers in my car, I arrived at her house somehow expecting her to give me a steer, an explanation, to tell me what to do. Looking back, I gasp at my cheek and naivety. Alison made me coffee and listened politely but it was clear that she had little interest in picking through such an untidy pile from the past. I would have to find guidance elsewhere. Then the moment passed.

There were also public memorabilia. My mother told me of visiting the Mitchell Library to enquire about Héloïse's bequests and of being overwhelmed when the librarian appeared pushing a trolley stacked high with heavy volumes. Embarrassing now, this sounded so far-fetched to my youthful ears that I assumed she was mistaken, that the trolley was carrying books for several readers. And Héloïse's recordings, somebody told us, were in the School of Scottish Studies. We had little idea where or what that was, but it sounded the right sort of place for her music to be.

Years passed with fitful explorations until circumstances combined to move me into action. Most simply, I got older. The pace of life slowed and I became absorbed by grandchildren whose very presence generated an urge to arrange that older family history into a form that they and their children might understand. And I turned to the internet. Immediately, it offered tantalising snippets: a concert in Singapore, another in New York; a Pathé newsreel of her being feted at a Druid ceremony; a website offering her records; a psychedelic folk band in New Zealand citing her as an influence; a fragment of her 1960s music sampled in 2003 by Martyn Bennett, the innovative young Scottish musician. Opportunity, motivation and means suddenly combined to make the task more exciting and, potentially, easier.

Cautiously, and realising that her life from 1896 to 1970 had covered a period of extraordinary social and political change, I began to assemble a simple chronology. It didn't take long to discover that although she had enjoyed a secure and privileged Victorian/Edwardian childhood, it was far from the suffocating existence that some modern depictions of that era suggest. Her parents seemed conventional yet unconventional, pursuing their own interests and often living apart. Although born in Glasgow, Héloïse's childhood had been nomadic, with long periods spent in Argyll where she and her siblings were left much to their own devices, often outside on the shore, in boats or scrambling around on hillsides. As I traced their movements, she became less of a stranger.

During my own childhood I had spent hours living wildly outdoors, alone with my imagination. I can invoke easily the sensation of sinking my fingers into wet sphagnum moss, soft, trickling, electric green against the nutmeg mulch of the woodland floor; or bracing my small shoulders for the heave of pulling over a tussocky nest of wood ants and peering at the insects bustling about with their fat white eggs. Behind our house, the smell of pine was ever in the air. The scent of creosote and warmed wood rose from the jetty that stretched into the loch and I would lie there belly down, mesmerised by the pebbles lying beneath the lap, lap of the ripples against the wood, so many shades of blue, brown and grey, some fringed with fine fronds of silky weed, all nudged comfortably close to each other. I longed to be a pebble.

I had not found people so accommodating. My only reliable friend in the tiny rural 1950s primary school was the daughter of a German prisoner of war who had married a local woman. We were an unlikely couple, she with her spindly little body and thready plaits and me, buttoned plumply into my cardigan. But we were inseparable.

She was taunted for being a jerry. I was taunted for being posh. I didn't understand the words but I knew what they meant. We didn't belong; we had no right to be there and at any moment, we might suffer for it. At playtimes we ran for the shelter of the woods behind the school hall where we prowled purposefully, intent always on building or shoring up a secure and secret den, trailing tangled fronds of bracken and fallen branches in our wake like feral princesses. We spoke rarely, preferring to crouch companionably in the bronzed, softly scented gloom offering each other crumbles of dried moss and ragged robin flower petals on platters of bark. Playing house. Silent fugitives.

At times, I'm still not sure whether I have a right to be here. Although I have never lived anywhere but Scotland, the legacy of my father's family and their Edwardian wealth casts a shadow sometimes across my life, making me reluctant on occasion to speak, hesitant still that I might be resented, that my accent may draw a sneer. I know this is silly. Isn't everyone marked by their accent? I should have got over it. I began to wonder whether exploring Héloïse's life might help me better understand my own existence.

In November 2013, I visited the Mitchell Library in Glasgow to see *The Russell-Fergusson Collection of Harps*, the nineteen volume collection which Héloïse had donated between 1955 and 1964. 'Do you want to see it *all*?' asked the librarian before returning with a trolley stacked with books and archive boxes just as Mum had described. In fact, on that first visit I did not see all of the collection but there was more than enough there to get me started. Lifting the lid from one archive box I found the four small grey envelopes sitting on top of her letter to Mr C.W. Black; the tapes that she had made in her car that drizzly September day in 1969, waiting nearly forty-five years for me to uncover them.

I sat with the letter before me and read it slowly. She had written it three months after I met her in Crianlarich and just three months before she died. It hit me suddenly how close she was to death at the time we met, how the breast cancer, for that was the primary cause, would have been eating away at her. Later, a doctor friend shared her recollections of cancer patients in the 1970s:

> When I was in medical school … I saw women who had horrendous cancerous growths that they tolerated. Usually with paddings in case they seeped, and did not want to even let the doctors look at them. They did not really understand about getting secondaries, seeing a pain in a remote part of the body as not connected. It is hard for us to imagine how afraid and uneducated people were about medical illnesses, never mind a frightening diagnosis such as C. The big C. People whispered the word, if at all.

Héloïse's letter filled my head with questions. Who were the Duncans at Ardencaple who had helped her with the tapes? Did they know she was ill? I struggled to retrieve any memory from that lunch in Crianlarich, wondering what she had discussed with my mother, whether there was anything that we could have done to help her.

My simple plan to document a rather colourful relative was brought up short by the magnitude of her collection and the emerging image of her lonely death. She deserved to be taken more seriously. The librarian made me a copy of the letter and agreed to find out whether the tapes had ever been heard. A few weeks later, she confirmed that they had lain undisturbed since Héloïse sent them to the library. The conservationist would examine them to determine whether they were in a condition to be copied. Hearing them became a possibility.

On the train home, I read and re-read the letter. It pulled me deeper into the mystery of her life. I resolved to listen to the tapes, to hear her voice, to understand what she had been so keen to share before she died. And I resolved that in the meantime, I would uncover her story, sieving through the memorabilia box, the letters and the cuttings, the photographs and the reviews, the library collection, the internet. I knew there would be gaps. Some I might have to fill with speculation or informed guesses; no doubt others would remain a mystery. But I would do my best to be true to her.

Chapter Two

Childhood

When their first baby, Héloïse, was born in July 1896, her parents William and Hélène employed a nursemaid to care for her. Aged twenty-two, Rebecca Mathieson, from Kilmonivaig near Spean Bridge, travelled more than a hundred and twenty miles south to take up the post in Glasgow. On arriving at Number Two Belhaven Crescent in the city's flourishing west end, the door was opened by Mary MacVicar, the young housemaid from Strath, near Gairloch, even further north. Both were native Gaelic speakers.

When Rebecca was not busy in the nursery or out with Héloïse in the fresh air, the two young women must have spent many hours together, Rebecca helping Mary while she washed windows, polished floors, waxed the furniture and shook out the rugs. I picture Héloïse, sitting in a warm corner with some toys as they fold the voluminous sheets, the monogrammed towels, tablecloths and table napkins that I still bring out on special occasions, watching them and listening to the rhythm of their voices. As those early months and years ticked by, she would have surely begun to imitate them, to practise the sounds and the syllables, to join in.

It is hard to ignore a child's first words. We respond almost instinctively, sharing rhymes, correcting a consonant, clapping when they get it right. As Héloïse echoed the sounds and rhythms of the Gaelic, Mary and Rebecca must have teased and encouraged her, reinforcing her efforts, unconsciously laying down the language with smiles and

11

cuddles. For Héloïse, Gaelic would have become close to what Julia Kristeva, the philosopher and psychoanalyst, has called 'the language of once upon a time', the language that narrates infancy, the 'prosody of words that lulled us to sleep as babies'.

Her parents William and Hélène were not Gaelic speakers but both had strong family links to Argyll which at that time was still a predominantly Gaelic speaking part of Scotland. Hélène Russell, whose father had been a partner in the Saracen Iron Foundry in Glasgow, was raised on the island of Bute in a large comfortable house overlooking the sea. William Ferguson was descended from a family of weavers from the eighteenth century settlement of Glenbranter near Strachur, also in Argyll. From the 1790s, two Ferguson brothers migrated to the United States and to Canada; a third headed to Glasgow, eventually finding work in the shipyards that were emerging along the river Clyde. A hundred years later, his descendant William was university educated and enjoying a senior position in Barclay, Curle & Co. Ltd., a large and successful shipbuilding company where, despite the fact that his mobility was impaired by the lasting effects of childhood rheumatic fever, he would become the company chairman before he died.

Thus, Héloïse's parents were part of the growing Victorian bourgeoisie in a Glasgow often deemed Britain's second city. They honeymooned in Paris, double-barrelled their surnames adding an 's' to Fergusson in the process, furnished their marital home at Belhaven Crescent with fine furniture, rugs and pictures, employed a cook and a housemaid and, two years after marriage, a nurse for this first baby, Héloïse. They fitted comfortably into Glasgow's prosperous middle class society. Hélène's father retired and her parents left Bute to live nearby in Cleveden; William's widowed mother and also his married sister Jane lived just a few streets away. A rather predictable pattern of life seemed to be on the cards.

Nevertheless, despite the household luxury and the sociability of fashionable city life, Hélène chafed to spend more time outdoors and yearned especially to be closer to the sea. William would not have been surprised. Between the pages of a family Bible, I found a pencilled note dated 2 February 1893 on which he had jotted down some thoughts on proposing marriage. Alongside calculations of the costs, he described what had attracted him most to this young woman from Bute. It was not her demure and gracious presence at balls and social events, although these were noted. Despite, or perhaps because of his own increasing disability, it was specifically her energy that he loved, 'her love of climbing hills and crossing fields', her revelling in being outdoors or on the water.

By 1900, the family would have needed little urging to leave the city. That August, a series of deaths in Glasgow, first thought to be typhoid, turned out to be bubonic plague.[2] There were calls to disinfect all trams and ferries, to disinfect even the coins in people's pockets, to ward off contagion. Belhaven Crescent was modern and affluent but the city was small and no one could be confident that the disease might not spread from the Gorbals where it was first detected. Due to the extraordinary sterling work of the Glasgow medical and health authorities, the disease had vanished by the end of September. Sixteen people had died. As I read about this outbreak, Ebola was ravaging parts of West Africa where its spread, in the early days at least, had been exacerbated by family funeral traditions where many people would attend a wake. This mirrored exactly the spread of the plague in Glasgow where contagion had been traced painstakingly through individuals who had visited the houses of the dead to pay their respects.

Unsurprising then, that the young Russell-Fergusson family spent increasing amounts of time in the west Highlands, renting houses close to the sea and favouring the villages of Port Appin and Taynuilt.

---

2 John Burrowes, *Great Glasgow Stories* (Edinburgh: Mainstream Publishing, 1998), p. 113.

A second baby named Marguerite was born in 1898. Then in 1903, a baby brother called Thomas Donald; my father, who was always called Donald.

It was while the children were young that Hélène developed a profound interest in Christian Science, a religious movement founded in 1870s America by Mary Baker Eddy and which was characterised often by the view that disease was a form of 'mental error', that the sick could be treated successfully through prayer. Baker Eddy promoted the belief that the material world was essentially an illusion and that reality was located more securely within the spiritual world. Through spiritual work and prayer, a Christian Scientist could not only distance herself from the evils of the material world but also, Baker Eddy suggested, could heal herself, and possibly others. Hélène became a committed believer. I wonder whether she had wrestled with the challenge of William's disability and its impact on their life together and had embraced Christian Science, initially at least, out of a desire to help him, to heal him.

The Glasgow branch of the First Church of Christ, Scientist was established in 1906 and it still flourishes. One dank November afternoon I visited its Reading Room where the archivist showed me the first membership book with Hélène's name neatly inscribed as one of the earliest members. Héloïse would have been ten years old; Margie, eight and my father just three. Unfolding a musty application form, I saw Hélène's signature and her agreement to the tenets and rules of the Mother Church. These ended with a promise 'to strive, watch and pray for that Mind to be in us which was also in Jesus Christ; to love one another; and to be meek, merciful, just and pure'. William did not join the movement, nor did my father, but Héloïse and Margie both became committed to Christian Science. Granny Hélène's faith remained strong and she continued to reject any medical intervention until she died in 1952. Possibly, that was one reason why Héloïse had kept her own final illness so private.

The 1911 census recorded no Gaelic speakers at Belhaven Crescent. Rebecca and Mary had moved on and a seventeen year old Swiss governess called Gertrud Apfel was living with the family, probably to tutor my father. The only trace of Héloïse attending school came from her earliest published writing in 1938–1939, in a series that she wrote for a Scottish paper called the *People's Journal*. It opened with a school anecdote:

> As a small child I stood among the others in a busy classroom eagerly scanning the results of the geography exam. The names were arranged in order of merit. My eyes travelled naturally to the top of the list but alas, the name was not there. Not even in the middle of it but at the very bottom. Two out of a hundred. The other children laughed. I was regarded as a sort of heroine. At that time I thought only of music and little dreamed that one day I would know geography as few people ever have a chance to do.

My sister Ruth reminded me of one of our dad's stories about school-days; not in Glasgow or Argyll, but in the town of Callander and his memory of sitting on an island in the middle of the river Leny, refusing to go in for supper. Digging into Stirling Council archives, I found the evidence. In September 1912, aged nine years old and not having attended school before, my father was enrolled in the primary department of McLaren High School in Callander. At that time, the town and its environs were bustling with tourists from around the world, attracted still by Victorian romanticism about Scotland and especially by the work of Sir Walter Scott, particularly his poem, *The Lady of the Lake*.

Héloïse's parents rented The Pass House, situated still on a ribbon of land two miles north of the town, bounded on one side by the road, and on the other by a steep drop above the swirling waters of the river Leny. There, the constant rumble tumble of the river and the wind in the trees would have made up the soundscape to Héloïse's teenage life; what she heard on waking, the fading echoes as she fell asleep.

On a cold March day in 2014, I drove to The Pass House, wondering who lived there now and whether I was bold enough to enquire. Built of red sandstone, a broad square tower rose above the entrance hall beyond which stretched the main body of the house, long and low, parallel with the river. My knock brought no response but as I walked past the series of windows overlooking the churning water, a pink cheeked woman emerged from the garden. Hearing the reason for my visit, Helen Carfrae put down the seed tray she was carrying, invited me inside and put on the kettle. She and her family had lived in The Pass House for over twenty years.

She led me into an oak panelled room, one of three which ran seamlessly into each other between folding doors that could close off discrete rooms or open up for larger gatherings and parties. Sitting with mugs of tea by one of the windows that overlooked the river, I described my father's recollection of playing on an island and shared my curiosity about Héloïse. Sure enough, below the house lay a tiny island tangled with trees and undergrowth which, without a bridge over the rushing water, would have been inaccessible for most of the year. The Carfraes had refurbished a little bridge that had been built in 1936 and it was possible, at least in summertime, to wade from the island to the opposite bank, where a popular woodland path followed the river north eastwards towards its source.

For the Russell-Fergusson children, the island must have been magical. As soon as a spell of dry weather reduced the depth and pace of the currents in the rich peaty water, I could see Héloïse and Margie hitching up their skirts, grabbing Donald's hands and wading across the slippery stones, their bare feet adept at finding a footing, to reach this private kingdom. There they stayed, challenging the calls to come in for supper. Maybe they played out *The Lady of the Lake*, built dens or waded stealthily through the shallow water to the opposite bank to observe the strolling tourists on the woodland walk. Perhaps they peered over the shoulder of the local artist John Howard Lyon, as he sat at his easel.

I have inherited two of Lyon's paintings, both painted in 1912 and which Hélène and William acquired probably as soon as the paint had dried. Entitled *Road, Strathyre*, one shows a small herd of cows ambling dreamily along the sunlit woodland path, the cowherd pausing on the brow of a stone bridge. The other, entitled *Pass of Leny*, shows the river in its full explosive glory, foaming downstream between high boulders and bare trees, the snow flecked shoulders of Ben Ledi towering in the background.

The Pass House felt peaceful and friendly. Somehow it was unsurprising to learn that Helen Carfrae was a piano teacher. It made it even easier to imagine the rooms filling with music as young Héloïse sat down to play there nearly a hundred years before. We said goodbye standing on the decorative floor tiles below the tower where I imagined William, just off the train from Glasgow, pushing open the door to stand beside us, leaning on his stick and listening to the music carrying from the drawing room. There were no family photographs from this period in Callander, nor any written accounts. Héloïse was not enrolled at McLaren High School. Yet the house, the island in the tumbling river, the wind in the trees, the pastoral paintings, had all brought me closer to her young life.

———

By 1914, my father had left McLaren High School to become a boarder at Fettes College in Edinburgh. William, still tied to the Glasgow shipyard, was keen to secure a permanent rural base for the family and his solution was to buy the house in Port Appin that they had been renting off and on for over ten years, along with the associated home farm.

Calling the house and the parcel of land Ardtur, he asked his solicitor to put it straight into Hélène's name, giving her the chance to live permanently in a place that she loved while inevitably, he still spent much of his time in Glasgow. In 1913, the magazine *The Shipbuilder* had noted 'Mr Fergusson's face with the kindly smile, is known to us all; and although, in a degree, he has lost some of his old nimbleness, yet the features of head and heart still remain unimpaired'. William was not a Christian Scientist but he was undoubtedly stoical.

Hélène must have felt elated. A 1904 photograph shows her with a windswept eight year old Héloïse and six year old Margie on her father's boat off the island of Lismore, just across the water from Ardtur. The children already felt at home in the house, had built dens in the woodland behind it, knew the layout of the garden that stretched straight onto the pebbled shore where they paddled in Loch Linnhe. To the north, stood a low stone walled pigpen, an orchard and rows of raspberry canes framing the path towards the home farm. To the south, past a sunken garden and through a shrubbery, lay the village hall where there were regular community gatherings and performances.

Hélène presided over a house of industry and order. She employed a cook, a kitchen maid, a housemaid and a butler, Gillies Crichton. She seemed determined to maintain domestic standards that reflected the family's wealth and status but otherwise, she pulled on her old clothes and was outside, striding up into the wood behind Ardtur with a local shepherd, picking his brains and drawing on local knowledge to work out how best to improve the water supply to the house. She invested in some Aberdeen Angus cattle and some Large Black pigs. She joined the Scottish Pig Breeders' Association, competing regularly and with some success at agricultural shows. A secretary, Margaret Glendinning, helped her with the paperwork which William had left entirely in her hands.

Crichton ran an immaculate household. Fresh flower arrangements stood in the hallway and the public rooms. Furniture, silverware and crystal gleamed. He supervised the serving of every meal, arranged the breakfast sideboard with warmed dishes of lamb's kidneys and bacon and oversaw the elegant dinners laid before the family and their guests in the evening. I was told that a visiting American ambassador had wanted to filch Crichton for the consulate in Edinburgh. If he went, it was not for long. Although not popular with the other household staff, Crichton seemed to be as devoted to Hélène as she was to him.

Unsurprisingly, Hélène had a boat. Robust and functional, it fell probably into the category of 'estate launch', used mostly for practical purposes. It was named *Nippa* (Appin backwards) although the family called it the *Paraffin Stink*. Occasionally, and with Crichton as companion or crew, Hélène would set out to rendezvous with her parents or brothers in various bays along the west coast. Crichton would be despatched to invite them aboard for afternoon tea before quietly and efficiently making a batch of scones. These trips were never recalled as family outings and although Héloïse and Margie, by this time in their teens, may have been at Ardtur, they were possibly disinclined to join their mother. It made me wonder whether Hélène and Crichton were lovers; my twenty-first century romanticism conjuring a John Brown and Queen Victoria story about a loyal servant and the stoical yet rather sad lady of the house whose distant and disabled husband could no longer meet her needs. Could that be true?

In June 2013, and with Héloïse's story niggling at the back of my mind, I had accepted my friend Tor's invitation to join him on his boat the *Briggen* for a leg of his annual summer trip from Inverness to the Inner Hebrides. His voyage in this sturdy, clinker built Norwegian motor vessel depended upon whatever crew he could muster, embarking and disembarking at quays and jetties along the way. So, with another friend, Moira, I went to meet him at Corpach Sea Lock where two immense black gates marked the doorway between the western end of the Caledonian Canal and the head of Loch Linnhe.

The weather held us back for twenty-four hours but at last we got the all clear, the lock gates opened and the *Briggen* chugged determinedly out onto the loch. The sky was a heavy whale grey and a fine drizzle shrouded the views. My friendship with Tor is longstanding. He is tall, bearded and bespectacled with a kindly face and, invariably, a seafarer's cap. Half Norwegian, he has a penchant for dark beer and late night conversations round the kitchen table. We meet mostly through our support for the peace movement in Scotland, organising a mobile café called The Jeely Peace that we take to demonstrations and other events campaigning for the removal of the nuclear submarines at the Faslane Naval Base. It is an activity over which I can be extremely bossy and Tor is admirably uncomplaining.

Once on the water, it was clear that our roles were reversed. Even if the sun had been shining and the sea like a millpond, this was not a trip for relaxing on a cushion, trailing my fingers prettily in the water. Tor brought a solemn urgency to the skills of navigation and he demanded a crew who were up to the job. Pretty quickly, I felt under duress. I had neither plotted coordinates nor considered the vocabulary of degrees and latitude since leaving school but finally, I made an accurate mark on the chart. This achievement, coupled with Moira having by far the best eyesight of the three of us which consigned her to look-out duty for the barely visible marker buoys, confirmed me in the role of navigator. Standing inscrutably at the wheel, Tor expected updates on the quarter hour and the pressure was intense.

Occasionally, one of us brewed coffee. Moira and I kept checking our watches and pondered the significance of high and low tides. I kept my eye on the chart and tried not to let my mind wander, my regular reports on our position becoming gradually more confident. Taking an exhilarating turn at the wheel, I felt a heady sense of power, staring across the hammered pewter of the water stretched around me, feeling the *Briggen* respond to the swell of the waves and to each small move that I made. Yet I knew that any sense of control amongst the swirl of the elements was illusory. There was certainly a lot of room to become a better sailor, but however skilled I might become, the wind and the waves had it.

Late in the afternoon, I plotted the course towards the shelter of Linnhe Marine in Dallens Bay where we would moor for the night.

The mist had lifted. The small bay with its handful of sailing boats lay tranquil in the summer evening, the silvery reflection of their masts like a flight of arrows darting into the still water. Celebrating the survival of good humour, we agreed on supper at the pub in Port Appin, scrambled into the inflatable dinghy and headed for the pontoon and a waiting taxi. Tor settled beside the driver who introduced herself as Tina. He talked about our trip and mentioned my family interest in the area. 'Ardtur?' said Tina. 'It's being renovated. We can drive up if you like.'

After a couple of miles, she swung the taxi up a rough driveway past some cottages and pulled up at a netted metal fence erected by the construction company, prohibiting access and warning of CCTV. 'Don't worry about that,' Tina said, 'come in and have a look.' We tumbled out of the car and shimmied like naughty children round the fence to crunch up the last few yards towards the house. Through the trees, Loch Linnhe glinted in the evening light. There were stacks of slates and other building material around the outside and an ugly extension at the back seemed to be in the middle of demolition. In every other respect, standing facing the water in that quiet and self-contained way of many Victorian country houses, Ardtur was quite beautiful.

Feeling unexpectedly self-conscious, I tried to take in the dimensions of the house, its overall footprint on the land, its shape beneath the sky, its proximity to the shoreline, touching the walls with my fingertips, peering through the dusty windows, even taking some photographs of what looked like beautifully proportioned rooms. I was pleased by this chance visit but uncertain what I wanted to get out of it. I barely noticed the garden, didn't run onto the shore. It would be on a later visit that I learned about the fruit trees, the pigpen, the sunken garden, the shrubbery. After all, we were on taxi time. I felt a little awkward, sobered by the stillness. It seemed suddenly silly to be there with Tor and Moira and Tina the taxi driver. Visiting the house had less to do with exploring its physical dimensions than with exploring my feelings, feelings that were still embryonic; and, tentatively, exploring Héloïse's feelings.

This was part of the heritage that had nurtured her, a place that she had left and to which she had returned, a place that had thrummed with life and that later had become eerily silent. It was the place that had laid down the curiosity and the fearlessness that I had been unearthing; her inclination to wander in the dense woodland of Washington's Rock Creek rather than follow advice to stay in the city; her compulsion to push through dripping foliage on a remote New Zealand hillside leaving others miles behind; her desire to sit late into the night with herders on an African plain, noisily sharing songs and then falling suddenly silent to watch a pride of lions walk to their drinking hole.

It was also part of the family heritage that had prompted the school teasing about being posh that made me feel, and sometimes still makes me feel, like an alien, unwelcome in my own land. Yet the place was calm and indisputably beautiful. There was so much that I didn't know about this family and their lives. I needed more time to work out what, if anything, Ardtur meant to me and why I might want to be there.

Feeling responsible for the detour, I insisted we head to the pub. We were a little restrained over the meal, tired perhaps, recovering from a day of acute concentration in the rather grim weather. But afterwards, full of good food and wine, we relaxed in the mid-summer dusk, mucking about on the jetty, laughing, taking photographs of each other with Lismore as a backdrop, waiting for Tina's taxi to take us back to Linnhe Marine.

Once aboard *Briggen*, we collapsed into our bunks. Settling myself, I remembered that the four spars of wood designed to support my mattress were one short. The previous night I had felt myself slithering like a grub in my sleeping bag into the resulting void or had woken with a start to find myself already there, fingers grasping for the edge of the bunk to heave myself back up onto the precarious mattress. I lay awake thinking about Granny Hélène and Crichton on the *Paraffin Stink*, wondering whether they ever spent the night on board. Did Crichton bring her hot water to wash in the morning, fry up some kidneys for her breakfast? Did they stand together, stretching in the morning light, welcoming the day?

In 2013, the June morning revealed a chill dank mist shrouding the land, the loch and the islands and after a hasty breakfast, we left the stillness of Dallens Bay, heading out of the Sound on an increasing swell. Moira and I scanned the flinty waves for the coloured marker poles to keep us on course, heading through the network of islands and shallows into the Lynn of Lorn that would carry us eventually down to Oban. 'There it is, Hélène,' Tor called, as we chugged past Ardtur. 'Look! There's your family's big hoose!'

I lifted my camera and stepped out of the wheelhouse into the drizzle. Tor was grinning at me. These wealthy antecedents were clearly jeopardising my peacenik credentials. Looking across at Ardtur, seen at its best from the water even in the dank greyness of the mist, I smiled back at him. But I didn't feel like being teased. My head was jumbled with the family stories, their mystery and their transience. That Russell-Fergusson family was a flicker in time yet Héloïse's story was making me curious. I never knew my grandparents, her mother and father. I met Héloïse only once. Yet I was intrigued by the emerging story; their nomadism, Granny Hélène's passion for being outdoors, William's hardiness despite his disability; his benevolence; Crichton, for goodness sake. As Victorian/Edwardian parents, they did not fit easily into a conventional picture. No wonder that caution seemed to have had eluded Héloïse.

Tor's invitation had brought me literally to the doorstep of Ardtur. The whole experience, the boat, the water, the weather and the land, swelled my commitment to Héloïse's story. Its strangeness and intensity was in danger of disappearing entirely if I didn't focus on assembling its disparate parts. We moored the *Briggen* off Kerrera and took the little ferry across to Oban harbour where Tor stocked up with supplies and we met Marco who would join him for the next leg of the journey. We sat with bowls of soup outside a café where, just before I climbed onto the bus heading south to Stirling, the sun came out. By then, I was looking forward to a comfortable night's sleep.

Almost a hundred years before, Héloïse had travelled south from Oban. Newly eighteen, she was slim and strong with her mother's straight nose and broad forehead and her father's warm brown eyes. Her glossy dark hair was caught loosely at the nape of her neck. Her smile was infectious and engaging. She was outgoing and confident, buoyed by the deep spirituality of her mother's religious belief, by her attachment to the natural world and, especially, by her passion for music. She had everything going for her.

Full of energy and probably on the glowing recommendation of a tutor, she had been offered a place at the Royal Academy of Music in London. She started in the autumn of 1914, just after war had been declared.

CHAPTER THREE

WORLD WAR I

While she attended the Royal Academy, Héloïse would stay with her uncle, John Ferguson, whose house was situated on the edge of Regent's Park at Number One, Gloucester Gate. His London born wife had died in 1894 and despite working with Ramage and Ferguson, shipbuilders in Leith, Uncle John, who was her father's elder brother by ten years, had remained in London, providing continuity and stability for his three children. By 1914, his eldest child Connie had assumed her mother's role in looking after the household and young Johnny, who had joined up as war broke out was a Lieutenant with the Hood Battalion. Fred, the youngest, has been hardest to trace.

As Héloïse unpacked and arranged her things in her room she paused to lean out of the window. The bustle and clatter of the London street replaced the crunch of pebbles on the shore of Loch Linnhe, the formal lawns and brightly planted flower beds in Regent's Park contrasted with the soft wildness of Ardtur. She knew that the Royal Academy of Music in its splendidly new, purpose-built accommodation on Marylebone Road, was situated just across the park. Each morning she could thread her way along the footpaths, observing the changing seasons that were so different in a city more than five hundred miles south of Argyll, anticipating her classes and sharing stories and experience with her new friends. Perhaps she hummed as she walked, rehearsing for her singing lesson with Madame Larkcom, for the harmony class with Mr S.H. Brathwaite or the demands of her piano lessons with Mr Reddie. Each day she moved contentedly from studio to studio before retracing her steps in the late afternoon back across the park to the family.

Within a year of enlisting, her cousin Johnny had been sent to the Dardanelles. He wrote to his father on 17 May 1915, saying:

> We have been ashore nearly three weeks now and we have had a pretty hot time of it. The day after we landed we were in the thick of it, and had a spell of five days trench work and one attack. We got awful shrapnel fire and one shell laid out the three men next to me and also went through my topee – which I hope to show you one day. We did not make much progress and lost a good many. After the five days of it, we had a night in reserve, which meant glorious sleep, and then we attacked again and advanced some way, and put in three days in the firing line and in the trenches we had captured. Without any boasting, the 2nd Brigade (The Hood, Howe and Anson Battalions) have made a terrific name for themselves, but at great cost. We went out to one attack with about 30 officers and 800 men and we finished the next day with 9 officers and under 400 men, so you can see what War means …

A week later he was killed. A book called *The Hood Battalion* contains a number of rather fuzzy black and white photographs, including one taken on 6 May 1915. It shows Lieutenant Ferguson sitting on the ground with a group of fellow soldiers, wearing his topee. There is a hole in it.[3]

Johnny's name is inscribed on the Helles Memorial in Turkey but John and William agreed that he should also be commemorated in Scotland. They must have discussed the best location: a site close to the shipyards that were so fundamental to the family perhaps; or a tribute to Johnny on the Ferguson family monument that stood already on Glasgow's Necropolis. But in the end, it seemed that their deeper roots

---

3   Leonard Sellers, *The Hood Battalion* (Barnsley: Pen & Sword Select, 2003), Plate 31.

in Argyll and their shared love of the sea decided them on Port Appin. William commissioned a war memorial plaque that would include Johnny's name, to be erected in the local Appin church.

Early in 2014, I visited Ardtur again, this time on my own. Searching for clues, I had been poring over faded photographs on a website dedicated to old Appin. The website's host Stuart Carmichael, seemed to know a surprising amount about the house and even about the Russell-Fergusson family. I discovered that he was the builder in charge of the ongoing Ardtur renovations, the builder whose CCTV cameras the *Briggen* adventurers had defied the previous year. Rather sheepishly, I admitted our intrusion. Stuart laughed and said that he would show me round properly on my next visit. Nevertheless, I felt shy driving up to Ardtur, an intruder, wondering whether I would really be welcome.

Stuart invited me into the house and walked slowly from room to room, commenting on what might have once been, on what was being planned or was already installed. The proportions were generous but family sized; the ceilings high enough for a good sense of space yet not overwhelmingly so. It was a house in transition, its floors dusty from plaster, not too far from completion. Upstairs, a bath stood ready to be unwrapped from its packaging. Fingers of electric cable wiggled from behind the skirting boards. And then up more stairs, narrower this time, into a warren of attic space linking several small rooms; a haven perhaps for Crichton and for Miss Glendinning, with bedrooms and a little sitting room.

Outside, through spring sunshine, Stuart showed me the orchard, the sunken garden and the path leading to the old community hall. We pondered the smallness of the semi-circular pigpen and why it was quite so close to the house. Stuart's grandfather had lived in Ardtur Cottage situated just off the driveway, and he had worked at Ardtur when my grandparents were there. Like Hélène, he had kept bees. We wondered about their conversations, what they had thought of each other, learned from each other. Ardtur seemed to be more part of Stuart's family history than it was of mine; his family had never left.

Then, seeming to have all the time in the world for a cautious visitor, Stuart revealed that he was an elder of the local church. If I would like to see the World War I memorial plaque, he had a key. We rattled down the road in his Land Rover and he led me through the vestry into the cool, dim body of the kirk. There was the plaque on the wall, erected in 1918. Underneath the inscription of over eighty individual names, it said:

> This Roll of Honour was presented by William Russell Fergusson Esq., of Ardtur, Appin in memory of his nephew, Lieut. Commander John White Ferguson, R.N.V.R. who was killed at Gallipoli, 7 June, 1915.

Some years earlier, Stuart had wondered why there was no equivalent memorial to those who served during World War II. Thanks to him, the church now boasts a second roll of honour. Much later, he would help me discover what Héloïse was up to during the years of that second World War.

As war was declared in August 1914, and my father and Héloïse departed; him for boarding school in Edinburgh and she for London, Hélène realised that she was pregnant for the fourth time. Aged forty-two, with her three children growing up, she had just started to relish the challenges of living permanently at Ardtur, to work with the seasonal rhythms of the small estate, to learn how best to raise a beef herd and her prized pigs. The pregnancy must have been at least a shock if not an unwelcome interruption to her new equilibrium. Certainly, it generated a swathe of tittle-tattle.

William's level of disability had increased so that he was using a wheelchair almost all of the time. When I was a teenager, picking up occasional snippets about the family, my mother had remarked drily that as a consequence and in order to conceive, Hélène must have taken the initiative sexually. Mum had raised her eyebrows and widened her eyes, hinting that this would have challenged conventional notions of propriety at the time. And there must surely have been whispers about the closeness of Hélène's relationship with Crichton. Clearly, she was damned if she had and damned if she hadn't. I looked closely at the rather stern woman standing proudly in a family portrait. Even if she had been feeling aghast inside, she looked like a woman who would have straightened her shoulders and faced the situation with as much dignity as she could muster.

It was a bitterly cold January in 1915. Aged sixteen, Margie was the only family member at Ardtur during her mother's labour. She went out for a walk but didn't want to go too far; she paced about downstairs, intermittently playing the piano or trying to read. Finally, on hearing the baby had been delivered, she bolted upstairs to see her mother. 'It was horrible,' she said, 'Mother just turned away from me. She wouldn't speak. I didn't know what to do.' A midwife may have been present although Margie never mentioned one. Because of her Christian Science beliefs, Hélène would have refused a doctor and, had it been on offer, would have declined any pain relief. Possibly torn and bleeding, she must have been utterly exhausted and would have preferred not to have been observed in such a vulnerable state by her impressionable daughter. Yet, Margie's bleak account of Denise's birth made me wonder about the relationships within the family, and again about her baby sister's paternity.

In London, despite the war and the deep grief that permeated every room and conversation since Johnny's death, Héloïse continued to study at the Royal Academy. In 1916, as her course neared completion, she composed and published a piece of music entitled 'Absence', which is lodged in the British Library. I wonder whether she composed it in memory of Johnny or of somebody else; or perhaps it was mourning all those lost by 1916. Getting hold of a copy was a challenge for although it was written nearly a hundred years ago, the library required me to get permission from the publisher, West & Co. Finding no trace of the company, I was referred to the Music Publishers Association for advice. The MPA acknowledged my request and then fell silent.

In the memorabilia box at home were two more pieces of music that Héloïse published around the same time. One, dated 1917, was entitled '*Three Short Pieces*', the first to be played *andante*, the second *allegro* and the third, *presto*. The other, dated 1918, was entitled simply, 'A March'. Neither had a title page nor a publisher's name, but both were credited to Héloïse Russell-Fergusson. Curiously, on both, the name Héloïse was scribbled over in thick black ink.

I found one photograph of her at the time. Perhaps home for the holidays, she was huddled around a kettle with some cousins on the shore at Lismore, a fairly typical Scottish picnic really, everyone well wrapped up but grinning. Another photo showed flames licking around a photograph that had been stuck atop a tall stick rammed into the centre of the fire. It was captioned 'The Kaiser'. There was a newspaper clipping too, telling of a fundraising open day at Ardtur which had included an impressive tableau representing the countries at war. It seemed everyone was doing their bit. Héloïse's sister Margie had joined the Land Army in 1917 and kept a diary that began:

> Before the war started, most girls of the middle classes did not know what work really meant. Their lives had previously been ones of pleasure and amusement, in fact, many of them had never given a thought to the serious side of things; but that is all changed now. Girls have come forward, rich and poor alike to offer their services to the Country, proving themselves capable of many kinds of work. They do it cheerfully and uncomplaining in most cases and many of them find it a welcome change from a life of ease. When war broke out, I was still at school, and it was not until two years later that I managed to get away to help. At first I was uncertain which branch of work to take up so being a lover of the country and outdoor life, I chose farming. I did not know anything about this work but was very keen to start.

For two years, living with about twenty other young women, Margie worked on farms in East Anglia. In all weathers and for long, long hours, they cleared stony fields, ploughed with horses, weeded and harvested. She loved especially the dairy work and in 1919, she went to work in the dairy at the Royal Farm at Windsor, where the cowshed walls gleamed with scrubbed tiles and she was expected to groom the cows each day as if they were horses. Early each morning, she delivered fresh milk to the castle, driving up in a Ford van emblazoned with a crimson coronet. Washing the van in the yard one afternoon, she looked up to see two men approaching her; King George V and the Marquis de Soveral. She wrote:

> The King came over and spoke to me and I had to essay a curtsey which being clad in breeches and sea boots was not a very elegant affair, and we had quite a long conversation all during which time the wet sponge which I had in one hand was trickling down inside my boot. His Majesty asked me many questions as to where I came from, how long I had been there and we had a mutual agreement that the best people came from Scotland.

In 1919, Donald left Fettes but Ruth and I were unsure what he did next. His father and grandfather had both attended university in Glasgow, followed by apprenticeships that covered the raft of knowledge and skills they needed for work at the shipyard; but there was no evidence of Donald attending university. Certainly, his handwriting was terrible but we knew that was because, as a youth, he had climbed over a fence without the safety catch on his gun and had shot himself in the shoulder and head with pellets. The incident was always mentioned with laughter but there may have been more to it. Perhaps he missed a key chunk of school or his rackety writing excluded him from taking his formal education further. I remember as a child sitting on his knee by the fire while he read to me, feeling with my fingers the pellets bobbling about just under the skin of his temple.

Looking at the few photographs from the time, we concluded that this good looking young man probably drifted between Scotland and London, driving fast cars and spending summers sailing with his Russell cousins in Argyll, or possibly in the south of France, apparently unguided and perhaps uncertain as to what he should do next. Eventually, in August 1923, William arranged for him to be apprenticed for two years to the Le Havre office of the Compagnie Générale Transatlantique where he did stints in various departments of the company and became fluent in French. He returned, not to work with his father at Barclay, Curle & Co. Ltd., nor with his Uncle John at Ramage & Ferguson in Leith, but with John G. Kincaid, Marine Engineers in Greenock, a firm with which there were more distant family connections.

Meanwhile, Héloïse had started performing professionally and had gathered some extracts from reviews onto a flyer publicising her work and availability: the *Daily Telegraph* had noted that 'she plays with an unbounding sense of atmosphere' and the *Glasgow Evening News* described Héloïse Russell, who, 'in works by Scarlatti, Debussy, Ireland, Goossens and Deodat de Severac … displayed talents of uncommon brilliancy for her age'. This was an encouraging start although I was curious as to why she had amended her surname. Perhaps Russell-Fergusson took up too much room on the page.

During the war years, business had boomed for Barclay, Curle & Co. Ltd. It had built Insect Class gunboats for the Royal Navy and had then become part of a larger Tyneside company called Swan, Hunter and Wigham Richardson. Inevitably, new orders for ships nose-dived as the war ended. At the same time, many of the social and political tensions that had been brewing in Glasgow throughout the war years spilled over. The city had become one of the most overcrowded in Britain with appallingly cramped, overcrowded and unsanitary housing conditions. A move to increase rents in 1915 had provoked outrage. The ensuing rent strike was massive; involving around 30,000 residents and led significantly by women, it was successful not only in the immediate term whereby the Rent Restriction Act 1915 benefited the whole country, but it prompted later legislation that would mark the beginning of council house provision.

Post war, the Clyde Workers Committee (CWC), a network of shop stewards which had formed in 1915 to defend workers' interests, and the Clydeside Independent Labour Party (ILP) demanded better wages and conditions. In particular, they sought a reduction in the working week from fifty-four hours to forty hours, a change which would not only have benefited the existing workforce but would have helped to provide employment for some of the thousands of demobbed servicemen. Their case was ignored and on Monday 27 January 1919, 70,000 workers went out on strike. On the Wednesday, a CWC deputation went to the City Chambers to ask the Lord Provost to put their demand to the government. Apparently fearing a workers' revolution, the government quickly sent troops, tanks and lorries by train to Scotland. On the Friday morning, 31 January, around 60,000 people massed in George Square outside the City Chambers waiting to hear the Lord Provost confirm the government's response. On hearing that their demands had been rejected with the government opting instead for negotiations with only the engineers' official trade union, the crowd erupted. The sheriff attempted to read the Riot Act but it was snatched out of his hands. What happened next has been described as a frenzied attack. The police began to baton the strikers indiscriminately and angry confrontations spread through the surrounding streets and onto Glasgow Green. The next morning Glaswegians woke to find armed and helmeted troops patrolling George Square, machine guns stationed on top of the Post Office and the North British Hotel and six tanks parked in the Cattlemarket. The official casualty list was nineteen policemen and thirty-four strikers injured. Six CWC members and six others were put on trial. Only two were convicted.

Was William in Glasgow at the time? Would he have sided with the government against the strikers? As a shipyard boss, that seemed rather inevitable but I could not know, absolutely, for sure. In the small archive relating to Barclay, Curle & Co. Ltd. in the Mitchell Library, I found a wages book for their Elderslie Works. Perhaps as a result of the strike action, wages rose between 1919 and 1921 although between 1922 and 1924 a significant number of workers' names either disappeared from the wages book or their wages plummeted. Unsurprisingly, there was no wages book for the directors. But the minutes of Barclay, Curle's AGM of 9 July 1920 had recorded that William, by then aged fifty-seven and in visibly declining health, had resigned from the post of managing director. The world as he knew it had turned and, whatever his views might have been, he had had enough.

The end of the war had heralded the introduction of votes for women over thirty. Hélène swiftly registered to vote in the Parish of Appin and Lismore. At the same time, she looked to her two older daughters and decided to take action to secure their futures. In conventional terms, that meant readying Héloïse and Margie to participate in the London debutante season, the succession of parties and social events for the emerging youth of wealthy families which included the presentation of young women at Court; a process which might draw forth suitable husbands. On 24 June 1920, Margie arrived from the dairy at Windsor Castle to sit solemnly in the centre of a formal photograph between Héloïse and her mother before their presentation. All three were dressed in ankle length pale silk, trimmed with lace. Hélène and Margie, brown as berries, looking directly at the camera; Heloise, her arm against her younger sister's shoulder, has her eyes cast down.

After two months on the lavish circuit of London events, the family headed north for the exuberant Highland social season that began in late August. Assembling at Ardtur, they threw themselves into attending the plethora of Highland games, sailing regattas and balls that were held from Portree to Inverness. However, any hopes Hélène might have had of finding husbands for her daughters were disappointed. Young men were, of course, in short supply but it seemed that even had one or two made an impression on or an advance towards either sister, both young women were predisposed towards an independent life. Margie, emboldened by the rigour and adventure of her wartime work, was veering towards her mother's passion for farming. Héloïse was determined to build her career as a musician.

There is no evidence to suggest that they didn't enjoy this conventional social whirl and, indeed, either or both of them may have set their heart on someone only to find their feelings were not reciprocated. But, rather like their mother, it is possible that they craved a more purposeful engagement with the world than marriage might have provided at the time. With Hélène as a powerful role model and a father who had encouraged their independence, the sisters had been brought up with few constraints and both seemed to bubble with vitality and curiosity regarding what the world had to offer, and what they could offer the world.

The combination of Héloïse's upbringing, broad education and financial security, meant that she was not short of confidence and it was evident that her parents would have supported her to do pretty much whatever she wanted. The challenge perhaps lay in deciding what that should be.

In 1920s London, artistic circles were humming with creativity and imagination but Héloïse did not seem drawn either to a conventional musical career there or to exploring a more bohemian lifestyle. I wonder again about the music lying in the British Library; perhaps the city held memories she did not want to revisit. Yet if she stayed in Argyll, the opportunities to perform and build a career might be constrained simply by geography and the idea of returning home permanently after enjoying two years of relative independence may not have seemed very attractive. Much later, writing in that first

People's Journal article in December 1938 in which she had laughed at her ignorance of school geography, Héloïse described the solution:

> It was while I was still a timid student at the Royal Academy of Music along with others who were to dazzle the world of music both at home and abroad later on, that my first great leap into the unknown came suddenly. Into the peace of a summer afternoon at my Highland home a telegram arrived. I tore it open. It was from London. 'Offer you position musical instructor well-known school, Washington, America. Urge instant acceptance. Sail immediately.' Holding the telegram in my hand, I repeated, 'Washington, America! Where is the atlas?'

The telegram cannot have arrived entirely out of the blue for the post of music teacher in Washington started five years after she had left the Royal Academy. But being a little flexible with the truth meant that she could offer her readers a seamless and more exciting story. And it was, without doubt, exciting. She was off to America.

CHAPTER FOUR

NEW WORLD, OLD WORLD

Héloïse waved frantically at her mother and Margie standing tiny as toys on the Plymouth dockside far below. It was September 1923 and with nearly two thousand other passengers, she had embarked aboard the *Paris*, ready to steam across the Atlantic bound for New York. As the ship hooted a final farewell and slid its 34,000 tons smoothly in the direction of France, she surveyed her surroundings. Completed at St Nazaire in 1921, the *Paris* was the largest and most elegant ocean liner of the day, luxuriously designed and equipped, with telephones in the first class cabins, Art Nouveau interiors and outstanding cuisine.

Within hours, Donald had joined her at Le Havre. Aged twenty, he had been apprenticed to the Le Havre office of the Compagnie Générale Transatlantique the previous month and here he was, a passenger on one of their newest and most prestigious ships. I imagine he had work to do, building his practical experience throughout the vessel with regular stints in the gleaming engine rooms and perhaps some testing tutorials on navigation. But whatever his reason for being there, he and Héloïse soon discovered that all the luxury in the world could not keep the hurricane season at bay. Héloïse wrote later about the voyage:

> I crossed the Atlantic on a luxurious French liner, but I am afraid her sumptuous appointments, especially the famous restaurant, were lost on me. I remained bundled up in rugs on the heaving deck most of the voyage, an undignified position for one who loves ships and whose

people have been responsible for the construction of many on the Clyde. Once, when we ran into a 90 mile an hour gale, it seemed best to die, but eventually we sighted the Statue of Liberty, America's first greeting to newcomers, and no landmark ever seemed so welcome.

Disembarking at Ellis Island where all migrants were given the once over, she finally checked in, somewhat dehydrated and weary, to the Pennsylvania Hotel in New York. In her room, an array of upfront instructions and advice both charmed and irritated her. She wrote:

A large homely looking Bible brushed sides with a menu from the Roof Garden. One was told what to do on every occasion, where to go. 'Does your frock need pressing?' asked an orange coloured folder briskly. 'Good morning, have you slept well?' murmured a slip pasted on the morning paper. 'What are you going to do today?' it continued. And there followed a list of suggestions. 'Try our salads!' commanded a pamphlet pinned beneath glass. 'Peanut, popcorn, pimento'. What marvellous names! I hummed a little tune to the words and opened the bathroom door. 'Do you need a shampoo?' shrieked a sea green folder, shaped like a bottle. 'Mind your own business,' exclaimed the traveller from Scotland.

Two days later, watching her trunk and bags being loaded onto the train at Grand Central Station, she considered her decision. She would have a full-time job and be part of a staff team. I could imagine her excitement tinged perhaps with some trepidation. Living with Uncle John in London had been a stepping stone to independence. Here, she knew no one.

The Lucy Wing Madeira 'Miss' School was situated at 1330, 19th Street just by the Dupont Circle in central Washington. It was an elite boarding school for the daughters of wealthy politicians, bankers and businessmen and it was proud of the academic achievements of its girls. Disappointed to discover that music and singing were regarded by the other teachers simply as useful pastimes, Héloïse took her work very seriously and she also practised assiduously to maintain and build her own skills. She joined the local concert circuit, giving occasional recitals both solo and for two pianos. Just before Christmas 1924 and billing herself again as Héloïse Russell (Scottish Pianiste), she played Mozart, Ravel, Arensky, Philipp and Rachmaninov in a recital for two pianos with a Katherine Ellis, under the patronage of a number of doughty Washingtonians, including Mrs William Howard Taft, wife of the former president.

Despite finding another Scot amongst the staff, someone else, much to the hilarity of the others, who used an egg-cup at breakfast time, she recorded no particular soulmates at the school. When not at the piano, she put on her coat to go exploring, asking colleagues where she could find parkland, somewhere approximating countryside. The head of the school frowned and advised strongly against venturing beyond the city streets but Héloïse craved natural surroundings, to feel earth and leaves underfoot, to hear birdsong, twigs snapping, wind in the trees. Scrutinising a local map she found Rock Creek Park just ten minutes from the school. Encompassing around two thousand acres of natural woodland, it had opened in 1890 as the first urban national park in the United States. It teemed with wildlife.

There, she could lose herself amongst the dense deciduous trees that obliterated the noises of the city. White tailed deer grazed in the shade amongst cinnamon ferns, squirrels bounded from her path and in the wetland at the water's edge, she was startled and then entranced to find eastern box turtles that moved slowly through the undergrowth, looking determinedly for grubs. She walked and dreamed. She talked happily with strangers, occasionally making herself invisible just as she had done with Donald and Margie in the woodland by the river Leny. She wrote:

> I often met solitary Negros in my wanderings. A courteous 'good day'
> would bring a friendly grin to their faces. Frequently, I discussed his catch
> with some lone tramp angling patiently in a stream or from the canal
> bank. Occasionally, my instincts warned me against an encounter and
> I would 'vanish' before I had been seen until the way was clear again.

One cold winter's day, she had gone downtown to buy music for a pupil when something caught her eye in a shop window. Embellished with swirling Celtic designs there stood, rather forlornly and without strings, a clarsach; a small harp that had been made in Syracuse, New York. Immediately, she sensed a powerful connection to it, writing later that 'it seemed no stranger' and arranged for it to be delivered to the school. Her colleagues popped their heads round the door of her music studio and chuckled at this unfamiliar instrument but, almost immediately, its impact on her was profound. She wrote:

> Playing (the piano) in my studio alone one night, one single chord made me suddenly pause. I do not know why. I was swept thousands of miles back to where the seabirds shrilled above the gale as they did centuries ago. The Hebridean people's songs! I lost all sense of time. I was spinning with them; milking. I was waulking the cloth although I HAD NEVER SEEN THIS DONE. I keened tragically on the shore with the rest when the lads failed to return. That had happened so often. I was quite, quite familiar with these islands although I HAD NEVER BEEN THERE!

Reading this account, I pictured Rebecca and Mary towards the turn of the century, talking and laughing as they tackled the domestic chores in Belhaven Crescent, young Héloïse always close by. She *had* been there. The sound and rhythms of Gaelic songs and stories, the young women's conversations, laid down during her precious early years, were surely hard-wired, buried deep down in her unconscious; never lost entirely. And combined with that 'language of once upon a time' were the childhood memories of playing on the shore below Ardtur, scudding between islands in her uncles' boats, aware always of the power of the winds and the weather, reinforced with the Gaelic heard in harbours, in the Ardtur kitchen, in the streets of Oban. In his book *Musicophilia*, Oliver Sachs remarked on the extraordinary tenacity of musical memory, speculating that 'so much of what is heard during one's early years may be "engraved" on the brain for the rest of one's life'.[4]

Héloïse's earliest musical memories then, with the imprinted sounds, sensations and security of childhood, had been struggling perhaps for sustenance while she was so far from home. She had explored parts of the United States, had ventured to Mexico where she had been pulled unceremoniously from a train for not having the right papers, had been teased by hotel staff in Virginia for always bringing wild flowers to her table in the evening; but she did not seem ever to have felt comfortably settled. Even while the harp stood stringless in her studio, she imbued it with character, naming it 'Harplet' and establishing a loyalty to this inanimate soulmate that would stand beside her throughout her life. Its sheer presence triggered an epiphany, established a sudden realisation of what she must do. She wrote:

> Fortunately for me there was no interruption that night. Keeping the chord under my still hands, I came slowly and reluctantly back to the studio. Was I not in America? But that music! It was everywhere. I must tell the whole world about a great vanishing art. And these people in the new world kindly they helped and encouraged me! The call of the Hebrides became increasingly strong. My American friends deeply appreciated the small repertoire I had collected. When asked out to parties, 'Harplet' was always invited too.

By the mid-1920s, published and recorded Gaelic songs and music from the Hebrides were readily available thanks to the work of collectors such as Frances Tolmie and Marjory Kennedy-Fraser. Indeed, Kennedy-Fraser and her daughter Patuffa had performed in New York in 1916, with a programme drawn from Kennedy-Fraser's collected *Songs of the Hebrides* from which Héloïse drew her early repertoire.

Her teacher was Mildred Dilling, an American harpist just two years older than herself who had already performed in Europe and

---

4   Oliver Sacks, *Musicophilia* (London: Picador, 2008), p. xii.

a few years later, would coach 'Harpo' Marx. Significantly, Mildred was also a devout Christian Scientist. She not only taught Héloïse the techniques of harp playing; she reinforced the powerful spiritual impact that the clarsach had already made on her. In an undated speech that she made to students at the Principia College for Christian Scientists, Mildred had noted that there are '13 places in the Bible where one is admonished to praise the Lord with the harp'. Then, showing the students an early African harp, she had said, 'There has been a lot of talk about turning swords into plowshares but some credit should go to that primitive man who turned his lethal weapon, the bow, into a harp which has been one of mankind's pleasures ever since …'[5]

With Mildred's tuition and encouragement, a basic repertoire and a sense of spiritual purpose, Héloïse and Harplet soon ventured beyond Washington to perform in New York. Margaret Fay Shaw, a young American already interested in the songs of Marjory Kennedy-Fraser and who would later become a dedicated Scottish folklorist, noted their meeting in her autobiography. She told of introducing Héloïse to a Scot whom she herself had met in the city only a few months earlier, hoping that he might teach her Gaelic. The man claimed to be the Chief of Clan Fergus of Strachur. He was 'wearing a kilt and a sort of military jacket and a great leather belt with a very handsome silver buckle. He had a bonnet with eagle-feathers and a dirk in his stocking. His cape was thrown open and his hair hung in rat-tails around his collar.' Shaw wrote that Héloïse had been 'thrilled to meet the man she took to be the chief of her clan and told him she hoped he would come to the concert. And so he did, but she got the bill for the box he had taken!'[6]

---

5   Utah, Harold B. Lee Library (HLL), Betty Bradley Papers on Mildred Dilling, MSS 7813.
6   Margaret Fay Shaw, *The Alleghenies to the Hebrides* (Edinburgh: Birlinn, 2008), pp. 37–38.

There was nothing amongst Héloïse's memorabilia about this encounter but I could understand the lure of meeting someone with family links to Strachur. I had gone there myself to look for Glenbranter, the remote glen above Strachur where our Ferguson forebears had been weavers. Making a detour on the way to meet Russell cousins in Knapdale, I pulled off the road and tramped for a while through brackened woodland on a fine burnished autumn afternoon, the turning leaves fluttering softly around me. Eventually, finding nothing that hinted of Fergusons, no swashbuckling men with bare knees and eagle feathers in their bonnets, no lichen covered remains of abandoned dwellings to prompt a deep melancholy nor even the rough edge of an eighteenth century button catching my eye amongst the leaves; and aware of the miles still to travel, I squatted to pee below a colossal beech tree, trusting that my DNA would refresh the many generations of Ferguson legacies that lay deep under the soil. Then I got back in the car and headed on my way.

It is impossible to tell the extent to which shared Christian Science beliefs cemented the friendship between Mildred and Héloïse but it is clear that Mildred gave her a great deal of support, indeed egged her on to pursue her new dream. Héloïse wrote later:

> Greatly excited by the songs, she (Mildred) advised me to present them in London as soon as possible. Still practising for my debut as a pianist, I was uncertain of taking the risk. The harpist immediately volunteered to share the programme. So I bade farewell to America and sailed for Europe. I was on the threshold of my career!

Returning to Scotland, Héloïse wanted to immerse herself immediately in the traditional music of the Hebrides. Travelling from Oban in a small steamer, she headed first to Barra, one of the southernmost islands of the Outer Hebrides, to meet Annie Johnston, the school teacher at

Castlebay and a well-known and highly regarded proponent of Gaelic language and culture. Héloïse wrote:

> Annie I found the most kind and congenial companion and the two of us often sallied on picnics, usually taking a large black kettle. She had songs for every occasion including a lilt to help the kettle boil. Few people have done more to foster the Gaelic language and no summer school at which it is taught would be complete without her presence. I found her a mine of information on Hebridean lore. She calls all the months of the year by colours, according to the periods in which the various flowers bloom. May is the white month, July the yellow, and August the purple.

Murdoch Morrison, the postmaster at Castlebay also taught her a traditional song, 'The Feather in the Cockerel's Tail', and later, on reaching Eriskay, she noted joyfully that, 'songs as well as stamps are supplied at the post office'. Around twenty years earlier, Marjory Kennedy-Fraser had visited Eriskay and learned songs from Duguld MacMillan the postmaster there when she was criss-crossing the Hebrides and recording songs which she would later perform with clarsach accompaniment and also publish. Kennedy-Fraser received considerable acclaim for her work at the time but was criticised too, and still is in some quarters for taking liberties in her efforts to translate the Gaelic into English and for corrupting their authenticity. But in the mid-1920s and new to the field, Héloïse was most probably oblivious to that debate and, as a newcomer to the clarsach, Kennedy-Fraser's published work certainly gave her somewhere to start.

Although Harplet was in her luggage, she mentioned the clarsach only once, when it might have been endangered crossing 'the great ford' between South Uist and Benbecula:

> Continuing north, I crossed the shifting sands of the great ford. This remarkable passage, which at high tide is a waste of raging seas, can be crossed at low tide on miles of sands. The driver of the waggonette was a well-known character in the Isles. I perched beside him on the box.

Harplet rested inside. Crossing a deep channel, the water rose until it was
up to the seats. It came swirling within two inches of the precious harp.
At another point we came across a tern, busily breakfasting off sandworms.
My driver swept off his hat, 'Good morning, Tern,' and he bowed low
from the box. 'I greet him every morning,' he explained to me.

Héloïse had a stout history of sailing on turbulent waters and of
tramping across sodden hillsides in inhospitable weather and she was a
contented and capable lone traveller. Moreover, she would have found
that the islanders were accustomed to visitors from the mainland
who were curious about their culture and traditions. In Ireland, and
then in Scotland a Celtic Revival had been in full swing since the
mid-nineteenth century, a variously political, cultural and linguistic
movement, promoting Celtic art and literature, infused often with
a romantic longing for a pure and innocent past and characterised
sometimes by a 'racial type'; in this case, the Gael, who appeared to
represent a glorious mix of stoicism, humility and courage with an
intuitive, almost mystical link to the natural world. Héloïse threw
herself into sharing in as many aspects of day to day Hebridean life as
she could, mostly outdoors:

> I watched the seals and crept out onto high ledges to observe the sea
> birds. I saw the wild geese brought back in boatloads from the northerly
> skerries, afterwards to be salted for winter menus. I helped stir the crotal
> dye in black pots on the hillsides and fished for spouties in the sands
> at low tide, digging my hand in, fingers first then giving a twist and
> drawing the long creatures out.

Stormbound and waiting for a late boat one evening, she fell into
conversation with a young man about the same age as herself. Héloïse
noted in her 1939 account:

> He was Mr Arthur Geddes ... author of the well-known book '*The Spirit
> of the Tartan*'. A great authority on our national dress, Mr Geddes has
> also done a lot for Hebridean music, especially the songs of the island of

Eriskay. We sat far into the night discoursing on tweed by candle-light. He showed me how the kilt was worn in bygone days. It was belted not pleated.

Arthur was the son of Patrick Geddes, the now legendary sociologist, ecologist and town planner whose work had influenced others quite profoundly both in Europe and in India where he had a close working relationship with the Bengali poet Rabindranath Tagore. Arthur had studied Tagore's work for his PhD, spending time with the poet, translating some of his work and accompanying some of his songs with the violin.

I pored over a copy of Arthur's translations of Tagore songs, trying to resist creating fantasies about this later meeting with Héloïse. After all, she had only alluded to Arthur's music yet I imagined him lifting his violin to play a snatch of a Tagore song, evoking a romantic similarity to the Gaelic songs they were hearing. Perhaps they discussed Tagore's spirituality; his poetry and music, his compassion, the reach of his influence. There was also the rather mind boggling candlelit demonstration of kilt wearing too, wrapping and unwrapping, belting and unbelting. In 1932, Arthur would write *The Spirit of the Tartan: a Song-Drama of the Gael* and later still, Héloïse would develop a kind of 'song-drama of the Gael' herself. Meanwhile, there seemed little harm in imagining the two of them quite delighted with each other's company, waiting for the storm to subside.

On Berneray, she found Seton and Audrey Gordon camping close to the water's edge, he a naturalist and ornithologist, she a photographer. The weather was appalling. Héloïse squelched across boggy terrain with them, knee deep in heather and with little shelter from the driving wind and rain, listening for corncrakes and wheatears. She crouched on the shore with Audrey, waiting silently for what seemed hours, to photograph porpoises and dolphins. At times, they took refuge in Héloïse's lodgings, hanging their dripping coats and hats in the porch, peeling off their socks to dry their feet before the fire. A musician himself, Seton was as curious about the traditions and the music of the Hebrides as he was about the wildlife. They would all meet again in musical settings.

The Reverend Kenneth MacLeod lived on the small island of Gigha. He had collaborated extensively with Kennedy-Fraser, helping to translate the Gaelic and developing many of the musical arrangements that would appear in her volumes of *Songs of the Hebrides* from which Héloïse would build much of her repertoire. Héloïse had been thrilled to meet him:

> It was worth visiting the islands alone to meet Dr Kenneth MacLeod.
> He gave me a unique collection of beautiful lilts and has been my
> inspiration and encouragement ever since. A very retiring man
> ordinarily, he has an absolute genius for the sound of words, and
> Hebrideans owe him a debt which can never be repaid. I was kept busy
> for days writing down the many songs which poured forth from him in
> a never ending stream.

Within the trolley load of archive boxes in the Mitchell Library I found a large brown envelope stuffed with loose leaves of paper, scribbled notes on the backs of envelopes, hasty jottings, questions to self, myriad references to sources and individuals that all seemed to stem from this visit to MacLeod. Not all of the handwriting was the same, and some of it was in Gaelic. There were words for songs too, rough notations of music, and what seemed to be the beginnings of reference system.

On a piece of paper headed, 'Circumstances of Noting', Héloïse described sitting in MacLeod's house one afternoon 'busy with words and songs' when he went to the kitchen to make them some tea, humming a tune. She asked him to sing the words but he denied knowing them. She reminded him that they were published in *Songs of the Hebrides* and started singing them herself but instead of picking up the song, he began another tune, 'one of Kirsty's,' he had said, describing it as being about 'an uncanny woman flying about looking for a good glen to settle in'. Héloïse wrote, 'I laughed and laughed … He looks so elfin on these occasions. One could almost expect a large uncanny woman to come flapping into the room!' Much later in my research, I would sit in the library beside a Gaelic singer as she pored over the scattered papers from this box, scrutinising the music, cross-referring, humming quietly to herself, beginning to make sense of it. That big brown envelope seemed to hold a story all of its own.

Finally, tired but possibly more relaxed and happy than she'd ever felt in America, Héloïse boarded the boat back to Oban. Her head birled with all that she'd seen and heard but a plan was emerging. She would take her professional lead from Kennedy-Fraser and put her musical talents, together with that profound and comforting sense of connection to the Hebrides, to good use: she would actively promote the music and the culture of the islands.

Her time in America had been spent, at least in part, trying to escape the commercial pressures of the early twentieth century that she had met on arrival in the Pennsylvania Hotel in New York; the brash, overt pressures to buy, to consume, to be a certain sort of person; to fit in. If she had to fit anywhere, the legacy of the Celtic Revivalists, who had craved a kind of spiritual reconnection with lives and language uncontaminated by the vagaries and vulgarities of the encroaching industrial world, seemed much more attractive.

CHAPTER FIVE

ARGYLL

As Héloïse was leaving for America in 1923, the Ardtur Estate Company bought Muckairn Castle near Taynuilt. It stood about twenty miles from Port Appin on a hillside promontory overlooking Loch Etive and the family had rented it, perhaps alternately with Ardtur, since at least 1904.

Built in 1897 by John Stuart McCaig, the early photographs show a large, plain house which William planned to transform to live up to its castle name. As a child, I was told that he had bought Muckairn because the last leg of his journey from Glasgow through Taynuilt to Port Appin became too arduous as his mobility difficulties increased. As I got older, I heard hints that he preferred the easy company of the nurses who looked after him at Muckairn to Hélène's rather grim work ethic at Ardtur. There may be truth in both stories but old photo albums are stuffed with pictures of cheery young relatives paddling, picnicking and visiting both Ardtur and Muckairn from 1904 well into the 1920s. Although Hélène's brothers had moved to England to find work, their passion for sailing brought them to Argyll as often as they could manage and despite Hélène and William appearing to live apart, there was no rift so serious to stop her family from spending time at Muckairn.

I have in my porch a sturdy, glass fronted, rectangular wooden box that houses the remaining mechanism for the twenty four bells that would have hung in the kitchen at Muckairn to summon the

49

servants. Each bell has its own little window through which I can see the faded red candy striped flag of fabric that would have danced when the bell was pulled. Each window is framed and labelled in gold. The labels correspond to the front and back entrances, to nine bedrooms, a boudoir, a dressing room, a smoking room, a dining room, a drawing room and two bathrooms. There is also a suite of rooms, presumably downstairs, labelled nurse's room, Mr Ferguson's bedroom, his personal sitting room and his bathroom. William proposed to live comfortably and in some style. Correspondence in the Barclay, Curle & Co. archive in the Mitchell Library shows that William habitually used the surname Ferguson for professional correspondence, suggesting, perhaps, that the marital decision to double barrel their names and to double the 's' in Fergusson, was largely down to Hélène.

While he was planning the refurbishment of Muckairn Castle, Hélène was struggling to keep the home farm at Ardtur viable. She was acutely aware of business fragility and of the challenges of maintaining a family income. Her father had clung to the trappings of wealth while his interests in the Saracen Ironworks were being seriously undermined by his former partner, and he had refused stubbornly to acknowledge that he could no longer afford the opulence with which he had surrounded himself at Cleveden in Glasgow. Since his death in 1911, Hélène had witnessed the continuing impact of this on her mother, who had fled eventually to live with her sisters at their guesthouse in Southsea. Muckairn Castle would surely be a drain on the family. William had virtually retired from Barclay, Curle & Co. They had a son yet to finish his apprenticeship and three unmarried daughters.

Making Ardtur productive must have seemed paramount. An outbreak of foot and mouth disease in 1924 had led the Scottish Pig Breeders' Association to cancel their spring show and sale which must have been a disappointment. Hélène had invested in a bacon factory in Stirling but it failed somehow to get the Ministry of Agriculture assistance that was available to similar initiatives.

Arguably, she shouldn't have worried too much about the grown up children for they were an independent bunch. Now fluent in French, Donald was working hard in Le Havre with the Compagnie Générale Transatlantique; Margie, although details are scant, seemed to prefer a modest lifestyle and was committed to working with the land; and Héloïse was determinedly pursuing a professional career as a musician and a music teacher. Denise, of course, was still a child.

———————

By the late 1920s, Héloïse had begun to venture into Europe with Harplet, keen both to perform her new repertoire and to learn about other forms of traditional music. On stage, she adopted a romantic Celtic persona, wearing a white silk robe reaching to the floor. As she raised her arms to play, the silk sleeves slipped back to reveal red velvet undersleeves. The robe was gathered at the waist with a slim leather belt threaded with lozenge shaped metal studs; on her shoes were embroidered Celtic symbols to illustrate the undying nature of the music. Before each song, she gave audiences a short description of what they would hear, determined that they should understand her rapture for the Hebrides and its precious culture and language. That meant learning enough of the language wherever she went, to make herself understood. She described her nerves before introducing a concert in Holland:

> It occurred to me that in presenting Gaelic songs to Dutch audiences, some descriptive remarks would be needed. I resolved to speak them myself. Could it be carried out? The hall was full. On the platform my chair was ready. In the artistes' room, surrounded by a number of excited Dutch people, I clung to my papers. Would I remember all these curious syllables? Firmly resolved, I left the notes on the table and ascended to the platform. An introduction in Dutch came first. Trembling I opened my mouth. Studying the audience, I saw their blank expressions change gradually to those of surprise and finally, understanding.

Flushed with this success she went on to learn enough German, Italian and Finnish to introduce the Hebridean scene for future audiences. It served her well. Having arrived one bitterly cold evening at the port of Åbo in Finland, she was crossing slippery cobbles in the dark to find her train to Helsingfors, when two women journalists approached her for an interview. Blue with cold, Héloïse described the three of them leaning against the wind and wrestling to communicate in English. Then:

> Suddenly I remembered. My Finnish! Learned with such labour over many weeks. I could practise on them. I started. The effect was magical. They produced fat notebooks and started to scribble. When I reached Helsingfors a few hours later, my patrons knew all about me. More had arrived at the station as it was said I spoke fluent Finnish! This was a good compliment to my poor efforts and a good beginning to an altogether delightful trip.

During one recital in Finland she observed Otto Andersson, newly appointed as the first professor of musicology and folklore at Åbo Akademi, sitting in the audience with his head bowed. She feared he had fallen asleep but it emerged that he had been taking meticulous notes and sought her out afterwards to sit talking late into the night. Although not an academic herself, she was discovering the extent to which traditional music and culture was the subject of academic study in other countries. Some years later, she was given a book inscribed to her 'with best compliments from the author' by Armas Otto Väisänen, who from 1926 had been head of the folk music department at the Sibelius Academy and would become professor of musicology at the University of Helsinki thirty years later.

Written in 1935, the book was about the Ob-Ugrian Harp. Along with an English translation, it is lodged in her archive at the Mitchell Library. The traditional religion of the Ob-Ugrian people, who lived somewhere between Finland and Russia, was based on animism and shamanism; the shamans used either drums or the *sangultap* or *shangur* which resembled a lyre, to call out the spirits. Héloïse's fascination with such deep rooted connections between music, spirituality and the natural world would emerge again and again throughout her story.

In 1929 she visited a number of German universities. She wrote later:

'Harplet' held court in the artistes' rooms where one evening a well-known German professor was even seen to hug him! I appeared twice at Berlin University during the course of a year. But the most pleasant memory I have of my visit to Germany was of the gay parties I attended after my concerts. My harp and I were invariably carried off to some restaurant by the professors and students where we drank beer (as everybody does in Germany), sang and talked far into the night.

I like this snapshot of a lively young woman, her sociability, her readiness to be 'carried off' and enter into the spirit of the occasion. And it seemed that the German public had liked her too. Reviews she saved from *Allgemeine Musikzeitung*, *Berliner Musikbrief*, *Germania* and the *Berliner Borsenzeitung* all praised her 'little harp', played to good effect.

Alongside the language learning, she developed another habit that would persist. Wherever possible, she visited local museums looking for the cultural contexts of indigenous music. Her persistence seemed to have been irresistible. Not only was she allowed to rummage in storerooms and take photographs but she struck up relationships which continued to enrich her knowledge. She was finding harps and harp-like instruments from different historical periods that reflected differing cultures and practices yet were all underpinned by something universal; the human compulsion to respond with music to the natural environment and to the social world.

Meanwhile, the alterations and refurbishments at Muckairn Castle had been completed. In March 1926, William hosted a party for the household and invited the local community in Taynuilt to come and celebrate his new home, fully renovated and with the addition of a conical, fairy-tale turret. The depression that was hanging like a pall over the country seemed to have made no noticeable impact on William's plans. Across the country, wages had been slashed, thousands of people had been put out of work and there would be a General Strike just two months later. But William appeared to be completely detached from Barclay, Curle & Co. and his former industrious city life. He and Hélène now lived entirely in Argyll, albeit in different homes and pursuing their independent interests.

Donald, by then working in Greenock, came up to take charge of decorations throughout the house. Crichton came from Ardtur to manage everything else. The ballroom glittered with coloured lights looping from a central chandelier between streamers, balloons and twinkling lanterns. Over a hundred guests danced on the newly laid parquet flooring to the music of Dr McNicol's local band before sitting down to a grand dinner. From his wheelchair at the head of the table, William extended a warm welcome, praising the community of Taynuilt and commending in particular Dr McNicol's support for local music. Peter Bruce, the stationmaster at Connel Ferry proposed William's health, declaring how proud he was to have known William over his twenty-five years of visiting Taynuilt. The speeches ended with Crichton expressing thanks on behalf of the staff for the splendid entertainment. The dancing resumed and 'merriment and laughter', according to a clipping from the *Oban Times*, went on until four o'clock in the morning.

His brother John was there, supporting William along with their sister Marie, but the reported jollity of the evening could not conceal the fact that Hélène, Héloïse and Margie were absent. Possibly, Héloïse was in America, for passenger lists showed me that she docked in Glasgow from New York that year on 20 June, recording her Scottish address as Muckairn Castle. Margie and Hélène may have been visiting the latter's mother, now very frail, in Southsea. Otherwise, if there was little animosity between them, it seems strange that Hélène was not beside William at this celebration of his new home. Perhaps that would have been a step too far.

Stuart Carmichael from Port Appin sent me a cutting from the *Courier and Advertiser* dated 19 November 1926, eight months after the Muckairn party, which reported a meeting in Stirling regarding the Scottish Bacon Curing Factory. It had been presided over by Lord Hamilton of Dalziel with the others present being the shareholders: Mrs Russell-Fergusson, Ardtur and Colonel Hay Drummond, Cromlix. The report noted that the shareholders could not put up the money to save the factory so the liquidator would endeavour to sell it. This provides compelling evidence that Hélène may have resented the expense of Muckairn's transformation, the whole idea of a 'castle' seeming ridiculous. Perhaps it was her frustrated business sense, alongside William's allegedly overly benevolent nurses, which made it impossible for her to stand graciously beside him as he welcomed his guests.

There is one later photograph dated 1927, taken at Muckairn. Entitled 'Oban Ball', it shows Margie and my father with some of their Russell cousins lazing on a garden bench, others perched grinning on a window sill just behind, enjoying the late August sunshine. The only trace of Héloïse that year was a leaflet noting her return from a successful European tour and publicising a recital of 'Hebridean Songs to the Clarsach' at St Andrew's Hall in Glasgow in aid of the Soldiers' and Sailors' Help Society.

A few months after that summer photograph was taken, Dr McNicol certified William's death at Muckairn at 2.30pm, on Monday 19 December 1927, due to a cerebral haemorrhage. He had enjoyed his new home for less than two years. My dad was already at Muckairn that afternoon, just arrived from Greenock perhaps, and planning to spend Christmas with his father. Aged twenty-four, he witnessed the death certificate. The *Oban Times* obituary was bland, recording William's commitment to Barclay, Curle & Co. but nothing about his love of Argyll. At the Barclay, Curle & Co. Directors Meeting of 21 December, the chairman Mr Thirlaway noted William's death in the minutes and spoke of his forty-seven year involvement with the firm, his capacity to build connections with other shipbuilders, his cheery disposition and his great courage, on all occasions, in the face of his physical condition. Condolences were expressed to the family.

So that was William Russell-Fergusson, my grandfather, an educated man, a grafter and a boss on the Clyde, a stoic, seemingly a respecter of independent women, a builder of fairy-tale turrets and, I would discover later, of modernist architecture. He died when his eldest daughter Héloïse was thirty-one, twenty-five years before I was born.

And the bell box from Muckairn Castle? It is in my house due to the kind of coincidence that occurred more than once during this search for Héloïse's story. I met a new work colleague who travelled from Taynuilt, over seventy miles away and for a while she lodged with me during the week, before she got a job closer to home. We became good friends, and in 2005, I went to visit her family and told them about my link with Muckairn. They brought me up to date. The house and estate had been bought by an American woman who was rarely there, was indeed absent that weekend, who kept the estate cottages empty and who, in the eyes of many local people, had failed to manage the land as they would have wished; they would have preferred a more informed and engaged owner with an evident active and benign interest in the community. Over a very good supper and several bottles of wine, we talked long into the night. Had we the money, we decided, we would buy Muckairn, restore good quality housing and set up a not-for-profit conference and retreat centre devoted to promoting social justice.

Following a too early breakfast the next morning, my friends left for work and I drove down the single track road from their house, heading for home. My head was full of our conversation from the night before, the possibility of creating new ventures in old places, about William with his fairy-tale turret, my father up a ladder stringing coloured lights, the craziness of it all. What were the cottages like when William was running the place? Was his ownership benign? He had certainly thrown a party. I felt compelled to swing off the main road and took my car crawling up the bumpy track towards Muckairn.

It was a glorious April morning, barely nine o'clock. A young deer lifted its head to look at me from behind the trees, the newly greening woodland and mossy undergrowth dappled by sunlight. I passed two overgrown and tumbledown cottages before the track rose towards the big house, set above Loch Etive. Driving cautiously round the back and finding no cars, I drove back to the front and parked. No one was at home. I stepped onto the damp grass in front of the curved driveway. A dilapidated wooden garden seat overlooked the dazzling cerulean blue of Loch Etive, stretched out far below. The sky was cloudless; the morning air, crisp and clean with just a hint of early warmth to come. I lowered myself onto the seat, enchanted. William and Hélène had surely sat there together, at least in the early days, washed with joy at the beauty of it all, watching their children run down to the woodland amongst the emerging daffodils.

My reverie was interrupted by a sharp noise. Someone was opening the heavy door of the house behind me. A small upright figure stood framed on the doorstep, the interior impenetrably dark behind her. I rose and walked awkwardly towards where she stood. Understandably, the American, for it was her, was concerned about this stranger on her property. I offered a weak explanation, an apology. She replied curtly that she had no time to talk for she was leaving shortly and sure enough as I drove away, cheeks blazing with embarrassment, a car came trundling up the track towards the house. When I got home I wrote to her, explaining the family connection and enclosing some old photographs. We had one rather uneasy phone call in which she invited me to visit if I was ever back in Taynuilt. It was kind of her, but something made me reluctant to take up her offer.

Before leaving Taynuilt that day I made another visit. Driving into the village, I detoured to the churchyard and found William's grave in a far corner. His father John Ferguson, a former Provost of Partick, was buried beneath a rather grand memorial on Glasgow's Necropolis beside his mother and three of his siblings but William had preferred, or had been given, this more modest resting place. Beside him, another mossy headstone commemorated his youngest daughter Denise. I stood on the damp grass and thought about the rest of the family. It struck me forcefully that there should be another stone; one that would commemorate Hélène and their children Héloïse, Margie and Donald. Their absence was another reminder of how easily they might disappear from history.

Fired by the importance of preserving family memory and a warming sense of my own benevolence, I drove into Oban. A couple of enquiries led me to a stonemason's yard in an industrial estate where I sat down to explain what I wanted. Within minutes, I realised I had been too hasty. The Russell-Fergusson name unrolled languidly before me, popping my balloon of enthusiasm. Stone masonry inscriptions are costed per letter. The combined four names were just short of a hundred letters. That was without their dates, without any commemorative remarks and without the cost of a piece of stone to write them on. Not to mention the possible costs of negotiating a space beside William and Denise from the Church or from the local Council. I swallowed hard at the fruit machine figures clocking up behind my eyes, thanked the stonemason for his time and got back in the car, chastising myself for being so cocksure, for such ridiculous romance.

Shortly after our awkward encounter, the American sold Muckairn Castle. Before she left, she arranged for the bell box to be delivered to my friends in Taynuilt asking that it be passed on to me. I would never know what she saw in Muckairn nor why her occupancy seemed so tenuous but I was grateful for the box; a thoughtful gift, a hint that she cared more than we knew about the history of the property that she had inhabited so briefly. Unsurprisingly, and despite the house coming onto the market, our inebriated enthusiasm to start a twenty-first century ethical business there never quite got off the ground.

William had been as devoted to Muckairn as Hélène was to Ardtur. Photographs show a long and happy family connection with the house and, in his will, he had declared:

> It is my wish that the Estate of Fearnoch and Muckairn which is the property of the Ardtur Estate Company be retained as a residence for my wife and family so long as any member of the family continues to reside in Scotland and that if, at the date of my death, the family do not wish to reside in said Estate, the Estate be let in order that, at a later date, the family or any of them, may have the opportunity of residing there if they so desire but without prejudice to my Trustees agreeing to a sale of said Estate if in their discretion they consider it advisable to do so ...

Despite these clearly elaborated wishes, the year after he died, Muckairn Castle was sold. My father was one of the Trustees along with his mother and three of his male Ferguson cousins. I wondered whether he might have wanted to keep it and was outvoted. Despite the sumptuous renovations, the property proved difficult to sell. A contemporaneous newspaper cutting headlined 'Going at £14,000 – But No One to Buy!' stated:

> This afternoon, Messrs Knight, Frank & Rutley, auctioneers, offered for sale one of the most beautiful estates in the West Highlands – Muckairn – for the above price, but there were no offers. The estate which is situated three miles from Taynuilt and ten miles from Oban, has a beautiful residence – modernised as recently as 1926 – standing near the shore of Loch Etive. The castle has an electric installation probably unequalled in any private residence in Scotland. The estate extends to 1,710 acres, and includes a considerable shooting area together with trout and sea fishing.

For his children, William had set up a Trust Fund invested loyally in War Stock. It would provide Héloïse with a small but regular source of income, and she seemed more determined than ever to pursue her professional path.

Chapter Six

The Clarsach

Mildred Dilling, the American harpist, was true to her word. She arrived in Scotland in the autumn of 1928 and performed with Héloïse and a cellist called Edwin Angless at Glasgow's McLellan Galleries. Héloïse sang a selection from *Songs of the Hebrides*, two of which included '*cello obligati* drawn by permission from Mrs Kennedy-Fraser's musical settings by H. Russell-Fergusson' and Mildred played two sets of harp solos. Although they gave only one concert there were three versions of the programme or, more correctly, three versions of the programme's cover.

The programme contents were identical; four pages of song words and two pages of advertisements. Each cover was printed with the title, *Songs of the Hebrides*, and it named the performers along with the date, time and venue. But each was decorated with a different and distinctly amateurish hand drawn illustration. On one a Celtic cross, on another a Celtic brooch and on the third, a row of three small Celtic symbols: a spiral, a cup and ring and a petrosomatoglyph, a pair of small footprints; all ancient symbols that can be found carved into rocks in various parts of Scotland including Dunadd near Kilmartin in Argyll, the capital of the Scottish kingdom of Dalriada in 500AD.

I am sure Héloïse had added these last minute drawings. Bent over a desk somewhere and probably in a rush, copying the images from a book just before the programmes went to be printed, she was determined the audience would carry home not just their memories of the music but some lasting visual reminders of its spiritual and cultural symbolism. The images tallied with descriptions of the Celtic symbols embroidered on her slippers and reminded me of those that I had seen stitched haphazardly onto Harplet's cloth bag in Glasgow Museums Resource Centre. The programmes had not been tucked away in the memorabilia box but had arrived on my desk via an email from Utah.[7] Mildred Dilling had taken all three of the programmes home with her, mementoes of her visit to Scotland.

The *Glasgow Herald* reviewer had not been impressed by the concert and saw the cello as surplus to requirements. Héloïse's voice 'lacked a variety of colour … to suggest really deep feelings' and there was only grudging acknowledgement that Mildred's solos 'held technique and artistry despite … the harp as a solo instrument … never having attracted the great composers'. It was not an auspicious beginning. Around three weeks later on 25 October, they performed at the Grotrian Hall in London. The *Times* reviewer, also confused by the presence of a cello, offered double edged compliments:

> The songs which Mrs Kennedy-Fraser had collected from the Hebrides exhale their sea-soaked atmosphere at any time and in any place. Miss Russell-Fergusson has the advantage – and strictly for this purpose alone it is an advantage – of not being a trained singer. She sings well all the same, so long as some extra-long phrase does not find out the limits of her technique. The simplicity of natural singing is the right medium for these magical folk-songs and when they are accompanied on the harp the illusion is made so complete that not even a *violincello obligato*, which adds greatly to the effect, can destroy it. A bass note on the harp, the bottom notes of the *violincello*, as in 'A Coastwise Song', from Lewis – and we hear the Atlantic booming outside in Wigmore Street. Miss Mildred Dilling plays not only the Celtic harp but the big modern instrument and plays them both extraordinarily well, with all the variety of tone colour which the somewhat limited character of the harp as such permits.

7   HLL, MSS 7813.

I suspect Héloïse was thrilled to share a platform with Mildred. Nevertheless, it was a little surprising that despite having already sung and played with Harplet in America and in Europe, she confined herself to singing, for Mildred undertook the entire accompaniment, playing clarsach as well as harp. Was it lack of confidence or respect for her mentor that led Héloïse to pass Harplet to Mildred, I wondered. Or had Mildred insisted?

The following year, Mildred was back in the UK where she and Héloïse played at a much more parochial event which sounded rather like a benefit concert for a friend. Held in Devizes in Wiltshire, the local *Western Daily Press* of 12 September 1929 noted that:

> A recital was given at the Town Hall, Devizes, on Tuesday by Miss Mildred Dilling harpist and Miss Russell-Fergusson. The latter sang folk songs. The recital was arranged by Mrs Thompson of Eastbourne House, Devizes in aid of the funds for the National Lifeboat Institution but the audiences were not large. The artistes were presented with bouquets by Mrs Thompson's children.

After that, all public trace of Héloïse's links with Mildred fizzled out.

In 1920s Europe, Héloïse had learned about the extensive collecting of folklore and of traditional songs and she must have been curious about the parallels to be found in Scotland. Although there had been academic courses in Celtic studies at the Universities of Edinburgh and Glasgow for some time, usually in combination with other subjects such as classics (Edinburgh) or theology (Glasgow), students were likely to study medieval rather than contemporary Gaelic texts, and folklore and music did not seem to be part of the syllabus. It would not be until 1947 that the Folklore Institute of Scotland, which transformed fairly rapidly into the School of Scottish Studies, was set up to bring some rigour to the collection, classification and preservation of traditional music and song.

Nevertheless, in 1891, an organisation called An Comunn Gàid-healach had been set up in Oban, devoted to the preservation and development of the Gaelic language. The following year, it founded a Gaelic Festival called the Mòd, modelled on the Welsh Eisteddfod and which would continue on an annual basis. It also promoted the Gaelic teaching and summer schools that Héloïse learned about from Annie Johnston in the mid-1920s. I wonder how Héloïse felt about her own knowledge and use of the language. Although she had that almost immersive grounding in her early years and the continuous association with Argyll she was not a native speaker and had not lived her life entirely within a Gaelic language and cultural embrace. Indeed, with her Gaelic repertoire drawn largely from Kennedy-Fraser, might she have been seen as, or felt herself to be, something of an outsider, an intruder even?

Even as I speculate, I wonder whether I am in danger of projecting my own feelings onto her, of being oversensitive about where she 'fitted' within Scotland's cultural context. She was simply absorbing new learning about the Hebrides into a personal mix of Gaelic influenced early years, her formal musical training and the intensity of her experience in America, much of which had been overshadowed by war and by living far from home.

Nevertheless, she had walked into an arena that was becoming something of a lion's den. Just as her interest in the clarsach was emerging, the powerful and romantic Celtic Revival period that had bridged the turn of the century had dissipated. By the 1920s the 'collecting' of Gaelic songs and their popular arrangement and performance, particularly by Marjory Kennedy-Fraser, was being challenged by critics who both scorned the dewy romance of the Celtic Revival and questioned the authenticity of such published music.

The argument was well illustrated by a public spat in 1926 between Christopher Grieve, the poet better known by his pen name, Hugh MacDiarmid, and Hugh Roberton, composer and conductor of the

Glasgow Orpheus Choir. Roberton had written enthusiastically about Kennedy-Fraser's work in the *People's Journal* magazine, asserting:

> Many of these Hebridean songs fall easily within the category of 'great'. That they are not all exactly as they fell from the lips of the people is not the sound argument many well-meaning Gaels think it is. … Kennedy-Fraser has done what only a fine artist can do. She has put the songs into what seems to her … the most artistic and permanent form.

Grieve responded in an essay published in *Contemporary Scottish Studies*, sneering first at Roberton's choice of publication and then quoting the article at length so that he might demolish it. In a systematic dissection of the inadequacies of Kennedy-Fraser's work, he invoked Bela Bartok's painstaking approach to collecting folk songs from Hungary, Romania and Slovakia, compared to which he regarded Kennedy-Fraser's efforts as 'a capitulation'. To call her work 'Hebridean', Grieve wrote, 'is misleading and unwarrantable and that … if, through it, "the name of Scotland is carried furth of Scotland and honoured" [as Roberton had stated], Scotland is accepting bouquets on false pretences'. He concluded that if a musical work was to be put forward as being of national significance and permanent artistic value, it must be '… capable of appealing to men as well as to seals, and dependent upon something of more consequence than scarlet robes for its vogue'.[8]

Kenneth MacLeod, who had sung to Héloïse in his Gigha kitchen, did not escape criticism either. Some suggested that in collaborating with Kennedy-Fraser he supported the bowdlerising of traditional Gaelic songs, had revelled too readily in romance and had been perhaps rather too taken with the associated publicity and acclaim.

It is impossible to know whether Héloïse was aware of these rumblings. Buying the clarsach in Washington and visiting the Hebrides

---

8   C.M. Grieve, *Contemporary Scottish Studies: First Series* (London: Leonard Parsons, 1926), pp. 274–281.

seemed to have been impetuous personal acts. If her journey to the Hebrides had been a quest for affirmation and a sense of belonging, then she had been richly rewarded by the beauty and challenge of the landscape, by the friendly reception she had received from people like Annie Johnston and Kenneth MacLeod and by the Gaelic language and the music that she absorbed there. She was not an ethnographer but she was drawn to the culture and history that were entangled with the songs, by the lived experience in the Hebrides and by the stories behind the music. And like Kennedy-Fraser before her, as a trained musician she was intrigued by the complexity of what she was hearing.

The first volume of *Songs of the Hebrides* contained an extensive introduction in which Kennedy-Fraser acknowledged that there could be several versions of the same song. She urged that when selecting a song, 'we should be careful to perpetuate the most strongly characteristic, the most faithful to the type, and to reject such as are at variance with the modal character of the air'. She aimed, she wrote, to bring many songs 'within the reach of singers who are accustomed to the support of pianoforte accompaniment and who, if they will learn to pronounce the original Gaelic, will find themselves amply repaid for their trouble'.[9]

In her efforts to be rigorous in choosing songs that she regarded as 'faithful' to the type, while trying at the same time to bring them 'within reach' of non-Gaelic speaking pianists, Kennedy-Fraser had set herself a seemingly impossible challenge; and a rod for her own back.

But to Héloïse, in the early stages of getting to grips with her clarsach and her own understanding of Gaelic language and culture, the volume must have seemed invaluable. The introduction was followed by a section entitled 'The Hebridean Scales' in which Kennedy-Fraser detailed her analyses of the music. It spoke to Héloïse not only as a

---

9   Marjory Kennedy-Fraser and Kenneth MacLeod, *Songs of the Hebrides* (London: Boosey & Co., 1909), p. xxi.

musician with a classical training but in a voice that was as enchanted by the Hebrides as she was. Perhaps also, the publication spoke to her as a woman, for that first volume of *Songs of the Hebrides* opened with a significant dedication from Kennedy-Fraser:

> To the women of the Hebrides, who were not only skilled in the spinning and weaving of fine linen and in the curious arts of the dyer, but who sang at their work and, singing, fashioned for themselves songs that are as rich in colour as the wools they steeped in lichen and heather, and as curious in construction as the tartans they designed – subtle too, at times as the interlacements of Celtic illuminative art – this attempt to preserve and restore some of their songs is dedicated.[10]

Héloïse was not entirely in thrall to the Hebrides during this period, nor did she restrict her professional activity to Scotland. Her love of the piano and her grounding in the wider world of classical music provided other opportunities. In her series written for the *People's Journal* in 1938–1939, she mentioned her debut piano recital in October 1928 with an orchestra conducted by Malcolm Sargent. And on 7 February 1929, under the auspices of the Guild of Singers and Players and billing herself as Héloïse Russell, she gave a piano recital at the Aeolian Hall in Bond Street, assisted by the Guild String Chamber Orchestra, conducted by John Barbirolli. She played Mozart's Suite for Strings (arranged by Barbirolli), Bach's Concerto for Piano and Strings in D Minor, Ernest Bloch's Concerto Grosso for Piano and Strings and Julius Harrison's Prelude Music for Piano and Strings, Op.16 (1912); this last composed originally for harp and string quartet.

The Guild had been set up after the war by baritone John Goss as a cooperative effort by artists to promote unusual concerts and help young composers and performers. Barbirolli, who had left the Royal Academy of Music just as Héloïse arrived, had helped to set up the

---

10 Kennedy-Fraser and MacLeod.

associated Chamber Orchestra which he later described as his 'first professional effort' as a conductor. The programme noted that Héloïse's next London appearance would be at the Wigmore Hall when she would be accompanied by two other Guild members: a singer called Sinclair Logan, and Marie Dare, on cello.

A little younger than Héloïse, Marie Dare was from Fife, and she had also studied music in London. At the Guildhall School of Music she had been an outstanding student, winning the instrumentalists' gold medal, prizes for composition and performing in 1918 as a young soloist at the Victory Concert in the Royal Albert Hall. Perhaps this concert at the Guildhall was their first performance together but it would not be their last. To Marie and Héloïse, the blend of cello and clarsach which had so baffled the early reviewers from *The Times* and the *Glasgow Herald*, was compelling, as natural a combination as the wind and the waves. Time and again, they played together. Often described as more retiring than Héloïse, Marie was equally independent and would go on to travel, compose, teach and play throughout a very successful and long professional career.

By April 1929, Héloïse had begun to set out her stall. Billed as Héloïse Russell-Fergusson, she gave another recital at the Grotrian Hall where she sang from *Songs of the Hebrides* to her own piano accompaniment. The *London Musical Courier* reported:

> Being Scottish, she created the right 'atmosphere' and her cultured singing enabled her to make just the right impression. She is a trained musician and a highly accomplished pianist, which help her to give the full musical value to these charming melodies ... and concert givers find her a valuable acquisition.

Advertising her first radio broadcast performance from Glasgow in August 1929, the *Press and Journal* described Héloïse as a new exponent of the clarsach, following Patuffa Kennedy-Fraser, Marjory's daughter, who, now married, was perhaps giving fewer performances.

In February 1930, Héloïse performed in Paris and then Holland where Marie Dare accompanied her on cello along with Rosa Spier, the virtuoso Dutch harpist. In October, she and Harplet were in Berlin with Rachel Neill Fraser, a Scottish contralto, accompanied by Eduard Behm on piano. Rather surprisingly, she also sang that summer without the clarsach in Cornwall, with violinist Sascha Lasserson and the Wadebridge Male Voice Choir and Amateur String Orchestra, raising funds for the Bodmin Hospital and Ambulance Service.

By November 1930, she was in New York at the extraordinary and innovative Barbizon-Plaza Hotel which had just been opened as the first 'music-art residence centre' in the United States with three separate halls for concerts, musicals, recitals, amateur dance and 'dramatic offerings'. It seemed a hugely imaginative undertaking, full of optimism and creativity. The *New York Times* reviewed Héloïse's recital there on 14 November, noting that she played the clarsach accompanied by Edgar Sittig on cello and Salvatore di Stefano on harp. She had, 'disclosed a fresh and authentic character in her native Scottish lilt and croon, as she staged each song with simple but picturesque effect'. Through what routes had Héloïse picked up Edgar and Salvatore? I asked the internet. There was no reply. I learned instead that the Barbizon-Plaza is now owned by Donald Trump.

A little later in Boston, the *Wellesley College News* reported that, 'Miss Russell-Ferguson … has gained for herself on the continent the reputation of a singer of charm and distinction. She will accompany her weird notes and thirteenth century Gaelic songs with her small Celtic harp and cello.' Sadly, no later review told me how the weird notes were received.

Back home and ever keen to ensure audiences had the chance to fully understand the magic of the Hebrides and the cultural context of the songs, she persuaded Kenneth MacLeod to join her at London's Aeolian Hall on 17 February 1931, to 'tell some legends of the Isles'. While *The Times* reported that the Rev. Kenneth MacLeod narrated some legends 'between Miss Russell-Fergusson's songs' it offered no opinion on their impact. Instead the reviewer was absorbed in 'the peculiar beauty' of the Hebridean folk-songs that Héloïse performed that evening, noting that the songs held 'a charm and fragrance suitable to their character', concluding:

> Not for anything in the world should she modify her frank style, but correct breathing would increase her vocal resources which she is artist enough to use to very good purpose. A whole evening of Celtic song with her has no monotony … she brings before us the life of the people in their croons and love songs and the misty sea-soaked atmosphere of the islands in the invocations and legends.

This frank, unaffected singing, albeit lacking in some technical respects, seemed to have characterised her style. An early flyer showed a young Héloïse seated at the piano above snippets from a number of reviews. The *Glasgow Citizen* heard 'qualities of tone and touch which showed a true musical instinct'. *The Scotsman* remarked on her 'easy platform manner' and her 'considerable judgement with respect to expressive values'. The *Glasgow Herald* noted 'a sensitive musical nature'. And a review from the *Daily Telegraph* of a concert at Chelsea Town Hall had enthused, 'Another of her virtues – and virtue it is by reason of its rarity – is the straightforwardness of her treatment.'

Notwithstanding these positive remarks, there remained guarded expectations about traditional Hebridean music. A 1933 review in the *Radio Times* suggested that she made Gaelic singing more acceptable only by 'translating' it for a general audience:

> Many native Celts of Scotland have a style of singing purely their own. Miss Russell-Fergusson, however, has, as it were translated Gaelic singing into international music. That is to say, she sings the lovely melodies of northern and western Scotland in the ordinary accepted manner.

Suggesting that the melodies needed translation to make them accessible would have needled some Scots, but I suspect Héloïse would have argued that she was, at least, providing an important platform for the music.

Certainly, I could find no evidence that she was criticised for her repertoire or cold-shouldered by others interested in protecting Gaelic heritage. On the contrary, quite early in her career, she was acknowledged by James Carmichael Watson, an academic in the world of Celtic studies and the grandson of the pioneering folklorist Alexander Carmichael from Lismore. In 1934, the year before he became a lecturer in Celtic at Glasgow University, Carmichael Watson published a book of the surviving eighteenth century Gaelic songs of Mary MacLeod, the 'poetess of Harris and Skye'. In the preface, his first acknowledgement is of Héloïse Russell-Fergusson 'at whose suggestion [the work] was undertaken'.

I wondered how they became acquainted. Héloïse was not a university student and anyway, James was fourteen years her junior. Perhaps the wider Carmichael Watson family, with Lismore so close to Ardtur, had known and visited Hélène and William, had perhaps influenced young Héloïse's interest in folklore, in Celtic symbolism and in the Gaelic language. And there may have been, even at that time, something about Héloïse's 'frank style' and straightforwardness that impressed young James for it seemed to be mirrored much later in his own preferred manner of communication.

In 2013, Professor Donald E. Meek, in giving the Angus Matheson Memorial Lecture at Glasgow University, described his delight as a student on first reading Watson's work:

> Like his father, he had a great gift for producing crystal-clear editions
> of modern and medieval Gaelic literature, which opened the door
> to understanding for those who genuinely sought enlightenment.
> Indeed, from my own experience, I would go as far as to say that
> James Carmichael Watson was the originator of the 'user-friendly' (as
> distinct from the standard 'user-hostile') edition that modern students
> so urgently needed … and still need today. I will always remember

> my very positive encounter with James Carmichael Watson's 1941
> edition of *Mesca Ulad* ('The Drunkenness of the Ulstermen') when
> I was concluding my Junior Honours year in Glasgow. It was like
> going into a room in which all the lights had been switched on, rather
> than unexpectedly switched off … as was so often the case with such
> editions … which seemed to do all in their (non-electrifying) power to
> discourage and confuse the students.[11]

Indeed, alongside her frank and open performance style, Héloïse's commitment to learn something of the language wherever she performed so that she could contextualise the songs, makes 'user-friendly' a particularly apt description of her approach.

So, the period from the late 1920s to the mid-1930s had been one of professional experimentation for Héloïse; sometimes playing piano, sometimes simply singing, sometimes developing her clarsach skills. In November 1931 she was in Stockholm performing with Harplet at the Music Academy and also at the Grand Hotel as part of the Swedish-American Society's Thanksgiving Party. She wrote that she had met Crown Princess Ingrid who was, 'not only beautiful and charming but keenly interested in my music'.

The previous month, she had been in Dingwall during the national Mòd organised by An Comunn Gàidhealach. That year, while the many competitions were running, a small group of enthusiasts, with the support of the president of An Comunn, established the Clarsach Society with the aim of actively promoting the instrument and encouraging new players. Although she was present at the inauguration, Héloïse did not become a member. All her activity to that point had been independent. She was happy to rehearse and perform with others but mostly such partners seemed transient, leaving her free to travel

---

11 Donald E. Meek, 'Glasgow and the Making of Celtic Studies in Scotland: From Magnus MacLean to Angus Matheson', http://meekwrite.blogspot.co.uk/2013/03/celtic-studies-glasgow-and-making-of.html.

and to follow up any opportunities that caught her eye. I suspect too, that had she joined the Society she might have wanted to be in charge, or at least to be a fully active member. Remaining detached gave her freedom and she would not let anyone down. Nor would she have to toe a line.

It was becoming clear that the clarsach was her instrument of choice. She participated in fundraising concerts for Mòds and some years later, she would donate a clarsach prize, the Scotia Trophy, to the national event. In 1932 she visited the island of Iona with Eleanora Cameron, the Clarsach Society's Vice-President that year, to see a memorial erected to the memory of Marjory Kennedy-Fraser who had died two years earlier. Eleanora had sent Patuffa a postcard, saying that she and Héloïse were enjoying their visit 'beyond words'.[12]

The clarsach was an instrument of some status which had been played throughout Gaelic Scotland, Ireland and Wales in ancient and in medieval times. Players, almost always men, usually enjoyed aristocratic patronage and, as bards, were recognised and highly regarded within cultural life. For a while, its popularity flagged but it revived gradually during the eighteenth and increasingly in the nineteenth century as interest grew again in the instrument's heritage and cultural symbolism. Harplet, which Héloïse had bought in Washington, decorated with gold and brown sprays of shamrock and interwoven Celtic designs, had been made in Syracuse, New York, possibly in response to the growing Irish diaspora.

In 1920s Scotland, harps were hard to come by. Indeed, the recently published history of The Clarsach Society records that demand

12 Edinburgh University Library (EUL), Material relating to Marjory Kennedy-Fraser and Helen Patuffa Hood, Coll-1407.

frequently outstripped availability and that there were recurring frustrations and activity around securing enough harps for the increasing number of potential learners and players.[13] As An Comunn and the Clarsach Society were encouraging the production of modern instruments in Glasgow and elsewhere in the 1930s, Héloïse could not shake off her curiosity about the smaller Queen Mary Harp, an early medieval instrument believed to date back to possibly the fifteenth century and to have originated in Argyll. Wire strung and without levers or pedals, it was simplicity itself. She turned for advice to the French born medieval instrument specialist, Arnold Dolmetsch who lived and worked in Haslemere.

Dolmetsch had studied music in Brussels before coming to London in 1883 where he attended the Royal College of Music and then taught at Dulwich College. He developed a passion for early music and soon became an acknowledged expert on medieval instruments, giving up teaching eventually to focus on building copies of fifteenth to eighteenth century keyboard and stringed instruments in his workshop in Haslemere in Surrey. His book, *The Interpretation of the Music of the XVIIth and XVIIIth Centuries*, written in 1915, was regarded by many as a milestone in the development of authentic performances of early music. An expansive bohemian character and the head of a very musically creative family he later founded the International Dolmetsch Early Music Festival that would be held annually in Haslemere.

By the early 1930s, Dolmetsch had begun to explore the medieval Welsh harp and its music, so Héloïse's approach would have been timely. He looked into the history of the early Scottish clarsach, took to his workshop and in what seemed a surprisingly short time, he was satisfied with the outcome which he presented to Héloïse: a small harp inscribed with the words, 'the first clarsach'. Enthused, he then

---

13 Stuart Eydmann, *In Good Hands* (Edinburgh: The Clarsach Society, 2017), p. 57.

embarked on making several more, refining his skill with each one. Increasingly pleased with the result and perhaps mindful of some of the rough edges of his initial effort, he wrote to Héloïse in July 1932 with a proposal:

> I made one clarsach amongst the others of a very fine piece of cherry wood. It looks most beautiful, is lighter in weight than the others and has a deeper more velvety tone. It has the right tuning pins – I very much desire that YOU should have this one. I would exchange it for the one you have of which I should remove the inscription.
>
> I should write a similar one on the cherry clarsach and we should be within the truth, for all these clarsachs were made at the same time and I have not delivered any although I have sold three. So you would still be the first! Moreover, the cherry one has not been shown to anybody and I shall keep it secret until I hear from you. Its colour is deeper and more golden. Is there a chance of your coming here soon?

The capitalised YOU seems to convey both respect and affection for Héloïse, his sensuous description of the colours and textures, the sound and the feel of this new clarsach alongside his desire that she collude in this secret exchange, hinting at the quality of their friendship. There is a photograph of the Dolmetsch harp in *The Russell-Fergusson Collection of Harps* in the Mitchell Library but she made no mention of whether there had been an exchange, noting simply that it was inscribed with 'This clarsach, the first of its kind, was made at Haslemere in July for Miss Russell-Fergusson by Arnold Dolmetsch' and adding, 'the shape resembles the ancient Irish and Highland instruments. 27 strings of thin metal set closely together to be played with the finger tips. Clarsach of cherry wood.' Did that mean the swap had been made? Then there is a further note, dated April 1952 and typed over an Arnold Dolmetsch Ltd., label, stating, 'Fifteen of these little metal stringed harps were made and distributed and three somewhat larger gut stringed instruments.'

Perhaps equally iconic at the time, were the Scottish bagpipes with their own far reaching, complex and sometimes controversial musical history in which Héloïse was invited to share in August 1933. She was one of a sixteen strong house party which the clan chief, MacLeod of MacLeod, invited to Dunvegan Castle on the island of Skye for the unveiling at Borreraig of a memorial cairn to the MacCrimmons, the legendary hereditary pipers to the Clan MacLeod.[14] I picture her at Dunvegan the evening before the event, sitting at dinner between Seton Gordon, for he and Audrey were also on the guest list, and Norman Heathcote, her host's nephew who had arrived with his sister Evelyn on his steam yacht which would transport the whole party to the memorial unveiling the following morning.

Héloïse awoke to the sounds of a piper playing below the castle wall. After breakfast, pipers paraded the deck while the party boarded Norman's boat to steam up Loch Dunvegan to Borreraig. There, the atmosphere gradually became hushed as the guests processed through the waiting crowd towards the newly erected memorial where MacLeod of MacLeod solemnly addressed the gathering. In the afternoon, a further memorial tablet was unveiled at Kilmuir churchyard and in the evening, Héloïse took to the stage in Dunvegan public hall where, with baritone Hugh Campbell, she provided the entertainment. Fred T. MacLeod who had been largely responsible for the day's events, wrote in the *Oban Times* the following week:

> At the conclusion of the unveiling of the cairn and the tablet, a concert was held in the public Hall of Dunvegan, over which the Earl of Cassillis presided. There was a very large attendance, the proceeds being in aid of the Hall Fund. The programme was wholly sustained by Mr. Hugh Campbell, a noted baritone, who sang groups of Irish and Scottish songs to the delight of the audience, and Miss Héloïse Russell-Fergusson, who in her singing of Hebridean songs to clarsach accompaniment was given

---

14 *The Oban Times*, 12 August 1933.

a fine reception. Miss Fergusson's singing and clarsach playing, together with the easy natural way she told the story of each of her songs, made a strong appeal to her audience.

It was nearly ten years since she had discovered Harplet in Washington; ten years of exploring and experimenting with her new learning from Annie Johnston on Barra and Kenneth MacLeod on Gigha; of expressing her passion for the Hebrides in Europe, in America and across the UK. This performance had not been for a city audience in Berlin, New York or London. It was in a village hall with a crowd of people that included many Gaelic speakers and singers, potentially her most critical listeners. I wonder whether she treasured Fred MacLeod's comments more highly than those offered in urban reviews.

I have been told since that the legend of the MacCrimmons may have been another Victorian confection, another example of cultural inauthenticity. But Héloïse was undoubtedly there in 1933, taking part, playing her clarsach in front of that audience and warming to their applause. It was all grist to the mill of revealing her story.

Chapter Seven

Family Comings and Goings

While Héloïse was caught up in this welter of professional activity, her mother was struggling to keep Ardtur going. The Aberdeen Angus herd and her beloved Large Black pigs were long gone and Hélène had switched to a small Ayrshire dairy herd, invested in some poultry and was nurturing soft fruit and vegetables as well as her beehives. An Ardtur Home Farm delivery van was taking produce round the local communities. By 1932, she and Héloïse were the only family members on the voters' roll at Ardtur. Denise may have been at home, or perhaps away at boarding school. Margie's whereabouts are unknown.

As for Donald, he had been spending as much time as he could in London, captivated by Elise Mainwaring, whom he would eventually marry. She was a photographic and catwalk model who had been selected by Kodak for their first life-sized, cardboard cut-out advertisement in the UK. Her ubiquitous figure stood outside chemist shops that stocked Kodak goods, attracting customers to buy film and to drop off spools to be developed. She smiled down into a box camera wearing a blue and white striped dress reaching just below the knee. Donald doffed his hat each time he came across one.

Elise had not set out to be a model. She had been learning millinery when a friend who worked at a photography studio suggested that she have her photograph taken. 'It was just for fun,' she told me, 'but then the photographer used the pictures to advertise his studio and plastered them over all the London Tube stations.' After that, her face was everywhere. She smiled from the cover of the first edition of *Woman's Own* magazine in 1932, holding up the three skeins of wool that came free with every copy. Her clear blue Optrex eyes gazed down from the back of London buses and she looked out from hoardings dreamily smoking a Craven A cigarette. Newspapers and magazines were full of her image, modelling everything from swimwear to furs. During the London Lord Mayor's Show of 1931, she stood centre stage as the Goddess of Light in a tableau that celebrated the age of electricity.

Probably in today's terms, she would have been a minor celebrity; rubbing shoulders with the well-to-do simply because of her beauty and the public exposure which prompted invitations to parts of society that otherwise would have ignored her. She was welcomed at cocktail parties and balls, wined and dined at Ciro's, Claridge's and the Savoy, invited out by a string of suitors and new friends. Despite the sudden financial independence which she celebrated by buying a little car she called Psyche, she still lived at home where my Nan was an uncompromising chaperone, insisting that the flowers and gifts that arrived at the door, sometimes beribboned boxes containing a new gown in clouds of tissue paper, would all be returned with gracious thanks.

Then, as part of the Daily Sketch Fashion Tour of Britain, Elise visited Scotland where she met Donald. An unusually informal photograph in an undated cutting from the *Press and Journal* shows her standing beside the open door of a car as another young woman steps out. Elise is smiling to her left where my father is standing, a newspaper in one hand, and a cigarette in the other. They seem to be in conversation. It looked as if he had just chanced upon her, as if the photographer had caught them all unawares. The caption read, 'The mannequins arrive: some of them reached Aberdeen for this week's

Fashion Parades at the Trade Exhibition just as the sun broke through after a shower.'

She chuckled to recall her first visit to Ardtur; the long train journey, the drive as dusk was falling, turning off the narrow road up the winding driveway to the solitary house overlooking the water. It would be hard to find a greater contrast with the home in the small London cul-de-sac where she lived with her brothers and her parents, my other grandparents. For despite the glamorous circles in which she moved as a model, her family was at the opposite end of the social spectrum from the Russell-Fergussons.

Elise had been born in Brixton in 1907. Before her second birthday, her mother was widowed with two very small children and Elise's earliest memory was of sleeping in a laundry basket tucked under the shop counter where her mother worked. In 1913, my Nan met and married Frank Pitt, a warm hearted London cab driver, and my mum soon had a baby brother. The family moved to Acton and took in a permanent lodger to help make ends meet. My Nan's stoicism and determination surely matched Granny Hélène's although I'm not sure whether they understood each other. Certainly for Mum, Ardtur was a sober household compared to the rollicking sociability in Acton where the whole family were part of the local dramatic society and noisy informal musical evenings were the norm.

Initially, she had felt a little awkward with the formality of the household; changing for dinner, Crichton tapping on the bedroom door bearing a glass of whisky for my father (never a drink for me, she complained), having to ring a bell if she wanted a cup of tea instead of wandering into the kitchen to put on the kettle. But Donald's mother and his sisters were unpretentious and did their best to make her feel at home. Perhaps they were relieved that Donald had found someone who might settle him down. As for the Russell cousins, they seemed quite delighted at this glamorous addition to the family. A series of photographs shows them partying in 1933 at a Russell house in

Colintraive in Argyll; lots of boats and booze and, I feel protectively, some slightly over-familiar embraces of my mother. Margie is in the photographs and Dad of course, but not Héloïse.

Their wedding was at St Columba's Church of Scotland in London's Pont Street in December 1932, my mother dressed in long sleeved, ivory coloured soft velvet, trimmed with pearl embroidery. Héloïse, Margie, Denise and a girlfriend of my mother followed her up the aisle, wearing dresses of mushroom lace edged with dark brown velvet and carrying deep red carnations. The newly-weds settled in Glasgow from where Donald travelled daily to work at Ardrossan Dockyard and Elise assumed the modest wifely role befitting her new status, never to model again. Pretty quickly, her brief and heady encounter with the world of glamour and importantly, with independence, had dissolved.

That summer, before Donald and Elise were married, Hélène took seventeen year old Denise on a women's study trip to Canada to learn about farming, under the auspices of the British National Union Party which was affiliated to the Scottish Conservatives and the Liberal Party. Interviewed about farming in Scotland by the *Calgary Daily Herald*, Hélène couldn't resist mentioning her eldest daughter Héloïse, 'a professional Gaelic singer who has appeared on the concert platform in New York and in Eastern Canada'. I can find no record of Héloïse performing in Canada but by then her travels were extensive. There are probably many more venues and concerts of which I am ignorant, that have not popped up in archive searches.

Hélène and Denise were joined on the tour by two women who farmed in South Africa. The four of them travelled across Canada together, visiting farms and learning about different techniques. Hélène listened intently to her companions and began to think seriously about her future. She read about South Africa and pondered the opportunities for farming there. Perhaps she should make a break from Argyll and have a completely fresh start. After all, Denise would soon be eighteen.

On their return, she swung into action. Denise would participate in the London debutante season the following May and be presented at court, making the formal transition into adulthood. In the autumn, Hélène would assemble the family for the Argyllshire Gathering and the Oban Ball where she and Donald would introduce Elise formally to Highland society. Thereafter, she would make a reconnaissance trip to Africa. I imagine Héloïse felt both aghast and thrilled at the idea of her mother contemplating a move; disengaging from Argyll must have seemed unthinkable, yet she knew well the allure of travelling, of adventuring, of exploring the unknown. The plan moved on well-oiled wheels. Denise was presented at court on 12 May 1933 and ten members of the family assembled at Ardtur in August to rehearse their dance steps and attend the Ball.

Over eighty years later, the Ball still takes place. I had assumed it was an annual fund raiser with pricey tickets but an event which anyone might save up to attend for a special night out. In fact, it was, and it remains an exclusive and very private party. Organised by the Argyllshire Gathering, which was established in 1871 and consisted of 'an association of gentlemen connected with the county of Argyll, for the promotion of an Annual Social Meeting', it appears little changed. Its first rule book stated that, 'membership shall be restricted, generally, to landowners of Argyllshire, their sons and brothers; discretionary powers being reserved, however, in exceptional cases, to admit gentlemen not having that qualification'. This remains the case although I hope at least that women are now welcome and equal members. Securing a ticket for a non-member at the Ball, however, still depends on an approved recommendation.

Buying Ardtur gave William and Hélène the chance to join this club. In Edwardian Argyll, it represented a particularly Highland cultural recognition of their social standing and the Oban Ball was a formal event, rather like the presentations at court, where socially approved contacts could be made for romantic or for business purposes. Nowadays, it may seem anachronistic but it appears to remain popular.

As the autumn of 1933 turned to winter, Hélène headed to London and boarded a ship bound for Cape Town. Unsurprisingly, Héloïse had decided that she must go too. I first thought she might be travelling as a companion for Hélène but on reaching Cape Town, mother and daughter parted company; Hélène to decide whether Africa should be her new home and Héloïse to find somewhere to play. Her persuasive skills worked their magic and the conductor of the Cape Town orchestra engaged her almost immediately to appear at one of their regular concerts. It was a splendid beginning. The large audience was receptive and before the evening was out, she had the whole house singing 'Loch Lomond'. 'Probably a first at a symphony concert!' she wrote later.

During the interval, the conductor had knocked on her dressing room door, 'Come back next week, will you?' he asked. The next week was a gala night. The hall was packed with Scots who had heard about the previous concert. The Governor General sat with his party in a box and led the applause and the call for encores. The previous week's reception had not been a one-off and in the following weeks it seemed that she was given an unqualified welcome wherever she went. Inevitably, she covered the colonial circuit but occasionally she visited mission schools for African children. There she found that the walls were covered so often with illustrations of heavenly harps that the children found Harplet completely unnerving. They preferred her to sing unaccompanied.

Following a concert attended by a largely Scottish audience, she was chatting informally when a little girl had piped up, 'I know those songs, I know those songs'. Her mother had laughed and said, 'But you've never heard them before!' The child solemnly tapped her forehead. 'I've always known them' she said, 'I can hear them in here.' This unbidden affirmation of cultural memory seemed to echo

Héloïse's own response when confronted by the clarsach in America; the disjuncture of place and a cultural prompt suddenly activating lost experience, lost memory. Sometimes, audience members might recollect some Gaelic. She wrote:

> At East London I had a particularly well organised concert as the arrangements were in the hands of Mr Currie, a well-beloved chief. Pipers opened the concert and I was escorted up the aisle on his arm. An old lady was brought round to see me after. She had not been out for years but had insisted on coming that night. And she recognised many of the songs. Tears of emotion were in her eyes. 'Ah, my dear, if I could only get back,' she said 'I will never see it more.' I was deeply touched. Such incidents have happened many times since. Should memories so poignant be awakened or rather left to sleep, I have wondered. These old people always insist themselves on coming and I learn they have never been the worse for their efforts. They have also sung songs of long ago to me in their own homes.

In Kokstad, KwaZulu-Natal, the local baker, a Scot, sent a box of oatcakes to her hotel. Cape Town Rotary Club invited her to talk at one of their regular lunches; the first woman to address them, she reported proudly. Elsie Hall, an Australian pianist who studied and worked in Europe before settling to play with the Symphony Orchestra in Cape Town, invited her to lunch. I wonder whether Héloïse heard Elsie on the BBC's *Desert Island Discs* programme in April 1969. By then aged nearly ninety, Elsie was interviewed about her career and invited to choose a luxury to take to her desert island. She opted for a billiard table, a cue and a set of billiard balls, claiming robustly that women never got a proper chance to play. I imagined her and Héloïse thirty-five years earlier, swapping views about music, culture, the position of women in society, potting a few balls before lunch.

The night that Héloïse left Cape Town pipers marched along the station platform playing 'The Road to the Isles'. The Scots in Johannesburg did the same. As a privileged white woman bringing romantic reminders to the Scottish diaspora, travelling across South Africa seemed as straightforward as taking the train from Oban to London. Nevertheless, bureaucracy nearly stopped her from crossing into Tanzania, at the time a British Protectorate called Tanganyika. She was held up at the border and her baggage severely scrutinised. She wrote:

> The young Scotsman was worried. He scratched his head. Overhead, the fans groaned in sympathy with our problem. It was a torrid morning. Even the brilliant blue sea at the end of an avenue of Flame trees looked hot. My ship was preparing to depart. I had arrived in Tanganyika that morning and Harplet was having difficulties. 'Are you sure that's what it says?' I asked again, incredulously. We bent over the printed sheets of regulations. 'Here it is,' said the young man. 'No musical instruments allowed in this territory.' 'Well, I can't go on without Harplet, so what is to be done?' I queried. He continued to read, 'Perambulators, pets, clothes hampers, tools,' he skimmed over the page. 'Tools,' we both suddenly exclaimed. The solution was found. Harplet entered East Africa as my trusty tool.

Across South Africa, Zimbabwe, Tanzania and Kenya, she remained relentlessly inquisitive about indigenous music and musical instruments, about the ways in which music reflected and was part of day to day life. Much later, she would record her research in *The Russell-Fergusson Collection of Harps* at the Mitchell Library, but writing for the *People's Journal* in 1939, she selected a traveller's tale more likely to entertain the non-specialist reader. It was a nocturnal adventure:

> It was really owing to my passion for native music. I was in the habit of visiting the night herd, who, armed with a spear and other weapons, mounted guard out among the crops to keep off the wild beasts. Like the other herders, he had a small fire and when night fell these fires gleamed like red stars all over the vast plain. He possessed a fund of lovely native tunes and I noted many of them down. This particular evening we arrived to find a group of natives who had heard there was to be a singsong and were determined not to miss it. We sat round the fire and

Kazimoto, a magnificent figure, stood upright with his spear at his side, continuously scanning the surroundings with his keen eyes and joining in the songs. The balmy stillness of the African night inspired us all to song.

I was just noting a particularly quaint ditty when suddenly Kazimoto stiffened. He became tense and immoveable, his spearhead against his cheek. The other natives stopped their song instantly. 'Simba,' breathed Kazi, pointing to the plain nearby. I knew enough to recognise the native word for lion. I saw a small light moving along. It seemed to be coming in our direction. Presently it stopped and there were two lights as the beast turned his luminous eyes on us. Simba was abroad! … Soon we watched three great beasts lope along. No mistaking a lion's stride. Occasionally, scenting intruders, they would stop and turn in our direction. But they were thirsty and fortunately we were not between them and the magic ditch full of water known as the Furrow without which every Shamba and the beasts also would starve.

She hoarded these experiences from Africa, the songs, the sights and sounds, the musical instruments. In 1956, she wheedled her way backstage at the Palace Theatre in London after a performance of *Ballets Africains*, the company founded and directed by Keita Fodeba. She wanted to meet the kora players, Daouda and Bakary, to see and talk with them about the kora, to examine the instruments up close, to learn the intricacies of how they were played.

I read about the kora online, described as a 'double-bridge-harp-lute' and then listened to the range of rich sounds that can be drawn from the complex stringing. The instrument is native to West Africa so perhaps it was only on that visit to *Ballets Africains*, twenty years after her visit to Africa, that she first saw and heard it. The *Russell-Fergusson Collection of Harps* includes enlarged photographs of Daouda and Bakary taken at the London performance. Ever practical, Héloïse had noted that they kept spare strings inside the calabash sound cavity and she went on to enthuse about Bakary's curtain song, writing that:

As he moved across the wide stage at the Palace Theatre [it was] beautiful, natural, primitive and unspoiled. He wore a loose cloak of rose and purple and held the instrument before him as he walked. His song came in snatches with effective and sudden diminuendo at the end of phrases which appeared characteristic of the idiom of the music. I learn that few play the Cora [sic] any longer in their district. It has been ousted by the modern guitar.

Before Héloïse left for Africa she had made three records of Kennedy-Fraser songs at the Kintore Studios in Edinburgh. On the first was ''Sa Choill Ud Thall' ('The Island Herd Maid') and 'Taladh Eiresgaidh' ('Eriskay Lullaby'); on the second, 'A' Chruinneag Leach' ('The Islay Maiden'), 'Iona Boat Song' and ''Strusaidh Mi Na Coilleagan' ('The Cockle Gatherer'); and on the third, 'Land of Heart's Desire'.

She would record again in the 1940s but it was not until 1966 that listeners would hear the influence of her African experiences. On 'Dance of the Drops', a track on her third EP, *An Treisamh*, she played an African mbira, or thumb piano, as well as Harplet. On the sleeve note, she described the piece as 'a happy dance' and to be sure, the warm tones of the mbira interplay with the clarsach like wind chimes on a summer breeze. She might have brought the mbira back with her, for the instrument's origins were in Zimbabwe and South Africa and she would have been attracted by its sound. I pictured it lying with the chanter, the folders of music and the old rug in the back of her car when it went to the scrapyard.

'Dance of the Drops' would have a lasting resonance. In 2003, the young Scottish musician Martyn Bennett sampled fragments from this track in an improvisation called 'Wedding' on his final album, *Grit*. The album pulses with Bennett's characteristically passionate and fearless blends of traditional Celtic and contemporary music amongst which 'Wedding', described by Bennett as a 'tone-poem' and including piano and viola, brings a delicate poignancy, all the more so because Bennett died shortly after its release. I am certain that Héloïse would have been pleased and proud to have been included.

Chapter Eight

Bardess of the Gorsedd

On their return to Ardtur, Héloïse turned to the neat pile of correspondence that Crichton had placed on her desk. One letter was particularly intriguing. She was invited to attend a Grand Festival (Bretagne-Ecosse) in Roscoff, Brittany, not only to perform but also to be invested as a Druidic Bardess in recognition of her contribution to Celtic music.

The event was a Breton spin-off from the Celtic Congress established in 1917 to promote the languages and cultures of those nations and regions with a distinctive Celtic heritage: Ireland, Scotland, Wales, Brittany, Cornwall and the Isle of Man. Héloïse would have delighted in this Celtic family with its similarities of history and culture, its mix of scholarship and mysticism, its solemnity yet lightness of spirit. It chimed with her attraction to the uncluttered life of the Hebrides, reaching back for what seemed a simpler, safer time. In the 1930s, this was not only a Celtic preoccupation. There was a pastoral craze in England that included moonlit walking, for communing with the land, celebrating ancient sites and folk traditions, drawing on Shakespeare, Chaucer, on Arthurian legends. It has been described as one element in a wider movement of national cultural salvage, born of the trauma of the Great War and which flourished in fear of the next.[15]

The Celtic Congress was not without a political edge with some members committed to achieving greater autonomy or independence

---

15 Helen MacDonald, *H is for Hawk* (London: Vintage, 2015), p. 118.

but, for Héloïse, I suspect that it simply validated her reverence for cultural traditions that seemed unpolluted by the pace and preoccupations of contemporary life, offering her the companionship of like-minded people and legitimising, if needed, her sense of romance. She accepted the invitation with alacrity.

The event had been planned by Francois Jaffrenou, a champion of Breton language and culture who, having attended the Welsh Eisteddfod in 1899, at which he had been awarded the status of Ovate and the name Taldir ab Hernin, set up the Gorsedd in Brittany and would become its Grand Druid. Taldir and his son Gildas had visited Scotland on several occasions, taking a particularly keen interest in traditional music as well as in the historical links between Scotland and Brittany.

And so it was, that at the end of July 1934, Héloïse found herself walking as part of another solemn procession; this time through the cobbled streets of Roscoff, swathed in early morning mist and led, not by pipers, but by a troop of horsemen bearing Breton flags. Crowds of people, many dressed in traditional costume, turned out to line the route that led up the hill to the chapel of Sainte Barbe and the Druid stone where the ceremonies would be performed.

An Oaled, a Breton magazine edited by Taldir, noted that the Scottish delegates included Audrey and Seton Gordon, the latter to be invested as a Druid in recognition of his contribution particularly to piping, George and Mary Dott and Neil MacCormick and his wife representing the Free Scots Party as well as Catherine Robertson and Annie and Denise Reid representing the newly established Scottish National Party.[16] The previous issue of *An Oaled* had included an article by Augusta Lamont of Inverchaolain, Argyll, describing its inauguration in April 1934 after the amalgamation of the former Scottish Party and the National Party of Scotland.[17]

---

16 *An Oaled*, No. 50, pp. 332–333.
17 *An Oaled*, No. 49, pp. 284–285.

As they reached the stone, the mist began to clear. Héloïse and the assembled Celts stood in silence. Beside her, Harplet was draped in mistletoe, a powerful Druidic symbol of healing, protection and fertility. Héloïse's name was called out and she mounted the plinth to stand beside Taldir. He drew a ceremonial sword from its scabbard, held it before her and asked, 'Is it peace or war?' She laid her hands on the sword. 'Peace,' she replied. With Taldir's help, the first Bardess of the Breton movement, Erwanez Galbrun, placed the blue Bardic sash edged with gold over Héloïse's head and across her shoulder. Héloïse turned to face the crowd. Speaking in French, she expressed her thanks:

> I appreciate this honour you have conferred on me, on the music of the Gaels, the Highlanders of Scotland and on this ancient instrument of Scottish music, the clarsach. It is truly amazing to consider what the members of the various branches of the Celtic race have in common; the key to international goodwill through the gentle music of long ago. As long as it exists and we can express it, we can help the world to quit its torments and become a happier place.

A snatch of the event was captured on a Pathé Gazette film clip entitled *Eisteddfod of Brittany*. Standing next to Seton Gordon, Héloïse can be glimpsed wearing a slim tartan kilt with a tartan shawl over her pale blouse, clutching the sprig of mistletoe. Then she is standing solemnly on the plinth by Taldir, touching the sword, being invested with the sash, then smiling and expressing her thanks to the crowd before being helped down. Wearing the kilt, with a plaid over his shoulder and draped in a white sash, Seton was initiated with three other Druids, all from Brittany.

A vegetable packing shed was decked out for the evening concert. The wooden crates were stacked around the sides or under trestle tables at the back, the floor swept clean and a stage set up, decorated with baskets of flowers. Coloured lights and bunting stretched in welcome from the doorway as dusk was falling. People crowded in from Roscoff and the surrounding towns and villages across the district of Leon, more than twelve hundred finally finding a seat or a place to stand before the official party arrived. They hushed at the sound of the pipes as Seton, wearing his Druidic sash and playing a solemn *pibroch*, led the Grand Druid Taldir into the hall followed by the Druids, Bards and Ovates. As the audience settled, Héloïse stepped onto the stage with Harplet in her arms. Dressed in her long white silk gown with the red velvet undersleeves and wearing her embroidered shoes, she played a selection from her repertoire, first describing each song in French.

George Dott noted that she sang beautifully while also being quite nerve-wracked by the audience walking about and buying ice-cream.[18] Taldir wrote less pragmatically about the event in *An Oaled*, describing an unreservedly rapturous response:

> The entire press has underlined the great talent of Miss Russell-Fergusson. *An Oaled* can add that she made the stern Leonards cry as they called her back for an encore. Now, according to Roscovite memory, there are no other examples of the Leonards being so completely carried away in the theatre.[19]

He also offered a rare, and rather endearing, description of Héloïse herself:

> The outstanding success of this singular artist from the Hebrides is connected not only to her special style and the unique interpretation of her playing but also to the natural appeal that emanates from her, and to her fine character. She is the most approachable and interesting woman to talk with; she's also the least pretentious you could meet. She expresses herself with extreme simplicity and on meeting important people she never talks about herself. She is very well-educated, she speaks French and is interested in the Scottish

---

18 National Library of Scotland (NLS), George Dott Diaries and Papers, GB 233, Acc.12987/55.

19 *An Oaled*, No. 50, p. 337.

movement. It was at her instigation that M. J. Carmichael Watson published recently the songs of Mary MacLeod.[20]

His son Gildas had been particularly curious about the clarsach. In a radio interview that he gave in 1988,[21] he described the success of Héloïse's 1934 concert in Roscoff and confirmed that they corresponded afterwards. She had sent him a series of photographs from which he tried to make a clarsach himself. His first attempt had been a bit of a disaster but after a trip to Wales and also to Dolmetsch's workshop in Haslemere, he drew up a design and finally made what he called his first Celtic harp in 1946.

A couple of years earlier, Taldir had been imprisoned in Quimper, convicted for his involvement with Breton nationalism, his alleged association with Vichy France and for harming national defence. While there, he had received a letter from Georges Cochevellou seeking advice about teaching his son to play the harp; Taldir asked Gildas to help them, which he did. The boy grew up to be Alan Stivell, a powerful figure in the revival of Celtic music from the 1970s, whose name was familiar even to me. I wondered whether Gildas ever told Héloïse of the success of the young harpist he had helped. As for Taldir, he was pardoned in 1946 and released.

Héloïse returned to France at the end of November 1934 to play at the premiere in Rennes and then at screenings across Brittany, of *Chanson d'Ar-Mor*, a short film directed by Jean Epstein. Set in a Breton fishing village, it was the first film to use entirely Breton dialogue. The film was relatively short and Héloïse's task was to establish an ambience of Celtic romance with an introductory recital of Hebridean songs selected to reflect love and loss, heroism and humility. *L'Ouest-Éclair* reported from the premiere that her voice had conveyed, 'the soul of a race closely related to our own'.

---

20 Ibid., p. 337.
21 Jane Freshwater, personal communication, 28 September 2003.

Three days after the Rennes concert and apparently unconnected to her film commitments, she performed in Paris where an enthusiastic review in *La Semaine* echoed her *Gorsedd* speech, describing her performance as an urgent reminder of the need for unity amongst peoples who had unconsciously submerged their Celtic past.

Returning to Ardtur just after the 1934 *Gorsedd*, she had performed at the Argyllshire Gathering Halls in Oban. Mid-August heralded the beginning of the Highland social season so the extended family would have been assembling at Ardtur for the games, the balls and the regattas that punctuated the weeks to come. Héloïse donated the proceeds of that concert to the National Mòd at Oban and the following year she gave a further fundraising recital at Gogar House in Edinburgh, courtesy of Eleanora Cameron of the Clarsach Society with whom she had visited Iona. Although her repertoire was drawn mostly from Kennedy-Fraser, on that occasion she had included some songs collected by herself. There was evidence that before setting off for Brittany she had been back to the Hebrides: the *Scotsman* review of a concert at the Lyric Theatre in Glasgow in 1935 noted that:

> Her unaccompanied songs, which comprised a group recovered by her last summer in North Uist, Eigg and Barra, were faultlessly rendered and made special appeal. These included Morar Reaper's Song from North Uist; Spinning Song from Eigg; Lullaby from Kenneth MacLeod; and Waulking Song from Peggy McCuish, Locheport.[22]

Meanwhile, the South African visit had helped Hélène to make up her mind and in the months that followed her return, Ardtur had been in some upheaval. Denise and Margie were busy helping their mother prepare for her new life in Southern Rhodesia, which would not achieve full independent status as Zimbabwe until 1980. This time the move would be permanent. Hélène had acquired some land

---

22 *The Scotsman*, 26 October 1935, p. 16.

near Umtali and was readying herself to set up a household and start farming. Crichton would go with her. This last fact had always fuelled my belief that there was something special between them; travelling across the world to start a new life together was surely a romantic endeavour. It was Stuart Carmichael in Port Appin who helped me to learn more about Crichton, that meticulous, attentive man so beloved of my grandmother.

Stuart not only showed me round Ardtur and the Appin church. He took me to visit Jenny, an elderly woman who had spent her life in the village of Port Appin. She was generous with her time and did her best to recall what she knew of the days when the Russell-Fergussons were at Ardtur. Her mother had worked briefly in the Ardtur kitchen as a teenager during a school holiday, but not for long. Crichton had raised his voice to her, preventing her from going on an errand for the cook and insisting that he was in charge of her activities. The strong minded teenager had left abruptly and had not returned to the house. The anecdote reminded me that Crichton had not been popular.

But when I put the suggestion cautiously to Jenny that there may have been a romance between Granny Hélène and Crichton, she buried her face in her hands and rocked with laughter, 'Oh, no, no, no,' she said, shaking her head vehemently. 'Go on, tell me,' I asked. She peeped through her fingers and then took her hands from her face. 'Crichton didn't like the ladies,' she said with a chuckle. Not just a bit of a bully, it seemed that Crichton may also have been unpopular because he was gay. If Hélène was pleased to be leaving behind a residue of gossip about her late baby, Crichton might also have relished a fresh start. I wondered what Hélène made of his sexuality. Perhaps they were silent accomplices. Perhaps he was bi-sexual. Perhaps she was oblivious to his private life.

Margaret Glendinning, Hélène's secretary, by now a good friend and confidante, was also going to Africa. Denise would go too and Margie would join them later. Heavy furniture, canteens of cutlery, tiers of crockery, bales of soft furnishings, trunks of clothes and books were all being packed. Ardtur was stripped of everything but the basics with which it could be let out in the summer. Seeing the house being emptied must have brought home the reality of it all. With Muckairn long gone, Ardtur was Héloïse's sole tangible connection with Argyll. It was home; its very existence possibly the reason why she had never thought to set up independently on her own. It might still belong to the family but now it would be let out, and would not always be available to her.

Moreover, although Héloïse had been a confident, independent traveller for well over ten years, her mother was surely her lynchpin, that strong, dependable and unconditionally loving person to whom she returned after each foray into the wider world, the person who most celebrated her achievements. With her sisters departing as well, the only immediate family member remaining in Scotland was my father, her brother, who was married and absorbed in his own life.

Perhaps seeking reassurance, Héloïse headed for London and settled into the familiar surroundings of the Forum Club in Grosvenor Place. Modest but comfortable, the Club had been established in 1919 as the London Centre for members of the Women's Institute. Marjory Kennedy-Fraser had performed there in 1922,[23] giving a recital organised by Rachel Neill Fraser who would perform with Héloïse in Germany some years later. It was a good place in which to gather her thoughts and consider her next steps. There was a thriving Scottish community in London, a branch of the Clarsach Society and cousins too. But perhaps she consciously resisted getting caught up in the humdrum of the latter's concerns for it was not long since Uncle John had died and her cousin Connie, now separated from her husband, was busy with two young children. Héloïse didn't need more family turmoil. She wanted to focus on her future.

---

23 EUL, Papers of Marjory Kennedy-Fraser, Coll-1036, Gen. 284.

She preferred probably to catch up with Marie Dare and others from her familiar musical world. They would have enjoyed her stories from Africa, about meeting Elsie Hall, breaching the male bastions of Cape Town Rotary Club, her descriptions of the music that she had heard and the instruments she had seen. Marie had also been travelling professionally, building an excellent reputation across Europe both as a composer and as a performer. John Barbirolli, who had conducted when she played with the Guild String Orchestra a few years earlier was now conducting partly with the Scottish Orchestra, partly with the Halle Orchestra in Manchester, and would soon depart for the New York Philharmonic.

Predisposed to be nomadic and imminently to be without even a notional home, Héloïse would have felt comfortable with independent, creative friends who travelled readily to wherever beckoned. If she had shared any feelings of despondency about the family leaving Scotland, I suspect Marie would have encouraged her to think ahead, asking, 'So, where next for you?'

Invigorated by her experiences in Brittany and her Bardic status and perhaps recalling her enthusiastic reception from the Scottish diaspora in South Africa, Héloïse started to research the possibility of visiting New Zealand and Australia, firing off letters to Caledonian societies, organisations and schools. Anticipating her visit, the *Evening Post* in New Zealand reported that Héloïse had visited the High Commission in London which put her in touch with Stella Murray, who:

> Always a very generous hostess, arranged two parties at her South Kensington home this week in order that Miss Russell-Fergusson might have the opportunity of meeting some well-known New Zealanders and that they should know something of her privately and as an instrumentalist. She gave a number of items from her extensive repertoire which consists chiefly of attractive songs in Gaelic with Hebridean settings. The harp is her instrument of accompaniment: her costume is either of Scottish tartan or a robe of flowing white silk cut on

Bardic lines. Prior to each group a descriptive account is given. For New Zealand, she was given introductions to leading people including Lord and Lady Galway.

Stella Murray was musically talented and socially active. In 1951, she would receive an OBE for 'social welfare services on behalf of New Zealanders in the UK', and after her death in 1965, the Royal Overseas League set up a Stella Murray memorial prize for New Zealand musicians studying in London. In 1935, she gave Héloïse the social connections she needed.

Hélène and Denise embarked at Southampton heading for Cape Town on 11 October 1935. Exactly two months later, Héloïse and Harplet left the London docks on board the *Remuera*, bound for Wellington.

CHAPTER NINE

HOME FROM HOME

Héloïse was looking forward to her first engagement in New Zealand, a performance at the Wellington Burns Club's annual dinner. No doubt she put in some practice on board the *Remuera*, perhaps entertaining fellow passengers, picking up contacts, gleaning what she could about her destination. But just as the long voyage was nearing its end, the British Empire was plunged into mourning by the death of King George V after a reign of over twenty-five years. British Pathé described him as 'more than a King, [he was] a father of a great family'. The Wellington Burns Club began to deliberate whether it should cancel the event and on 23 January 1936, the *Wellington Evening Post* reported on its decision:

> The committee of the Wellington Burns Club has given considerable thought to the question of whether the Burns anniversary evening, on Saturday next, should be postponed in view of the death of the late King, but has been advised that, as the function is to be purely one of commemoration, the arrangements should not be cancelled. The usual toast list will this year be suspended, and all song and poetry will be confined to the work of Burns.

Héloïse's contribution was cancelled. Undeterred, she paused to secure a few contacts in Wellington and then headed for South Island, making the long journey down to Dunedin. It was a good move. On the platform at Dunedin's magnificent railway station, the chiefs of eight Scottish societies stood resplendent in full Highland dress to welcome her. With their support, she built a schedule of performances in concert halls, schools and prisons, staying with Scottish hosts at sheep stations and in rural towns. She felt entirely at home, although occasionally and despite the strong Scottish diaspora, not everyone was familiar with where she came from. More than once, she claimed, a radio announcer introduced her as 'visiting from the New Hebrides'.

In New Zealand, there was no challenging new language to frustrate her when she was describing the origins of her songs. Communities welcomed her like a long lost family member and the terrain was similar to Scotland with burns and open fields, small settlements and isolated dwellings that could easily have been crofts. Yet the high, craggy mountain ranges, the wide stretches of crystal clear sparkling water, the wilderness dense with luxuriant ferns and rich with unfamiliar wildlife and birdsong took her breath away. She determined to explore and learn as much as she could. Pacing herself carefully, she mixed her performances with speaking engagements from Dunedin to Christchurch and deliberately cut out time to immerse herself in New Zealand's extraordinary natural beauty.

She kept a detailed diary of two particular excursions in the Otago District of South Island, illustrating the pages with photographs. She sent the diary as a round robin letter to a group of friends addressed first to Mrs Norman McLeod in Buckinghamshire who would forward it to Mrs J. May, c/o the English Speaking Union at Dartmouth House in London, to Miss H. Lloyd in Guildford, to Marie Dare in London and finally, to Margie, c/o the family solicitor in Glasgow with the instruction that she should keep it. Not as intimate as some of her personal letters to Margie, it is nevertheless vivid and revealing. On the first trek, she was accompanied by a female companion who may have been known to all the diary recipients for Héloïse identified her simply and with familiarity, as J.

Their journey started by boat from Lake Wakatipu near Queenstown. She and J were escorted by a Major MacKenzie from what seems now to be called the Walter Peak High Country Farm but which, at that time, was called the MacKenzie homestead. The diary begins:

> 7am. Much too early to get up. But one's friend Adventure suddenly whispered 'the Trip – today have you forgotten?' And so I speedily got up and donned the riding clothes which had been waiting for this moment! I heard the purr of the motor launch that Major MacKenzie was bringing from her moorings. By 7.30am we were all aboard and the various bags and bundles containing stores lay in the cabin. What fun we had had packing them all and writing 'sugar', 'tea', 'candles', 'flour' etc. on the smaller bags which in their turn were put into large sacklike ones to be loaded on the horses. The Lake was beautiful in the early morning light and we got a good view of the MacKenzie's homestead nestling beside it, under the towering Walter peak, nearly 6000ft above sea level. This is the largest sheep station in the Southern Hemisphere and although there are thousands of animals one hardly ever sees them on the huge hill faces. Shepherds are constantly ranging over the peaks, peaks that look absolutely inaccessible from beneath and they have huts for the shepherds to shelter in. Each hut has a supply of stores, utensils, blankets etc. and we were actually to stay in one later.

From Elfin Bay at the top of the lake, they took to horseback. Entranced by the unfamiliar cries of paradise ducks and tui birds Héloïse's small party trekked through valleys and gorges for a good six hours before it stopped finally for the night at a shepherds' hut. She wrote:

> Soon the fire was blazing and I noticed that the sun was going to slip behind the opposite side of our valley so suggested to J that we inspect our quarters. One look at the straw pallet littered with bedclothes which had been used by everyone since Noah, decided us and we stripped them all off, revealing the straw mattress ...

> Major M is a splendid cook – soon the fish was sizzling in chunks and I was allowed to hold a frying pan over the fire with some things

like banana fritters in it. I nearly exploded into rapture at the whole proceedings. The sun vanished and a rich afterglow filled the valley. The splash of the river below sounded faintly and the noisy gurgle of a merry little burn rushing down beside the hut set me humming a *port-à-beul* tune.

When the fish was done to a turn, the banana fritters turned into potato chips (to my secret admiration, tinged with the shame of ignorance!) and we sank down upon some sacks near the fire and ate and gossiped round the fire and finally the men went off. We washed in the icy burn, creeping down to it in the darkness with the aid of a torch. My favourite piece of soap eluded me and I sought under stones for it in the starlight and brought it up only to have it slip down and be swirled down to the next pool! It was a very warming game and I repaired up the bank wet and happy to find a disconsolate J sitting on the bed thinking it was cold. So we shovelled some of the campfire into our apartment – alas for clean hands.

A faded photograph shows Héloïse, now aged forty, standing relaxed and comfortable in riding breeches, looking healthy and strong. She was passionately interested in her surroundings, determinedly optimistic and evidently quite sanguine about the unexpected. The diary reveals her transparent joy, not just in trekking for hours through what must have seemed like virgin territory but in the tiniest details of labelling the bags of supplies, sleeping in the bunkhouse, holding the frying pan over a fire.

I looked up the meaning of *port-à-beul* and shivered a little. It describes in Gaelic, an unaccompanied song, literally a song from the mouth. A few months earlier, lying comfortably entwined with my small granddaughter, she had asked for a story. As I moved to find a book she threw a restraining arm around me, demanding, 'No, no ... tell me a story *from your mouth*!' Already she knew the difference between the real deal and the second hand. She wanted my authenticity, my soul. It is a good phrase.

It was bitterly cold when they woke in the shepherds' hut as the sunlight had not reached their side of the valley. Héloïse clambered undaunted to wash again in the burn and after a breakfast of more sizzling fish, the group set off on horseback towards Lake Howden. After a while, Major MacKenzie reined in his horse and they paused to contemplate the skyline of spectacular peaks. Héloïse wrote with some astonishment:

> We were passing along the Ailsa Range, magnificent mountains, lofty and peak like and about all nameless. Major M asked me to choose one to bear my name! Fancy choosing a mountain! I couldn't make up my mind but finally chose the one on the left here [photograph pasted onto the page]. I don't know its exact height but our hut was over 2000ft up and the bush line here is about 3000ft and it is very much higher than the bush line. It revealed a glacier too. I was just gloating about it all when we suddenly plunged into bush again so thick that one hardly saw the sky – composed of multitudes of birch trees with tiny leaves also innumerable ferns and mosses and hanging moss.

Had Major MacKenzie been teasing her? Was the mountain his to name? Surely it had an indigenous name. I contacted the New Zealand Geographical Society which referred me to Professor Mike Roche at Massey University in Wellington. He sent me a link to the Land Information of New Zealand Gazetteer and also told me that place naming in New Zealand became organised thoroughly with its own Act of Parliament, only after World War II. The Gazetteer showed that while there is no Mount Russell-Fergusson, there are four Mount Fergusons on South Island. None has been named 'officially'. So, given the diary and the photograph and the evidence of no official naming, it seemed reasonable to assume, at least until an authoritative contradiction appears, that one *is* named after her. Professor Roche did not disagree.

J had not slept well in the hut and found it hard to warm up in the chill of the morning. She had set off on her horse wearing every garment she had, looking from behind, Héloïse observed bluntly but probably with considerable accuracy, like a large clothes bag. After a long day's trek to reach Eglinton Valley, she and Héloïse finally got on a bus to Te Anau where they were to prepare for another excursion from Lake Manapouri to Doubtful Sound. J perked up as they drove along, becoming quite illuminating about different sheep breeds and husbandry, but it was the last time she got a mention. The next day it was agreed that the trekking conditions were too strenuous for her and J was left behind.

Thus, as the only tourist, Héloïse set off on the second trek. She was accompanied by three men whom she described in her diary as 'the Guide, the pert little Engineer and the handyman, Malcolm'. She was convinced that Malcolm was a Celt and imbued him with a string of heroic qualities. Struggling with the steep climb, she described him coming up the trail behind her:

> I let him pass and heard his soft Highland tones, 'I always take it easy here,' and continuing, 'in fact I sometimes sit down a while'. I realized he was trying to prevent me pressing the pace and appreciated it, but nothing would have induced me to stop then. The remarks were typical of Malcolm and of his race.

> Later, trying to gauge the height of a magnificent tree fern with my eyes aloft for one moment, I fell down and still later, revelling in all the beauty I looked at the sunny little river I'd reached, fell down again. I then decided it wasn't worth it and plodded on to the halfway hut. Said Malcolm, 'You're travelling fast this morning (encouraging).' Me: 'I would have been here sooner but I fell twice.' Malcolm: 'Oh, well, but it's easy to do that now, I fell once myself going over.' What a gallant understanding creature, this 'handyman' who carries the biggest pack and is treated with slight contempt by the others.

After their evening meal, the Guide and the Engineer left the hut to see to the supplies while Héloïse and Malcolm talked beside the fire. She must have seemed a sympathetic listener, for he described how the slump had forced him to give up a smallholding where he had raised sheep, cattle and horses, including the Greenstone pony that Héloïse had been riding the previous day. She didn't write further about his personal catastrophe, but mused instead on the tedium of having nothing to do, depicting the three men almost as vagrants rather than tourist guides:

> The fireplace was littered with footgear and socks etc. drying. Two candles were stuck on saucers on the wooden table. Malcolm wielded great black kettles or billies and slowly washed up and I became vastly intrigued with the fact that I had nothing to do and realised the lives these people lead, having no belongings. All I had in the world at that moment was in a tiny pack in the adjoining room and it offered no scope for action. And one couldn't go out because of the flies!

Knowing how to help with washing up may have been as novel to her as frying potatoes but she didn't seem interested in helping Malcolm. I wondered whether her response would have been different had she been a man; would she have pursued or recorded more of the conversation, rolled up her sleeves at the sink? Imagining my father in her place, I wasn't sure. Granny Hélène would probably have engaged best with Malcolm; comparing notes about the cost of feed, the impact of the weather at lambing time; the horror of being forced to sell beloved stock. Of course, Héloïse may have done all of that. She just neglected to tell us about it.

In the morning, their journey started on foot from the north arm of Lake Manapouri along a flattish woodland trail. Héloïse selected Brahms' song, 'Wie Melodien zieht es mir', to carry her footsteps as she tramped along, bursting aloud into snatches of it every so often. As they started a long, steep and rough climb through dense bush she struggled to hold the melody and often had to stop to catch her breath, taking the chance to soak up her surroundings, listening to the birds, marvelling at the furled necks of the young tree ferns emerging like a string section from the undergrowth. Two days later, when the little team retraced their steps over the Saddle back to Lake Manapouri she chose a different, unnamed tune which she described as, 'gay enough to drive me on, but not too breath-taking to hum when the climbing became really steep'. She described the long, strenuous trek that ended only after darkness had fallen:

> Shortly after wriggling through a steep stony cleft it seemed one must have reached the top but after a flattish grassy walk it became apparent one was in a high cup like little plateau, surrounded by still higher hills and then quite suddenly, one reached a hut! I learned we had come 6 miles and had 5 to go. 'Was it steep?' 'Oh, a bit of a climb mebbe,' said the dear tactful (lying) Malcolm. It was nearly 3pm. I felt impelled to plod on. We climbed to 2200ft. Malcolm disappeared behind with his huge pack. I got a second wind but the toil was as great as ever. And everything was frightfully steep and very wet and dark. The big tree ferns were more profuse. I daren't look at them; footsteps were all that mattered, I was saturated and muddy and had been in 'over both ankles'. There was nothing but the dense silence of the bush, the hanging drippingness of wet mosses and ferns and the faint roar of the Livia River rushing down to the sea – and my darling song never once deserted me and one revelled to be alone in this great wild place.

The trek was broken with a day on board a boat exploring and fishing around Doubtful Sound. Basking on the sunlit deck in her bedroom slippers, relaxed and relieved after the days of strenuous climbing, Héloïse gazed in awe at the towering rock faces that plunged sheer and straight into the water with no perceptible shoreline. What she described as her 'large travelling shoes' lay drying in the sun on the deck. Later in the diary she observed, 'No one cleaned my shoes during the entire trip.' I laughed aloud. Was this an in-joke with her circle of friends? Or genuine bewilderment from a woman who could easily mistake a frying potato for a banana and who had lived only in houses or hotels where daily shoe cleaning was provided as silently and automatically as clean bedlinen and hot meals?

Later, she spent a day on the Franz Josef Glacier and wrote to Margie in May 1936 to say:

Then I flew over the Alps to the Tasman Glacier, a marvellous flight and we were told we were amongst the first women to land there. We rose 10,000ft and had a marvellous view of the dense bush, giving way to rocky hills and higher, giant snow peaks and ice fields. I've never seen such a sight. Away to the south and north there stretched the great snowy peaks, it was a cloudless day and the ice and snow glistened in the sun. I had 4 days rambling at Mt Cook (the place we landed at) and they were blissful. I was out from morn till night and took a thermos and went along trails and over rivers on tiny suspended bridges and up the baby glaciers and listened to the thunder of occasional avalanches and grilled in the hot sun. Now we are having winter but it is very bright and will be warmer as I go north.

In between and on the road, she was engaged to speak about the Hebrides as much as to perform with Harplet. She headed north slowly, addressing Women's Clubs and Institutes as well as the Auckland Rotary Club where, as in South Africa, a female speaker was a novelty. The weather became cooler. In one college, the boys sat in overcoats, mufflers and gloves with rugs over their knees, while she shivered on a cold platform in her long white gown. Her robes were getting tatty with suitcase life and she planned to get some new ones made in Australia. But she remained enraptured with New Zealand, and wrote to Margie on 26 August 1936, saying:

I'm in the throes of having a small holiday now and have just been to Tongariro, the winter sports place. It was such fun watching the skiing, people lying in the snow in heaps with their skis sticking up in the air helpless with laughter and the air full of the cry 'how do I get up?'! I had some lovely days tramping the high tussock covered plains or climbing about the huge mts having lunch on black rocks popping out of the snow. I was out, complete with thermos in mist or hot sunshine. The winter in this country is a joy. No fogs, no gloom, sun shining somewhere always although it has been cold too. In the daytime it is usually brightly sunny. I've just had a bout of concerts at the Bay of Plenty and there were flowers of many kinds, and lemons growing in profusion on the trees. The NZ 'bush' is evergreen so one doesn't get bare winter effects – arum lilies are a weed! Spring is coming, the trees are yellow with fragrant mimosa, most beautiful straw hats appearing in the shops, it seems so funny in August!

After spending ten months in New Zealand, she arrived finally in Australia in November 1936. Her persuasive skills, exerted on a Miss Nancy Jobson who had opened a finishing school called Hopewood House set in glorious grounds almost mid-way between Sydney and Canberra, secured the auditorium for a recital of Hebridean songs before an audience of invited guests. As a route for setting up more engagements, it paid off.

By 9 December, she was performing at the Christmas gathering in Melbourne of the British Music Society of Victoria where the programmes were threaded with tartan in honour of her visit. She may have been tired, but *The Age* reported that, 'she sang the songs with a lovely freedom that brought to her listeners all the wild throbbing beauty of the windswept islands'. Three days later she was entertaining a gathering of the Clan Cameron on board HMS *Orama*. A week before Christmas, she was at the Forum Club in Sydney with an audience that included the Lieutenant Governor and his wife and a range of dignitaries dressed in considerable finery. This first Australian foray had been successful and she would be back.

Margie had written to say that all was well with the family. Hélène was settling happily into a new kind of farming in Southern Rhodesia backed up by Crichton and Margaret Glendinning. My parents' marriage had had hiccups but seemed to be on a more even keel. Héloïse was relieved. She had found a Dutch agent in New Zealand who would organise the next part of her tour.

CHAPTER TEN

GAMELAN AND TINKLING TONES

Almost exactly a year after she had disembarked in Wellington, Héloïse arrived in Bali. It was early January 1937 and the streets were more than usually full of noise and colourful festivities. As part of the Dutch East Indies, Bali was celebrating the very European marriage, over seven thousand miles away in The Hague, of Princess Juliana of the Netherlands to the German Prince Bernhard of Lippe-Biesterfeld. The royal couple had met at the Winter Olympics in Bavaria just a few months before and had enjoyed a short if rather tense engagement period. The Nazi government denied visas to several German wedding guests and Prince Bernhard was hastily granted Dutch citizenship just six weeks before the wedding. It was impossible to tell how much Héloïse knew or understood of the fomenting unrest in Europe but it must have been in the air.

After her easy acclimatisation to New Zealand and Australia, Bali was intriguing and exotic. She was bewitched by the sights and smells and especially by the sounds. Following crowds down a dusty street towards a public square she heard for the first time the delicate, persistent rhythm of gamelan music. The musicians sat on stools or cross legged on the ground before an array of gongs, bamboo flutes, drums and xylophones. She told Margie that the rhythm was perfect. 'No conductor, no written music, an utterly relaxed, almost careless atmosphere and yet,' she wrote, 'each village orchestra has a repertoire covering a symphony!' She spotted a small boy who was lighting a cigarette when a gong player had suddenly handed him his beater. Nonchalantly, with the cigarette still in hand and without missing a beat, the boy had sustained the rhythm. Héloïse watched in awe. It set the tone for the rest of her visit.

She would surely have met Walter Spies in Bali. A gifted painter and musician, by 1937 he had lived there for over fifteen years and he was deeply absorbed in its art and music both as a researcher and creator. He was the go-to European for information about Balinese culture, just the kind of person that Héloïse, with her insatiable curiosity, would have approached. A few years earlier, Spies had begun to collaborate on some research with Beryl de Zoete, a dancer and researcher from London who was studying Hindu based dance and their book, *On Dance and Drama in Bali*, with a preface written by Arthur Waley, was published in London by Faber & Faber in 1938.

Héloïse's annotated copy sits on my desk. Not gifted to the Mitchell Library, she had kept this hefty volume with chapters covering myriad types of Balinese dance and illustrated with over a hundred photographs, almost all of them taken by Spies, close to her. Slipped between the pages is a thin sheet of paper with some faint handwritten notes describing aspects of her journey. She had also torn out seven pages from the October 1939 issue of the *Geographical Magazine*, on 'Art and Life in Bali' by Dr F.C.E. Knight and folded them inside. The physical and spiritual links between music and everyday life, whether in the Hebrides, Africa or Northern Europe already fascinated her. Now, she was intrigued to learn how Balinese dance movement also reflected belief and daily experience.

Nearly twenty years Héloïse's senior, Beryl de Zoete lived intermittently in London with Arthur Waley but she travelled and researched widely and had written extensively about music and dance. An online photograph of Beryl showed her sitting outdoors in Bali, her hair in a short bob, bare legs stretched before her, ankles crossed. Wearing a loose, backless, halter necked dress and with papers on her knee for note taking, she is gesturing towards a young male Balinese dancer posed in front of her, one leg and one arm raised. I could picture Héloïse observing her, being similarly relaxed yet determined in her own research, seeking responses and information from the musicians that she met.

I have few photographs of Héloïse, apart from publicity ones and the blurred snap from the trek in New Zealand. Almost all the personal descriptions I have heard were from her later life and in Scotland, where she seemed rather buttoned up. I can't be sure whether that reflected the climate, her temperament or her age at the time.

In Bali, clothes were light and the mood was relaxed, the place humming with imagination and cultural activity. During much of the 1930s, the anthropologist Jane Belo was there with her Canadian husband, the composer and ethnomusicologist Colin McPhee. Perhaps taking a lead from Spies, McPhee wrote extensively about Balinese music and would later influence Benjamin Britten. Belo was writing a book called *Trance in Bali*. The place was electric, not only with creativity but also with sexual tension, for in 1938, Spies would be arrested along with others in a crackdown by the local authorities on homosexuality. The following year, McPhee, also gay, divorced Jane and returned to spend time with Britten and W.H. Auden, amongst others, in New York.

Héloïse had stumbled into a moment in time in Bali. It is tempting for me to try to entwine her personal and emotional life within this intriguing world, not only in Bali, but wherever she travelled, particularly when her insatiable curiosity led her off the colonial beaten track. Although I am sure the beaten track would have had its own idiosyncrasies, she would have encountered almost everywhere, echoes of bohemianism; men and women exploring new and creative forms of self-expression, who were experimenting with and leading alternative lifestyles, culturally, socially and sexually. Clearly, doors opened to her readily, inviting her to perform. She was a welcome professional colleague. She was passionate, creative, determined and funny yet there seems to have been something missing. She must have met like-minded people who shared her passions, whom she found attractive and who found her equally to be so. Yet, my search for any deep personal connections or romance seemed to be proving fruitless.

Fleetingly, I wonder whether she was prudish. The tenets of the Christian Science Church urged adherents 'to love one another … to be meek, merciful, just and *pure*', which could lead, depending on interpretation, to a somewhat cloistered life. Yet coupled with her broad sense of spirituality and of romance, such tenets may have engendered an open mindedness to the sexual lives of others regardless of her own. Her upbringing had been characterised by the freedom to be adventurous, both literally and in terms of her dreams and aspirations. From her teenaged readiness to study in London, the fearless encounters in the woodlands of Washington, the partying with professors in Germany, her trekking in New Zealand, it was clear that Héloïse was no shrinking violet.

I wonder whether her solitary lifestyle was due to a love lost during those early London days, perhaps as a lasting consequence of war; or whether she had actively rejected a conventional marriage, or even an unconventional one, choosing deliberately an uncluttered freedom to pursue her passions and ambition. I question whether she was gay; wonder what else might explain the apparent absence of a lover, of an important confidante in her life. According to all that I have been able to unearth, she was sociable, communicative and fun. At the same time, she drew deeply on rich sources of spiritual and emotional fulfilment, often immersing herself entirely in the natural world and in music. She revelled in being solitary, most especially outdoors, absorbed in an inner life, alone with her imagination amongst the elements. Maybe that was enough.

Not long after Héloïse died and quite inadvertently, Margie revealed something of her own innocence and pragmatism about sex and marriage. With only two years difference in age between them, Margie's remarks may have echoed Héloïse's experience and views. It was in the early 1970s when, aged twenty, I told Margie that I had moved in with my boyfriend. She fixed me in her gaze and asked, 'Are you sleeping with him?' I nodded, anticipating moral rebuke. Without hesitation, she followed up with, 'What's it like?' There was what seemed like a very long pause. I stuttered and laughed weakly. We were both embarrassed. Then she laughed as well, hugging me, and we walked arm in arm down the echoing concrete stairs from her first floor flat in Helensburgh to go for lunch. Driving home, I squirmed at the awkward exchange. That question from an unmarried woman born in 1898 seemed to reflect not only innocence and curiosity but a humbling trust and openness towards me. I wondered whether both sisters had felt that in the absence of a desirable suitor, they would simply focus on their spiritual love of God and express their passions through work and creativity.

Fifteen years later when I told Margie that the boyfriend, by then my husband and the father of my children, and I were separating, she looked at me first for signs of distress and then became thoughtful. Accepting the facts without obvious judgement and implicitly urging me to move on, she seemed almost to be thinking aloud when finally, she said, 'Men have never known what to do with us Russell-Fergusson women.' It was a profound statement. I should have probed, asked what she meant, sought the stories of how many men, how many reflective conversations, how many relationships lay behind that remark. Héloïse may have held precisely the same view and Margie could have given me insights into the myriad experiences, the early feminism that had infused their lives. But in that moment, as ever, I was thinking about myself, my children, about my own life.

Of course, it may have been the other way round. Perhaps the Russell-Fergusson women had never known what to do with men. Hélène led a very independent life which some observers may have thought was neglectful of her husband. But from the outset, William had recognised Hélène's need not just to live in the country but to be actively engaged with it, indeed it was one of the reasons he loved her. He seemed to support her independence wholeheartedly. Inadvertently, it may have been William who set unfeasibly high expectations of any suitor in his daughters. Only Denise married, but then she was of a later generation.

Back in Bali, Héloïse sat outside entranced by an evening performance of the Kecak Monkey Dance-Drama based on the Ramayana. Awed by its power, by the sounds and the spectacle, she wrote to Margie, 'I have never witnessed such a unique scene anywhere. We were right in the heart of a native village, listening to the most incredible ART.' In de Zoete and Spies's book, it is described primarily as a dance of exorcism:

> The words are less words than power-giving sounds; reiterated bird-like cries, lonely wailing voices, hoarse ejaculations, murmured bouts of fierce dialogue … to seek a consecutive theme in the wandering voices is a vain quest. If we feel impelled to find an explanation of what is complete in itself it is because we are unused to this abstraction of emotion in movement, though familiar enough with it in music.[24]

Beryl was also a proponent of Dalcroze Eurhythmics, a method of teaching musical concepts through the natural rhythms of movement. The book had minutely detailed observations of the execution of Balinese dances, stressing not just the importance of rhythm but of blurring the distinctions between music, drama and dance. This interconnectedness of human creative responses to the world must have resonated with Héloïse. Everything she was seeing, hearing and reading in Bali reinforced her understanding of the intrinsic links

---

24 Beryl de Zoete and Walter Spies, *Dance and Drama in Bali* (London: Faber, 1938), p. 85.

between people, their living environments, their sense of spirituality and the urge for creative self-expression.

Yet the trip to Indonesia meant that while at one moment she had plunged into the thrilling unfamiliarity of Balinese life and culture, at the next, she had to fulfil her very European obligations. She moved deftly between the two while at the same time she pursued her personal research into the music and musical instruments of the country. In the volume, Harps F (Players), in *The Russell-Fergusson Collection of Harps*, there is a photograph of an instrument that looks like a small upturned boat. There is an accompanying note from Dr Karl Halusa at the National Museum of Indonesia, dated 9 February 1937, that reflects possible conversations they had had. He wrote:

> I send you photographs of the Javanese instrument kowongan (a kind of beetle) or 'tudung' (hat). This is played by herdsmen. The kowongan is used not only as a musical instrument but also as shelter against sun and rain. There are several strings tuned in slendro. On some are a small peg made from bamboo or wood to make the vibrations unquiet. The sound resembles a gong. There are also streaks of bamboo to imitate the sound of the Javanese drum called kendang.

She travelled through Java and Batavia (now Jakarta) to Singapore and back again, giving recitals and radio broadcasts and addressing another Rotary Club lunch to which, remarkably, 'ladies' were invited. She performed in concert halls, schools and one afternoon, on board the British naval ship HMS *Dorsetshire*, which she described to Margie:

> It was such fun, arranged in the open with many flags etc. and the men all around the platform and also perched up on turrets and guns. Half of my audience seemed to be in the sky. They were mostly south county men but responded to a man to the songs. I had a delightful letter from Capt. Murray afterwards about the men being unusually attentive and remarking that 'none had gone away' during the fray.

[cont'd]

This amused me as I had not failed to notice the ship's band drawn up ready to step in when the men became restive with the lone female who had come to entertain them. The officers, whom we met at the English Club next evening suggested I go to the 'Hermes' (aircraft carrier) when she is in Singapore because she has a more suitable place for Harplet to sing in – this, I discovered is the aeroplane hangar! We shall see.
PS I forgot to say that my Dutch agents here are so pleased with Harplet that they have offered me concerts in Sumatra and I will also tour Malaya then go to Bangkok, Angkor, Hong Kong.

Inevitably, her concerts had been to largely European audiences:

My first concert in Java was a great thrill. It was wonderful to sing once more to Dutch people. The Hebridean songs did their work thoroughly and several hundred people listened with unconcealed curiosity. Few had any idea of the ancient culture of Scotland. No one had ever seen a clarsach before. 'Does everyone in those islands play that little instrument?' asked an earnest listener. I had to assure him that they did not, as yet, though perhaps, some day – I explained each song in Dutch although this was not absolutely necessary owing to the people's good command of English. It was thrilling to read in the press next morning, 'If this art could be understood by all today, there would be no more war.' Surely the old Highland songs could gain no finer tribute than that.

Amongst the memorabilia is a review of a concert she gave in Tientsin and a colourful label for its Astor House Hotel. But her letters made no mention of China despite her bringing home labels from The Grand Hotel and the Hotel du Nord in Peking. By then, she must surely have been aware of the tensions in Europe and, more immediately, she was particularly close to the on-going conflict between Japan and China which would lead to full-scale war breaking out between the two countries that August. Yet in May 1937 she had travelled to Japan via Korea, visiting unnamed friends who lived off the beaten track in a house surrounded by rice fields and within easy reach of hill climbing. She wrote only of climbing through wild azaleas, lily of the valley, irises and forget-me-nots to rest finally on a hilltop with a picnic lunch before striding downhill and then up the next peak where the friends sat companionably with a flask of tea and gazed at the panorama.

I was curious about such friends but there were no details. Maybe she tapped into a network of Scots or of musicians who were happy to welcome a like-minded visitor to their homes; a cultural forerunner of Airbnb. Then, out of the blue, I received an email from the Netherlands. The writer enclosed a photograph of Héloïse at a guesthouse in the mountains above Batavia in January 1937 and another photograph of the message that she had written in the guestbook before leaving, which said:

> A rare experience of Beauty and Harmony, up in the hills, with a garden, music and wonderful kindness of a charming host and hostess and children. Greetings from the Clarsach of Scotland [a little drawing of Harplet], also Scotia (H. Russell-Fergusson).

She had been accompanied there by a Mrs May, possibly the same Mrs J. May, addressee c/o the English Speaking Union, to whom the round-robin diary of the New Zealand trek had been sent. Perhaps too this was the mysterious 'J' who had found the trek rather too tough but who had an impressive knowledge of sheep. Héloïse's letters revealed nothing about 'J' but she had mentioned this guesthouse when writing to Margie:

> We've just spent a most amusing weekend in the mts with a Dutchman (fan of Harplet) and his family and we had music all the time. Though a business man, he played piano exquisitely and we revelled in sitting peacefully in the chalet listening to him.

The sender of the email, the granddaughter of the exquisite pianist, told me that her grandparents' guesthouse was not a business but was used only for the convenience of friends. So perhaps the notion of a musical 'network' was not so far off the mark.

In Japan, Héloïse broadcast from Osaka and wrote to Margie that she loved the clattering of wooden sandals on the street, the women looking like butterflies and the men so elegant in kimonos. Her letter went on:

> My first appearance is in Tokyo next week. I enclose a notice, and have been fortunate to secure the impresario, Strok, to present Harplet as he can get the Japanese audience I want. European music is really only beginning here – I am busy in spare moments slogging at my Japanese, and have absolutely no idea how the Hebridean songs will strike Eastern people. Now I really must stop this ramble. To add to our occupation, 2 big bundles of Daily Telegraphs just arrived. We tried to hear the coronation in a small radio shop in a Korean town but nothing but static was to be heard, such a disappointment. Did any of the family go? I can picture Denise in the front row by chance and not design.

Awsay Strok was an American impresario who had introduced many European and American artists to Far Eastern audiences. A native of Riga, he began his career as a cellist with the old Shanghai Symphony Orchestra and then acted as an agent for others including the violinist Jascha Heifetz, the cellist Gregor Piatigorsky, and the pianist Arthur Rubenstein. The back copies of the *Daily Telegraph* would have been full of the constitutional upheaval following the abdication of Edward VIII in December 1936, and the lead up to the coronation of George VI on 12 May 1937. Denise, now twenty-one, was nowhere near the front row at the coronation. But she was no longer in Rhodesia either. She was in Aberdeenshire and a member of a local dance troupe called the Dancers of Don which had been set up by the Honourable Elizabeth Forbes-Sempill, a slight, boyish looking young woman of around twenty-five, glimpsed with Denise in a newspaper photograph.

Meanwhile, setting the newspapers to one side, Héloïse had to spend more time than expected on learning enough Japanese to introduce her performances. She described the challenge in the *People's Journal* series:

I had no idea how Japanese audiences would react to Hebridean lilts. Arriving in Japan, I wished to rehearse them and finding a sympathetic and talented Japanese woman, I confidently started my efforts. To my horror, she looked absolutely blank. I repeated it slowly and then loudly. Normally, no Japanese would laugh at one to one's face, it would be considered grossly impolite. But finally this modern Japanese could control herself no longer and she burst out laughing. And so did I, when I discovered the reason! In Japan, the women speak with high pitched tinkling tones and use a different style of speech to the men.

My professor had gravely translated my remarks in solemn professorial style which proved irresistibly funny to Japanese ears. 'Can any of it be used?' I asked in despair. My instructor gently broke the news that it must all be redone and relearned. With but a short time before the concert, I had to work day and night in order to be ready. We had a dress rehearsal in the hotel ballroom which possessed a platform. The great room was full of waiters with here and there a waitress in her graceful kimono, arranging the tables. 'A good opportunity,' said Miss Yamada, undaunted. 'See if they can understand.' I mounted the platform with trepidation. 'These songs come from the Hebridean Isles,' I announced loudly in my most tinkling tones. I continued my remarks in despair, feeling as if I could sink into the floor. But wonder of wonders, the air suddenly became charged with curiosity. Waiters stopped to gaze at me and then at each other, bewildered. Rice bowls were forgotten and thatched cottages took their place. They understood!

A memory flashed into my head from the day I met Héloïse in Crianlarich in 1969. She had told me the best way to learn a new language. 'You have to say it aloud,' she'd said, 'shout it out, really.' She told me how she'd hired a canoe and paddled down the Thames from near its source all the way to London, while practising her Japanese or Finnish or Italian at the top of her voice. I found further details in the *People's Journal* where she'd written:

I started at the source of the river near Cricklade, when it was in flood, in a small Rob Roy canoe with a double paddle. Not until I pushed off did I realise that the water was almost up to the little farm bridges across the stream. Impossible to stop! The flood was bearing me down at a speed of many miles an hour. The first bridge came into sight. One small low arch. Lying down flat in the canoe, I steered for it and hoped for the best. There was not an eyelash to spare! I cleared the tiny arch and rushed downstream exulting. At Boulters Lock, Henley, I must have looked a mere speck and from high above me, spectators looked down in amusement. I ran into a regatta by mistake and was rammed. I was chased by a swan and drenched by a speedboat. Caught by the strong tide, I spent an afternoon on Hammersmith beach where my canoe was surrounded by admiring urchins! I paddled 149 miles in all.

I wondered whether she had spoken in Japanese when she was invited to perform for the Emperor's brother Prince Takamatsu, and his wife. Curtseying before them, she had been disappointed that the Prince was wearing a lounge suit but delighted by the Princess's kimono of egg-shell blue embroidered with sprays of cherry blossom and an obi of heavy cream silk tied with a scarlet cord. Héloïse was surely in her Celtic robes.

Once back in Australia, her diary filled quickly with radio talks and performances, concert hall recitals and speaking engagements in schools and colleges. Along with Scottish singers Duncan Morison and Sidney MacEwan, she was welcomed by Clement Hosking to perform and to speak with The Sydney Folk-Song Choir. Hosking was well regarded as a singer and conductor and his interests included a fascination with Hebridean songs and those from Wales and from Cornwall, where his grandfather had lived. When he declared a desire to visit the UK, a fund raising committee quickly arranged a folk festival at the New South Wales Conservatorium which included some 'ancient bardic songs sung to harp accompaniment by the Sydney Folk Song Choir, clad in robes of druids, bards and ovates'.[25] Having enjoyed

---

25 Clement Hosking, *Fine Song for Singing, A Celtic Odyssey* (Sydney: G.M. Dash, 1950), p. 32.

Hélène Russell-Fergusson, standing, with Héloïse (reclining),
Marguerite and Hélène's mother, Marie, c.1901

William Russell-Fergusson, 1863–1927

Ardtur, Port Appin, Argyll

On the shore at Ardtur, 1916. Margie and Uncle John behind
William in chair, baby Denise and two unidentified others

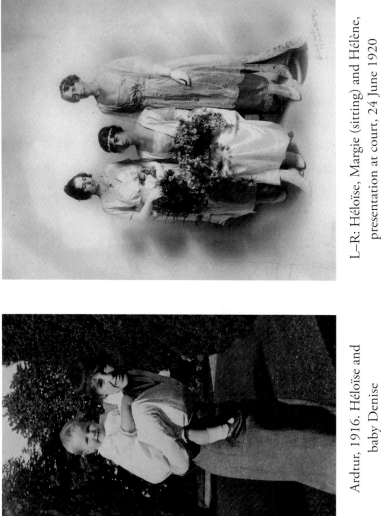

L–R: Héloïse, Margie (sitting) and Hélène, presentation at court, 24 June 1920

Ardtur, 1916. Héloïse and baby Denise

1924

Playhouse

1814

N Street

MONDAY

DEC. 15

at 4:30

RECITAL FOR TWO PIANOS, By

KATHERINE ELLIS and
HÉLOÏSE RUSSELL
(Scottish Pianiste)

UNDER THE DISTINGUISHED PATRONAGE OF:

THE LADY ISABELLA HOWARD

MRS. WILLIAM HOWARD TAFT

MISS LUCY BRICKENSTEIN	MRS. FREDERIC DELANO	MRS. ROBERT JOHNSTON
MRS. ERIC BUXTON	MISS LAURA HARLAN	MRS. JAMES MITCHELL
MRS. GRAHAM CHARLTON	MRS. FREDERICK HOLTON	MRS. WALLACE RADCLIFFE
MRS. HENRY GETTY CHILTON	MRS. WALTER HOWE	MRS. DAVID L. WING

Tickets on Sale at
T. Arthur Smith, Inc.
1306 G Street

Reserved $2.20

Unreserved 1.10

Flyer for Recital for Two Pianos at the Playhouse,
1814 N Street, Washington, 1924

Hélène and Denise aged eleven, standing outside Ardtur, 1925

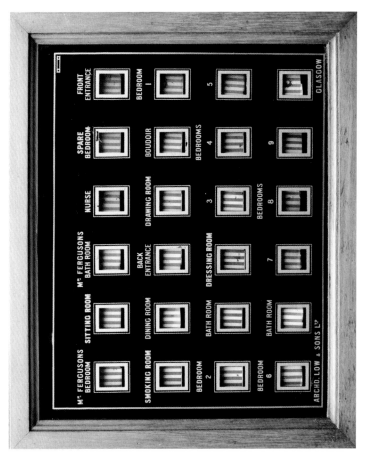

Bell box from Muckairn Castle, Taynuilt, 1926

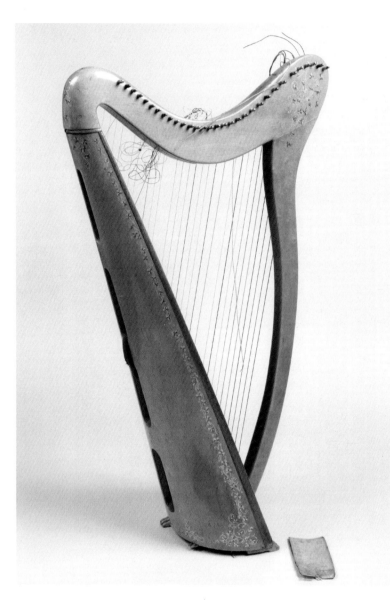

'Harplet' (© CSG CIC Glasgow Museums Collection)

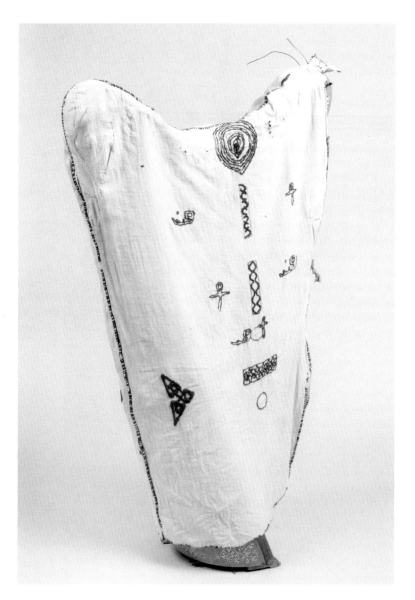

'Harplet' in its embroidered bag (© CSG CIC Glasgow Museums Collection)

Songs of the Hebrides—

HÉLOÏSE RUSSELL-FERGUSSON

An Attractive Singer of Folk Songs
" *Times* "

All Communications :
PORT APPIN, ARGYLL.

General flyer of Héloïse Russell-Fergusson with 'Harplet'
and press opinions, 1920s

McLellan Galleries programme, Friday 12 October 1928, with hand drawn illustrations

AEOLIAN HALL

NEW BOND STREET · - W.1

TUESDAY EVENING

FEBRUARY 17

at 8.30

𝕳ebridean 𝕊ongs

to the

𝕮eltic 𝕳arp

RUSSELL-FERGUSSON

assisted by

JULIA WOLF *Harp*   **MARIE DARE** *'Cello*

KENNETH MACLEOD

will tell some Legends of the Isles

" A fresh and authentic character. Stages each song with simple but picturesque effect."
New York Times.

" A superb performance." *Patric Farrell, Director Irish Theatre, New York.*

TICKETS (including Tax) : Reserved 8/6 and 5/9.   Unreserved 3/-

A limited number of Tickets at 2/4 will be available for members of Scottish Societies
May be obtained at the BOX OFFIC⸱ ⸱ ⸱ ⸱Hall, usual Agents, Libraries and of
IMPERIAL CONCERT AGENCY, Empire House, 175, Piccadilly, W.1
Telephone : GERRARD 9523

Application for tickets by post must be accompanied by a stamped addressed envelope

VAIL AND CO., PRINTERS, LONDON. W.1

Flyer for Aeolian Hall concert with Kenneth MacLeod,
Marie Dare and Julia Wolf, 1931. Note holes where
Héloïse's name has been removed

Wedding of Donald Russell-Fergusson and Elise Mainwaring, December 1932. Héloïse is second from left, Margie on the right and Denise standing by the best man. Other bridesmaid unknown

Héloïse, with 'Harplet', being invested as a Bardess at the Grand
Festival Celtique et Gorsedd des Bardes, Roscoff, July 1934
(© CSG CIC Glasgow Museums and Libraries Collection:
The Mitchell Library, Special Collections)

Héloïse, third row, second from the right, with other Bards, Bardesses, Ovates, Druids and associated dignitaries at the Grand Festival Celtique in Roscoff, July 1934 (© CSG CIC Glasgow Museums and Libraries Collection: The Mitchell Library, Special Collections)

Brooch made of hammered pewter, which Héloïse wore when she was invested as a Bardess in Roscoff in 1934

elbows!:- It looked at me reproachfully, & was so funny with only the ears showing above the brush!. However later on we were all amalgamated again, & rode on at a faster pace to make up the time - The photo shows my horse & me 'wondering in one of our last moments, & the difficulties of following a trail in that type of country -

We were passing along the Ailsa Range, magnificent M⁵, lofty & peak like, & almost all nameless - So major m. asked me to choose one to bear my name! - Fancy choosing a Mt.! I couldn't make up my mind, but finally chose the one on the left here -

I don't know its exact height, but our hut was over 2000 ft. up. & the brush line about here is 3000 ft, & it is very much higher than the brush line - It revealed a glacier too! & I was just gloating about it all, when we suddenly flung ed into brush again, so thick that one hardly saw the sky - composed of multitudes of birch trees, with tiny leaves, also innumerable ferns & mosses & hanging moss. Here is my Mt as I first saw it, also my horses ears in the foreground! - The

Page from Heloise's round robin letter from New Zealand
with attached photographs of her on horseback and of the mountain
she said was named after her, 1936

COWDRAY HALL, LONDON, W.1

TWO

R
E
C
I
T
A
L
S

APRIL
18th

APRIL
23rd

at

8. p.m.

S C O T I A

(Bardess of the Gorsedd)

interpreting

HEBRIDEAN SONGS to the CELTIC HARP

with

Marie Dare ('cello) & Maria Korchinska (harp)

Management: Imperial Concert Agency. London, W.1

Flyer for Scotia (Bardess of the Gorsedd), 'Interpreting Hebridean Songs to the Celtic Harp', Cowdray Hall, London, with Marie Dare and Maria Korchinska, 1938

Extract from the book of words and music compiled by Héloïse during her visits to Kenneth MacLeod and which is lodged in the Mitchell Library, Glasgow (© CSG CIC Glasgow Museums and Libraries Collection: The Mitchell Library, Special Collections)

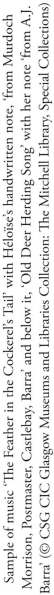

Sample of music 'The Feather in the Cockerel's Tail' with Héloïse's handwritten note, 'from Murdoch Morrison, Postmaster, Castlebay, Barra' and below it, 'Old Deer Herding Song' with her note 'from A.J. Barra' (© CSG CIC Glasgow Museums and Libraries Collection: The Mitchell Library, Special Collections)

The Dolmetsch clarsach

Inscription on base of Dolmetsch clarsach. It reads:
'This clarsach, the first of its kind, was made at Haslemere in July 1932, for Héloïse Russell-Fergusson by Arnold Dolmetsch.' Later, the new owner had added, 'Héloïse used this instrument as an ornament she never played it. In 1946 it was sold to Felicity Campbell.'

Children collecting scrap for the war effort, 1940
(Perth Museum and Art Gallery)

Right: Héloïse and 'Harplet',
1950. *Below:* Héloïse and
Andrew Faulds in *Tir-nan-Og*
at the Cygnet Theatre,
Edinburgh Festival, 1950

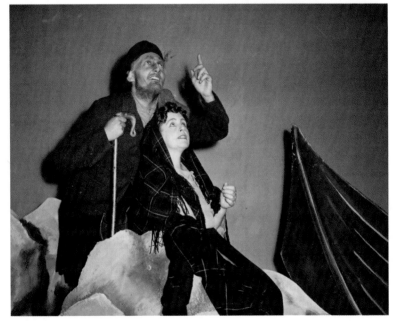

Have you heard

The

Celtic

Harp?

In peak performance, with a haunting
vocale

UNIQUE RECORDS

Composed and played by Russell-Fergusson

CROI **Ceol Clarsaich**
The Sea   The Sound   The Lochan

CRO2 **Highland Harper**
Drifting Wrack   Sea Rain   Spring River

CRO3 **An Treisamh' (the Third)**
Jabble   Dance of the Drops   The Welkin

CRO4 **Seascape**
Seascape   Gay Molaidh   Ostinato

From
CLARSACH RECORDINGS, OBAN, SCOTLAND
All EPs   Price 12/6 per disc

Flyer advertising Héloïse's four EPs in 1968

Portrait of Héloïse by Cathleen Mann, entitled *Singer with a Clarsach (Gaelic Harp)* (© CSG CIC Glasgow Museums Collection)

her own bardic event only a few years before, Héloïse may have lent some suggestions for this performance and she certainly supported his venture, providing, with others, letters of introduction to people in the Hebrides before Hosking departed in August 1937.

Otherwise, and although tempted to explore the natural beauty of Australia, Héloïse stuck to her performance schedule first between Sydney and Melbourne, then to Adelaide and Perth. Australian society life was recorded meticulously in the daily papers, many of which have online archives. She was a guest at the Annual Scottish Ball of the Robert Burns Society of Australia held in Redfern near Sydney in August 1937 and 'Madame Scotia', a name suggested to her by an elderly Scots woman in New Zealand, was entertained at morning tea (11.00am *on the dot*, said the paper) by Miss Mabel Marryet, president, and other members of the Lyceum Club, in September.

In Perth, she saw Arthur Rubenstein performing in the Winthrop Hall at the University of Western Australia, possibly as part of a circuit devised by Strok; a few days later she was one of several guests of honour at the Karrakatta Club Hall for the awards ceremony of the Royal Schools of Music Club. By late September 1937, no doubt tired from the relentless travelling and performing but with her sense of humour intact, she wrote to Margie from the Alexandra Club in Melbourne, sharing anecdotes and making preparations for her return:

We are getting into spring here now and it was quite summery in Sydney before I left. I've been very busy with daily broadcasting and one day I did it twice, morning and evening, the first time in my career. It was a hectic day and as I went to a lecture on Egypt by a friend in the afternoon, I had only had two minutes to get there.

Alas, in my haste I rounded the corner into the building, felt myself slipping in all directions and fell down into the liquid rubber solution as new lino was being spread! You never saw such a mess and as I was taken away by the workmen to be cleaned before the wretched stuff started to solidify, I would have bounced anywhere! Of course, I was late for the lecture and arrived literally soused in petrol and apologised to the Secretary. She said, 'Oh dear, you had better not go near anyone smoking!' I hadn't thought of that! Everyone at the lecture looked about them and politely sniffed and wondered where the petrol was … Something like you (or was it Denise?) who travelled to Appin with a cheese! Everything I had on practically had to go and be cleaned and my frock had just been done and my gloves were new of course. What a day. I simply shrieked with laughter at most of it.

Transforming her catastrophe into a bouncing ball almost obscured the fact that she was going to a lecture on Egypt. In the foreword to *The Russell-Fergusson Collection of Harps*, she specifically acknowledged Dr Hans Hickmann, 'at one time Curator of the Musée du Caire, Egypt' and there is a copy of Hickmann's *Le Metier de Musicien au Temps des Pharaohs* in her archive with his name, written by Héloïse, on the cover.

Hickmann was a German musicologist whose profound interest in traditional Egyptian music and musical instruments led him to settle there in 1933. The *Russell-Fergusson Collection* includes a volume devoted entirely to Egypt, filled with photographs and text that range from ancient wall paintings and early depictions of harps to more recent Egyptian examples. There is a photograph of the tomb of Ptahhotep, a vizier of the Egyptian fifth century, renowned for the maxims he wrote to advise younger generations, one of which Héloïse had written on the reverse of the picture:

> Do not let your heart become proud because of what you know;
> Learn from the ignorant as well as from the learned man;
> There are no limits that have been decreed for art,
> There is no artist who attains entire excellence.

It seems to sum up the values that she cherished; humility, respect and openness towards others and, rather reminiscent of Tagore, it urges artists to celebrate the infinite nature of the possibilities that lie before them. Two of the volumes contain larger photographs and some publicity leaflets. In one, there is a yellowed cutting from *The Sphinx*, published in Cairo. It is a favourable review of two concerts that she had given three weeks apart but frustratingly, it is undated. Her letter to Margie noted that she would stop at Port Said but her journey continued within ten days, not long enough for the two concerts. She must have returned at a later date. The letter had continued:

> I begin concerts in Adelaide the day after I get there, at a Boys College and I love these occasions. The boys are so interested and easy to hold and the masters always so surprised and no one realises I know all that is going on and the struggle the Head had with himself before engaging me as they always fight shy of female entertainers, saying they cannot hold the boys.

> By the way, have you been in London lately? Will you be down before 19th November? I have written for a room to Curzon House but have no idea if it still continues and haven't had a reply. Could you pop in and confirm my arrival, if you happen to be down? I arrive at Pt Said on 'Chitral' (P&O) on 31st October and stay with Mum until 9th November when I sail from Pt Said on 'Naldera' and arrive in London on 19th November. Where will you be again? Do let me have a line as I must see everyone as soon as possible! I have no immediate plans on arrival. It will be strange to be back in London.

Throughout the nearly two years of travelling, her letters to Margie had been upbeat, offering detailed descriptions of her surroundings and many anecdotes. I wonder whether all her letters had been in that vein; whether she included different news, different thoughts when writing, say, to Marie Dare or to other friends. Looking at the historical context, they must all surely have been increasingly alert to the possibility of another world war.

CHAPTER ELEVEN

MADAME SCOTIA AND MADAM SCRAP

Arriving finally in London, Héloïse checked into Curzon House, the club which had replaced The Forum as her favoured base. It might have felt strange to be back but she started hatching plans with Marie Dare almost immediately. And perhaps it was at Marie's suggestion that they approached a renowned Russian harpist to join them in a recital at the Wigmore Hall on Saturday 15 January 1938.

Maria Korchinska had a whiff of intrigue about her. Shortly after playing at Lenin's funeral in 1924 she had left her post as Professor of Harp at Moscow Conservatoire and arrived with her family in Britain. Three years later, Arnold Bax, the British composer who would go on to become Master of the King's Music, dedicated his *Fantasy Sonata for Harp and Viola* to her. Having lived in Ireland as a young man and also as a frequent visitor to the west coast of Scotland, Bax professed a deep affinity to Celtic culture and claimed in his memoirs that at one point, he had begun, '… to write Irishly, using figures and melodies of a definitely Celtic curve'. So to Héloïse and Marie, his endorsement of Korchinska may well have lent her a tenuous Celtic connection, at least by association.

The recital was held under the auspices of London impresario Wilfrid von Wyck. Billed simply as Russell-Fergusson, Héloïse led 'an interpretation of Hebridean Songs to the Celtic Harp', with Marie and Maria accompanying her. A hint of mysticism surrounded Russell-Fergusson for whom, the programme noted, 'the irresistible beauty of the Folksongs of her native land, many of which she had heard from childhood, came to her with their "Impetus of the Infinite energy to be glad" (Tagore)'.

Héloïse had been steeped since childhood in the spirituality of Christian Science and perhaps from an early age she had also read Tagore's poetry which was increasingly popular amongst western readers at the turn of the century. Or maybe she learned first of Tagore from Arthur Geddes during that stormy evening in the Hebrides, talking about his time in India. The quotation on the 1938 programme came from the last chapter of Tagore's Sadhana, where he wrote, 'In all our thoughts and deeds we must be conscious of the infinite. … In all our actions let us feel that impetus of the infinite energy and be glad.'[26] It does not seem too far removed conceptually from the fundamental Christian Science belief that:

> There is no life, truth, intelligence, nor substance in matter. All is
> infinite Mind and its infinite manifestation, for God is ALL-in-all.
> Spirit is immortal Truth; matter is mortal error. Spirit is the real and
> eternal; matter is the unreal and temporal. Spirit is God, and man is
> His image and likeness. Therefore man is not material; he is spiritual.[27]

Tagore's original phrase, 'and be glad', had been substituted on the programme with, 'to be glad'; either a misremembering or for Héloïse, a fortuitous misprint for it captured perfectly her joyous response to Hebridean music. Two thirds of the programme comprised songs from Kennedy-Fraser while others were attributed to Mrs Malloch, North Uist, Janet MacLeod, Eigg, Kenneth MacLeod, Gigha and Annie Johnston, Barra. On the reverse of the programme were listed three

---

26 Rabindranath Tagore, *Sadhana, The Realisation of Life* (New York: MacMillan, 1915).

27 Mary Baker Eddy, *Science and Health with Key to the Scriptures* (Boston: The Christian Science Publishing Company, 1906), p. 468.

string titles by Marie Dare, published by J. & W. Chester, London: Three Highland Sketches for Strings; Phantasy String Quartet; and Le Lac (Solo for Violin, Viola or Cello).

The following week, on 26 January, the Aeolian Hall in New Bond Street advertised a concert of Hebridean Songs to the Clarsach by Scotia (Russell-Fergusson), accompanied only by Marie Dare. *The Scotsman*'s London music critic stated the next day that Héloïse had held the audience spellbound and that after her 'exquisitely played harp accompaniment, no one in tonight's audience will ever be reconciled to a beautiful traditional Gaelic song sung to a pianoforte accompaniment'. *The Times* critic mused that her name change was 'intelligible in the light of the world tours she has recently undertaken', acknowledging implicitly the mouthful that is Russell-Fergusson, and although complimenting her 'fresh tone and direct simplicity', warned that she broke up her singing with too much verbal explanation; a consequence perhaps of her compulsion to share every small detail with her overseas audiences.

Around the same time, there is a faded clipping from gossip pages written by a Mrs Gadabout in an unnamed paper, that describes Bardess Scotia as the guest of honour at a supper party hosted by Mrs Norman MacLeod following a concert at the Aeolian Hall; possibly the same concert and the same Mrs Norman MacLeod who was the first addressee to receive the New Zealand diaries. The report noted that an enthusiastic London-Highland audience had welcomed Héloïse in her white robe with blue and white embroidery, scarlet undersleeves and matching red embroidered slippers.

In April 1938, she and Marie teamed up again with Maria Korchinska for two recitals at the Cowdray Hall in Cavendish Square. This time, the programme acknowledged songs from Annie Johnston, Barra, Miss Amy Murray and A. Mure McKenzie as well as Kenneth MacLeod and Kennedy-Fraser. 1938 was also the year of the Empire Exhibition in Scotland. Glasgow's Bellahouston Park was transformed into a theme park of grand avenues, magnificent pavilions, fountains and fairground rides. The Royal Scottish Country Dance Society laid on a series of exhibitions including five shows by the Dancers of Don, the troupe from Aberdeenshire of which Denise was a member. Hopefully, Denise enjoyed at least a cup of tea with Héloïse in the refreshments tent, for Madame Scotia sang on 28 May at the Concert Hall in the Park as part of a programme that included William McCulloch, entertainer, Matthew Nisbet, vocalist and the Glasgow Select Choir, conducted by Archibald M. Ross and accompanied by Wilfrid Senior.

A few months later, in February 1939, a Celts and Scots Night was held at the Queen's Hall in London. Denise drove down from Aberdeen with the Dancers of Don to take part and Héloïse was surely there too, if not to perform, then to support her sister. The event was organised by Margaret Morris, whose renowned creative and therapeutic dance techniques were not far removed from the Dalcroze Eurhythmics favoured by Beryl de Zoete; linking expressive movement to natural rhythms and using nature as a source of inspiration. Morris had become enthralled with the romance of the Celtic world after moving from Paris to Glasgow with her partner, the Scottish artist J.D. Fergusson and after the war she would establish the Celtic Ballet Club which in the 1960s became the Scottish National Ballet. In a later account of the 1939 Celts and Scots Night, the leader of the Dancers of Don mentioned Héloïse specifically, saying:

> One of the dancers who came from Argyllshire was the sister of Madam Scotcia [sic] who sang Gaelic songs and accompanied herself on the clarsach. She was an artiste with a worldwide reputation and gave recitals as far away as Japan. I think her most enchanting experience was when she sat on the shores of Appin and played and sang and the seals came up to listen to her, captivated by the music.[28]

---

28 Sir Ewan Forbes, *The Dancers of Don* (Aberdeen: Aberdeen University Press, 1989), p. 13.

Delving into the story of this dance troupe, I was startled to learn that the Honourable Elizabeth Forbes-Sempill, the leader of the Dancers of Don, seen in earlier photographs with Denise, had been wrongly gender-assigned at birth and had struggled with what he called 'the ghastly mistake' made by his parents and the medical profession when he was born in 1912.

Still named Elizabeth, he was studying medicine at Aberdeen University when the Dancers of Don performed in London in 1939, and he would practice as a GP in Aberdeenshire for many years. Aged around forty, he requested a warrant for birth re-registration and transitioned formally to male. The Aberdeen *Press and Journal* of 12 September 1952 contained the simple announcement that 'Dr E Forbes-Sempill henceforth wishes to be known as Dr Ewan Forbes-Sempill'. His patients were reported to have been universally supportive and a few weeks later, Ewan married Isabella Mitchell, with whom he had set up the Dancers of Don so many years before and who had also been his housekeeper.

His story had a happy ending, for the couple reportedly enjoyed a loving relationship for nearly forty years thereafter. But it made me reflect on how lonely and anguished this miscast youngster must have felt at times, growing up in the baronial Craigievar Castle in Aberdeenshire almost a century ago. I wonder whether Denise had been a confidante, whether she and the Dancers of Don had been a source of support and comfort for Ewan, or whether he had felt compelled to keep himself to himself.

The Celts and Scots Night had been a resounding success and the director of the International Institute of Margaret Morris Movement had written to Elizabeth Forbes-Sempill, saying 'your feet and those of your troupe as well, are an education to *all* dancers …' My casual research revealed that Margaret Morris Movement remains popular in pockets around the world and also, so coincidentally that I could not ignore it, that there was an imminent weekend school in Dumfriesshire to which, even as a complete novice, I would be welcomed. When I told my daughter I had signed up for a weekend of dance she regarded me with the gaze of an indulgent parent, 'Will it be rumpty-tum or whee-whoo?' she asked, floating her arms in the air. I just hoped to absorb something of the atmosphere that might have enveloped Héloïse and Denise that evening in London.

I joined a small group of dancers and tutors, most of whom knew each other from past gatherings, drawn together by their devotion to Morris's precepts regarding physical exercise and aesthetic movement alongside a rather esoteric consciousness of colour. The venue was Kilquhanity, a comfortably shabby country house with converted outbuildings where the relatively recent departure of the previous residents, the pupils of a free school, was evident in the treehouses balanced precariously in unexpected corners of the grounds. The mornings were bright and frosty and I joined happily if clumsily in dancing sessions and in a painting workshop.

By the second day, my confidence had increased. Comfortably anonymous, I found myself moving freely and unselfconsciously amongst the other women within the large dance studio, stretching out my legs and arms to the music, reaching, twisting and bending with an unfamiliar lack of inhibition. Very gradually, a growing sense of exhilaration, of expressive freedom started to overwhelm me and unexpected tears began to well in my eyes, borne it seemed, of an emerging timid joy that was expanding my being. Something inside me was readjusting, was reconfiguring my engagement with the world.

Very occasionally in my remembered life, I have heard music or watched performances that were hugely affecting, or met an individual whose words or behaviour would connect profoundly with something buried inside me. I know such experiences are symbiotic, that I am partly responsible for their impact; that they reflect how open I happen to be at the time to the words and ideas, to the sensual rush of sound, shape or colour. At such times I sometimes feel unhinged, hoisted high and almost bodily from my accustomed vantage point on the world, rescued from impending stagnation so that I might see things afresh.

The dancing dug more acutely into my being than I could ever have anticipated. It seemed that all the reading and thinking about Héloïse, the struggle to understand her experience and complexity, had opened up some unfamiliar part in me; had brought me to a place where the connections between music, my body, my senses and my deepest feelings were brought together starkly and unexpectedly. Was this how it felt, fleetingly, to be her? I left Kilquhanity sated with information and with experience, needing a period of stillness in which to think about it all.

I couldn't be sure whether Héloïse had ever met Margaret Morris or Fergusson although they had more than one acquaintance in common. In 1961, Marie Dare wrote the music for one of Morris's ballets, entitled *The White Moth*. Years before that, in 1928, when Fergusson went to New York where he had an exhibition at the Kraushaar Gallery, he received a letter addressing him as 'Dear Clansman' and inviting him to attend a lecture on aviation. The writer said, 'I have the honour (or shall we say the misfortune) to be the representative of the Fearghusian kings of Dalriada, otherwise known as Argyll …' and signed off as 'Clannfhearghuis of Stra-chur'.[29] There can be little doubt that this was the same colourful character that, according to Margaret Fay Shaw, had blagged a box at Héloïse's New York concert a couple of years earlier.

From the books and pamphlets supporting the Margaret Morris Movement course, I learned that Morris was a pacifist, as were her close collaborators, composer Erik Chisholm and the artist William Crosbie. Along with Fergusson, this was a group of intensely creative individuals working on their own and collectively in quite

---

29 Margaret Morris, *The Art of J.D. Fergusson* (London: Blackie Academic and Professional, 1974), pp. 162–163.

transformative ways, frequently exploring and reflecting Celtic art and mythology and apparently sharing a peace loving view of the world. During the war years, they were all living and working in Glasgow. But neither the memorabilia box nor press archives offered any hint that Héloïse's personal life intersected with theirs; she remained frustratingly enigmatic. Was she really such a loner?

———————

Not long after the Celts and Scots Night, shipping records showed that Héloïse docked in London from Malta on 17 March. Her trip there was confirmed by a rather scrappy draft programme in the memorabilia box which had been printed at the 'Times of Malta' by Progress Press in Valletta. Annotated heavily in pencil by Héloïse, it was for a forthcoming recital by Bardess Scotia at Little Scatwell, a large house in Inverness-shire owned by Hugh MacKay Matheson and his wife Katherine. The couple also had a house in London at which the London Branch of the Clarsach Society had been inaugurated.

I imagined Héloïse, her skin tanned from hill walking in the Maltese early spring sunshine, sitting overlooking the sea while poring over the details of the programme. It comprised mostly Kennedy-Fraser songs but concluded unusually with what was essentially a nonsense song, 'Brochan Lom', taken from a collection called A' Choisir Chiuil and after which she had added in brackets, (Strathspey and Reel). The concert was planned to take place on Saturday 16 September 1939 but much water was to pass under the bridge before then and whether it ever took place remains a mystery.

As everyone broiled in the June heat and the outbreak of war became all the more imminent, Héloïse, Marie Dare and Maria Korchinska got together for two last performances at the Aeolian Hall. The reviews were mixed. *The Scotsman*'s critic remarked that Korchinska's harp was, 'apt to sound like a fettered Wagner' compared to the small Celtic harp which had 'a primitive sound in keeping with the nature of the Hebridean songs'.[30] Previously critical of her wordy introductions, *The Times* reviewer appreciated Héloïse's rather spare commentary, saying:

> Miss Russell-Fergusson … manages to convey a good deal of explanatory comment in very few words, plays her own accompaniments on the harp and in a word, transplants the wild flower of the islands to a city garden without doing it violence.[31]

Then, despite or perhaps because of the increasing likelihood of war, Héloïse travelled back to Brittany. It was the fortieth anniversary of Taldir's first trip to the Welsh Gorsedd which had triggered his dedication to promoting inter-Celtic links. *An Oaled* noted that on 31 July 1939, the mayor of Vannes, M. Maurice Marchais extended a warm welcome to those who had come, mostly from Wales, for the three day festival. And he addressed particular thanks to Miss Scotia Russell-Fergusson, whose 'delightful harmonies' would entertain them.[32] A radical local paper, *le Progrès du Morbihan* noted on 6 August that in bringing greetings from Scotland, Miss Scotia had expressed the view that nationalism was simply a noble cultural expression; that it went beyond frontiers. Possibly Héloïse was more politically astute than I gave her credit for; she may have been trying to cool the hot water in which Taldir would soon be embroiled. Certainly, she was using the platform to make her accustomed plea for peace.

A month later, on 3 September, war was formally declared. Héloïse headed north to Port Appin, from where her mother was preparing to return to Southern Rhodesia and Denise was heading back to Aberdeenshire. There, the *Press and Journal* would publish a picture of her with a group of others in 1941, proudly taking delivery of a new

---

30 *The Scotsman*, 17 June 1939, p. 18.
31 *The Times*, 16 June 1939.
32 *An Oaled*, No. 70, p. 294.

mobile canteen being gifted to the Aberdeenshire A.R.P. and of which she would be the driver.

Hélène boarded a Union Castle ship called the *Llanstephan Castle* at Southampton in early October. Painted a depressing dark iron grey with black ports and gunwales, it crept out of the harbour as part of a convoy of about sixty vessels of all shapes and sizes. For three or four days they stayed close together before continuing independently. Hélène was frustrated by the black-out, writing, 'ports shut at 6.00pm and opened around 7.30 – so there is little air; no one may strike a match or smoke a cigarette on deck after dark'. She declined the invitation issued to all passengers to take a turn on the bridge to look out for submarines. Aged sixty-seven, she didn't think she would pick them up quickly enough. On 30 October she wrote home from Johannesburg. The voyage had taken twenty-seven days, they had sighted two U-boats, had some 'hazardous experiences' and she had felt 'mercifully preserved' when Table Mountain finally came into sight. Travelling home to Umtali, she noted that she 'came up on the train with Richard Tauber & Co who are giving some concerts here – they don't seem to like him much. … It might be a good time for H but I will find out more.'

I know nothing of Margie's wartime whereabouts, but I know that my father Donald had left Ardrossan Dockyard and was organising naval supplies somewhere near Bristol and that my mother was billeted in Otago Street in Glasgow as a driver with the American Ambulance Corps. She loved the female camaraderie of that billet and made many good friends. Since her parents were in London and she had more reason than most to look forward to a trip south, she was often allocated the long and hazardous journey through the blackout. Arriving in London, she would collect wounded Scots and drive them to locations nearer home. As a child in the 1950s, sitting beside her as the car trundled up and down the old A1 road between Scotland and London to visit my English grandparents, she would reminisce, pointing out the side roads that had led to wartime hospitals and convalescent homes.

Since their marriage, my parents had lived in Glasgow but my father had also been renting Sallochy, the old schoolhouse by Loch Lomond. Like his mother, he preferred rural surroundings and needed especially to be near water and to get out in a boat. Towards the end of the war he bought Sallochy, although unlike his father, he did not put it in his wife's name. Instead, and perhaps to prepare my mother for the self-sufficiency of permanent rural life, he gave her a copy of Elizabeth Craig's *Enquire Within*, a book which advised housewives on almost everything; from mending broken sash window cords and rehanging doors, to table etiquette, keeping chickens and child psychology. My sister and I were yet to be born.

The flyleaf records, without romance, 'For Elise, from Donald'. The book was stuffed with ecologically friendly ways to clean items with vinegar, borax, ammonia or tea leaves and included extensive gardening advice. Mum kept chickens and grew vegetables. Prisoners of war were mustered to dig potatoes in the adjoining field. And there were always fish in the loch and in the burn.

Granny Hélène was known to be a skilled angler but I never saw my father fish with a rod. I have memories instead of tramping with him on darkening winter afternoons to guddle in the burn; learning how to plant my feet firmly in the water below a boulder or rocky outcrop and slide my arms without flinching into the icy pool, fingers extended to feel tentatively for the fish as they lay still. I wondered whether as a child, he had guddled with Héloïse; and whether she had fished during those bleak war years.

Between 1940 and 1944, no electoral registers were kept and those between 1945 and 1949 record her simply as being at Port Appin. The register for 1950–51 records her living at Ardtur Garden Cottage and it is possible she had been living there since Hélène left for Africa in 1939.

Determined to make a practical contribution to the war effort Héloïse volunteered as a salvage organiser. She approached the task as systematically and energetically as a concert tour, applying her persuasive tactics to everyone from the smallest child to the wealthiest of landowners, setting up financial incentives for children and adults alike.

Pretty quickly, she was nicknamed 'Madam Scrap' which, I suspect, was due to a combination of her relentless enthusiasm and the likelihood of her rarely taking no for an answer. On my visit to Port Appin, Jenny recalled Héloïse urging the children to find scrap metal wherever they could and, if necessary, to press adults to help them to bring it to the green outside the village shop and heave it into the shape of a fish. 'And then to go and find more and more to make it into a whale,' said Jenny, stretching her arms wide, emulating Héloïse standing in front of the class in Port Appin School, enthusing the children. Each time enough had piled up to merit collection, Héloïse would call a lorry to take it to the depot in Oban and by the end of the war, with the money raised, she had funded over seventy post office savings books for local children.

Children were very involved in the war effort. I have read of them also working with adults gathering sphagnum moss for its natural disinfectant. It was dried out on great dust sheets spread outdoors and then taken into the greenhouses of a big house to be picked over painstakingly with tweezers to remove bugs, beetles or bits of heather and peat before being put into bags and sent to one of the hospitals for wound dressing.

Héloïse visited the primary school regularly. As well as urging the children to keep their eyes open for scrap, she encouraged them to contribute to a monthly drawing competition. Setting a topic which had some connection to the war and perhaps hoping to promote conversations at home about the war effort, she awarded a generous half a crown each month to the winner and posted the pictures in the local shop. Ian Ross, a couple of years older than Jenny, told me proudly that he had won it twice; the second time for a carefully crafted picture entitled 'Hitler at his worst'.

Twice a week, she climbed into her car and set off to collect paper salvage on a round trip to Duror and Fasnacloich Glen. She had set up an arrangement whereby anyone with paper to be collected would hang a badge in their window so she knew when to stop. On picking up the paper, she would hand over a raffle ticket in return. When her car was so stuffed with paper that she could barely squeeze herself into it, she drove it to the collection point in Oban, unloaded the bundles and bought National Savings certificates with the proceeds, which she raffled amongst the contributors. On these trips she kept her eyes open for scrap metal, for anything that might be salvaged and put to good use. Ian Weir, growing up on a farm nearby, recalled her 'coming in with a breeze' and offering his father 10/- for his old AJS motorcycle and sidecar, lying half-hidden in the long grass, overgrown with nettles. I imagine many a farmer turning round to see her striding across a field or down a hillside, pointing out a long forgotten piece of broken machinery and calling out to ask whether she could take it away.

From time to time, she broadcast a concert on Scottish radio or donned her long gown and played in the village hall, but mostly she pored over the books, notes, illustrations and photographs that she had gathered on her travels, reading and re-reading, intrigued by the differences and similarities between the harps and harp-like instruments that she had seen around the world and by their reflections of culture and of history. An intuitive scholar rather than an experienced academic, she may have struggled at first to impose order on the complexity of the connections she was making but she was rigorous and persistent. She began to develop a detailed catalogue that would become the master document for *The Russell-Fergusson Collection of Harps*.

Sitting at her typewriter one evening in late October, she heard a knock at her door. The gusting wind ushered in a swirl of autumn leaves and children, including Jenny. It was Halloween, although Jenny couldn't remember the year. Hoping for sweeties or coins or both, the young guisers followed Héloïse into her sitting room, where she listened to their poems and songs, humming along and clapping her hands at their performances. Jenny remembers that it was a small house, so it was probably Garden Cottage. Héloïse left the children to look at the piles of books and pictures and to tap on the keys of her typewriter while she scoured the little kitchen for something to offer them but apart from a bottle of Rose's Lime Juice, her cupboards were bare. She diluted the cordial and poured it carefully into glasses before carrying the tray through to the sitting room. Remembering this paltry offering, Jenny smiled wanly and excused Héloïse's lack of hospitality, saying that she thought Héloïse was unaccustomed to visitors, let alone children.

It seemed that Héloïse was regarded by the community as a rather solitary figure. Clearly, the name Madam Scrap was a response to her indomitable salvage activity but I wonder whether it also reflected something more subtle, the empty kitchen cupboard illustrating a meagreness of lifestyle which was noticeable, even in war time.

The youngsters had wrinkled their noses at the acidity of the drink and set off into the autumn night, unimpressed too, by the shilling Héloïse had popped into their hands, hoping for a more hearty welcome at the home farm.

In September 1943, she took part in a fund raiser for the District Nursing Association held at Ronachan House on the Mull of Kintyre. Her contribution was prefaced by Kenneth MacLeod, by then in his seventies and the master of ceremonies, speaking on 'The Place of

Music in Gaeldom' and 'Musical Ghosts'. The *Campbeltown Courier* noted that:

> In Dr MacLeod's view the Celt was so full of music himself that he found musical qualities not only among the songbirds but in other quaint and questionable directions. His view found support in the musical illustrations which followed. Miss Russell-Fergusson delighted her hearers with her marvellous reproduction of the 'wood notes wild' in such gems as the 'Lark's Call' and 'Crow's Tune'.

The following month, she performed with Marie Dare at the Central Hall at Tollcross, Edinburgh, where *The Scotsman* admired the way in which Marie Dare had 'fitted her modest contribution deftly into the fascinating pluckery of the clarsach'. But overall, such performances seemed few and far between. At the end of December 1944, the *Glasgow Herald* reported optimistically that the Dunedin Association had issued a prospectus detailing seven recitals that would be held in Glasgow throughout the following year 'for the encouragement of the Scottish creative arts and presenting Scottish music and poetry'. The programme of music, poetry and lectures was kicked off by Hugh MacDiarmid and concluded with a performance by Héloïse. A more mismatched pair of bookends it would be hard to find.

Thus, Héloïse busied herself practically and intellectually during those war years, but it was difficult to gauge how she would have been feeling. World War I had shattered the youth of her generation and barely twenty years later and notwithstanding the oft lauded 'wartime spirit' of community support and cheery cooperation, this second war with its gasmasks, evacuated children, never-ending death toll, strict rationing and encircling U-boats must have generated moments of darkest despair. The first aerial bombing in 1940 had been an attack on the airfield at Wick in Caithness and there were active naval, army and air bases up and down the Scottish coasts. Although far from the blitz bombing of cities, Argyllshire was neither a peaceful nor a safe haven.

And Héloïse was alone. I wonder how and with whom she found comfort and security. Christian Science would have urged her to believe that any difficulty, personal or global, reflected 'wrong thought' to be overcome through spiritual thinking and prayer. On the Christian Science website I found a lengthy address about the war written at the time by Martha Wilcox, a prominent American Christian Science teacher, which stated:

> As Christian Scientists we are primarily engaged in demonstrating the divine Principle, Love, in whose universe war does not exist … we should not be dismayed at man's apparent helplessness. These days are teaching us, universally, the need of divine help. The call of this hour is that man shall return to God, or Truth, because Truth is the only remedy for human ills, and as Christian Scientists we should be giving more attention to spiritual values and moral excellency than ever before … There is no limit to the good we can do, when once we refuse to accept the limitations which so-called mortal mind would impose upon us.

Héloïse may have drawn spiritual strength from such a speech but surely, at times, that must have been hard work. As she made her cheery visits to the school, drove around to collect paper or worked at home on bringing order to her years of research, she may have reflected on the overall impact of her pre-war work: all those recitals, talks, and sustained efforts to promote the experience and positive characteristics of Hebridean life. Had she managed to influence others? How best might she continue to 'do good'? If her spiritual beliefs provided the impetus for the flamboyant energy of Madam Scrap and the intensity of assembling her research, they would surely underpin how she reviewed and developed her approach to performance.

She had always offered verbal introductions, that narrative context describing the enmeshed links between people, their environment and the music they created and which she believed to be at the core of life in the Hebrides and in so many other places that she had visited.

Many audiences had enjoyed that storytelling as much as her singing. In Tientsin, for example, a reviewer had written, 'Not the least part of the charm was the "word pictures" with which she prefaced each song.' In some respects, the narrative had become almost as important to her as the music itself. It was perhaps logical for her to regard it now as a route to continue actively promoting a more harmonious world, for structuring the process, entwining the history, culture and songs into a more coherent whole, to develop and enrich the medium and thereby, the message. To extend, as Wilcox urged, 'the good we can do'.

Héloïse's increasing fascination with the universality of the relationship between music, nature and everyday lives would become evident in *The Russell-Fergusson Collection of Harps*. In it, I learned of the Javanese kowongan, a musical instrument played by herdsmen which could also be used as a hat against rain or sun; about the ganzavar five string harp played to accompany the work of Matakam smiths in northern Cameroon and at the Malinke smelters in Guinea; alongside, the Hebridean waulking songs that gave a sustaining rhythm to the monotonous work of softening newly woven tweed, all revealed exactly the same kind of relationship. And everywhere, there were musical paeans to the natural world, lullabies for restless babies, songs of love, of tragic loss, of celebration and of grief. Her copy of *On Dance and Drama in Bali* evoked not only the hypnotic sounds of gamelan but also Beryl's confident assertions about the intrinsic connections between drama and music. Héloïse turned over in her mind how she might build a song-drama, a performance that might begin to illustrate such connections, to remind people how much is shared, how little separates us.

It seemed that she was checking back with MacLeod too. An envelope postmarked February 1945 with notes she scribbled across it while talking with him, lies amongst the collection of papers about MacLeod which is in the Mitchell Library. I searched the memorabilia box for more details of those war years. Apart from a few newspaper cuttings, there was nothing except a kettle which I had seen so often I had forgotten about. It was sturdy and functional, made of a dense, dull copper and on top of the handle, the inscription, J.S.B. to H.R.F., 1944. How intriguing. Who was J.S.B.? Had she enjoyed a significant relationship; a specific brief encounter or perhaps something more lasting with J.S.B.? Yet Héloïse, I remembered, had not been the only person in the family with the initials H.R.F. There was a slim chance that the memorabilia box included items from her mother. I couldn't know for sure which H.R.F. the kettle had been intended to please.

CHAPTER TWELVE

COMPOSING AND RECORDING

Shortly afterwards, I was bemused by some other initials. I went to the British Library in London in search of 'Absence', the piece of music that Héloïse composed in 1916. The Music Publishers' Association had confirmed that the publisher, West & Co., had gone bust in 1914 and that there was no current West & Co. on their books. This welcome information permitted the library to give me a copy of the music and although I remained baffled that the company had gone bust in 1914 while 'Absence' was published in 1916, I didn't quibble. Awed to be visiting such a grand institution, I took along the several required forms of identification and was directed to the Rare Books & Music Reading Room where I could see the music.

The issue desk overlooked a large room of silent individuals bent over rows of long tables, intent on their reading. I found a vacant seat and opened the hefty volume which I had been handed. It contained sixty pieces of music which the library had bound together, all published during the same period. There was 'Let's Go over to France' with words by J.W. Illingworth, music by Ernest H. Feather, published by Clark Mills in New York; 'Goodbye Kid' with words by Arthur Anderson, music by Hugo Felix, published in London; 'My Indian Maid' words and music by H. Federoff, with a rather racy illustration on the cover, published by Maryland Music. And there was 'Absence', words, Anon., music by Héloïse Russell-Fergusson, published by Ward & Co. The title, her name, the publisher and the cost, 2/-, were printed on the cover. She had signed the cover carefully, with the two accents applied neatly to her first name and with her full hyphenated surname. Inside were three pages of music. At the top of the first page, by the title, was printed, 'Dedicated to M.C.S.' I began to read and felt very quiet inside:

> Something is missing in the sky and sea,
> Something is missing in the daisy's grace
> Something has vanished from the mystic charm
> Which erstwhile haunted each familiar place.
> The East wind drives the white surf to my feet
> From North and South the merry winds blow free
> The South wind whispers songs I once held sweet
> But not one brings a message back to me
> But not one brings a message back to me.
> Ah, something is missing in the sky and sea
> Something has stolen from the sun its gold
> And something dumbly waits within my heart
> Until the hour of parting all be told.

I was glad of the embracing silence of the Reading Room. Héloïse had selected this anonymous poem and composed the music in her last year at the Academy when she was just twenty, during the second year of that brutal, blistering war that was filling London's smoggy streets with grief and with wounded men, and the daily papers with long lists of the fallen.

The librarian made me a photocopy to take home to Scotland. Unrolling it there on my own desk, it felt precious, as if this was the music's first outing in a very long time. Curious about the source of the words, I entered the first line into a search engine and was rewarded with a February 1914 edition of a Connecticut newspaper called *The Day*. It had a 'Gems in Verse' section which included 'Absence' and cited the author as 'unknown'. So it seemed that the anonymous verses had a wide resonance at the time. I left it at that, for of greater interest was the dedication to M.C.S. The initials corresponded to nobody in the family, nor anyone that I had come across while researching Héloïse's early life. I contacted the archivist at the Royal Academy of Music who had already helped me learn about Héloïse's time there. She explored the student and staff names from the period, those attending the Academy, those who had graduated, gone to war or had been lost in war. There was no M.C.S.

I shared 'Absence' with Sally Garden, a Scottish mezzo soprano whom I had met on account of her knowledge of Marie Dare. She emailed me a few days later saying:

> Briefly, the 'Absence' setting, which is aimed at the amateur 'drawing-room' market, is competent, fluent, and wonderfully passionate! Your aunt seemed to know something of the pain of separation, perhaps a first love affair? ... If I may, I'd like to tuck this song into my repertoire, it would make an ideal encore piece for me – rich, dark, indulgently romantic and short – a wee Scottish gem to sign off with!

So, just short of one hundred years after it was written, Héloïse's composition 'Absence' might have a public hearing. I turned to the pieces of sheet music in the memorabilia box; *Three Short Pieces* that she had written in 1917 and 'March', written in 1918. On leaving the Royal Academy it seemed that she had been keen to compose and publish her music and I was curious to know what it was like. Encouraged by Sally's feedback, I needed to find others who could play the piano and might offer some commentary on her music; people who might even play the pieces to me. I got some copies made to share around.

Héloïse had first recorded music in the 1930s. Before heading to Africa she had booked time with Beltona Records at the Kintore Rooms at 74 Queen Street, Edinburgh and recorded three discs of Kennedy-Fraser arrangements although one, 'A' Chruinneag Leach', she had arranged herself. In April 1947, she and Marie Dare recorded four Kennedy-Fraser and Kenneth MacLeod arrangements in London, making two records using the Special Record label. It seemed that Margie had helped out and may even have funded the enterprise, for Héloïse wrote to her in London:

> Dearest Marg, The records came yesterday and are quite intact and this is just to thank you again, my dear, for making them possible. They will <u>always</u> be there now – I wonder if you have heard them? They are really not bad, tho' you will realise that all recording and broadcasting needs a separate technique which I don't consider I have got – hence that high note in the 'Ship at Sea' – reverberating – and other defects very apparent to me – but perhaps not to others. I <u>do hope</u> you feel pleased about them, my dear. I will send the box back and you can send the others by degrees, to be entitled.
>
> No more news except this brings my love. It is one of my exhausted days – when everything seems to fail – and I just can 'sit' waiting for bedtime. However, I've been doing quite a lot and am grateful. It is this domestic slavery that gets me down. I was <u>grand</u> in London! With love, dear, Héloïse

For the first time, a letter hinted of Héloïse feeling weary. In May, the woodland around Port Appin would have been bursting with the heavy blossom of hawthorn, the exotic colour of rhododendrons and azaleas, the soft beauty of bluebells and primroses and Loch Linnhe sparkling through the trees throughout the increasingly light evenings. Yet her spirits seemed in the doldrums. Her world had shrunk and she could not get used to domesticity, such as it was. She yearned perhaps to go touring again, to be surprised by the new, to be intrigued by what was different and, especially, to feel valued. She may have harboured nostalgia too, for her mother's reassuring presence, for Crichton's quiet attentiveness or even the comforts of the Curzon Club.

I suspect, although I could be wrong, that Héloïse's sense of being 'grand' had less to do with the trappings of wealth and social status than with missing the buzz of the professional world and of performance. For there had been a kind of grandeur to her Celtic romanticism; the names she used, the silk and velvet of her draped robes, the mystique of the clarsach, the embroidered symbols, the sheer joy of making music and sharing her songs and stories with an appreciative audience. She was nourished by applause. Audiences from New York to Tokyo had made room for her and made her feel worthwhile. Who was she now? Madam Scrap, whose energy and activity had contributed so much to the wartime community in Port Appin, was redundant. Rationing was still in force. Big houses were falling into ruin. Madame Scotia had become something of an anachronism. Who needed her? What was she for? Sharing this private feeling of despair with Margie was all the more painful to read because it was so rare.

The memorabilia box under my desk contained at least one of these early records although I had no means of playing it. Then out of the blue, late in 2011, I was contacted by Bill Dean-Myatt who, although English and living in Walsall, was compiling a *Scottish Vernacular Discography, 1888–1960*. He knew about Héloïse and had some of her music already but he wanted to know more. That November, he was visiting Scotland and we agreed to meet. It was an opportunity for me to rifle through the memorabilia and to unload some of it. I wanted to keep the personal letters and papers for the family but it seemed silly to hold onto records that I couldn't play. Bill seemed the ideal recipient.

On a wet and windy night I drove to rendezvous with him near Glenrothes, about an hour from home. Peering through the windscreen wipers, I wondered more than once why I was driving through the dark to discuss Héloïse with a stranger. But talking with Bill was easy, he was genuinely interested in her as well as being entertaining company. Over fish and chips, I told him what little I knew, showed him some of the flyers and letters and gave him the records. It was my first real attempt to discuss Héloïse with anyone since the abortive encounter with Alison Kinnaird so many years earlier.

Within a couple of weeks, Bill had sent me a crackly CD of all of Héloïse's early recordings. At last I could hear her voice, with even a handful of spoken words of introduction. There was the diamond cut elocution, the rather compressed vowels that I knew could make people wince, and there was the clear, joyous sound of her singing. The CD included the recordings from 1933, from 1947, two others with Marie made possibly in the late 1940s in London, and two recordings that Bill thought may have been made privately at Rae Macintosh Studios in 1950s Edinburgh. Of course, I had yet to learn that there were further tapes, the ones that Héloïse had made in her car, parcelled up and sent to the Mitchell Library in Glasgow a few months before she died. But once I started to write her story, I listened to Bill's CD regularly, my ears becoming accustomed to her voice. I hummed along a little.

The Mitchell Library also holds a large portrait of Héloïse. Entitled *Singer with a Clarsach (Gaelic Harp)*, and painted by Cathleen Sabine Mann, Héloïse had gifted it to the library in 1956. It shows her seated at her clarsach; dark hair centre parted and gathered at the nape of her neck. She is dressed in the white silk robe described during her European tour, the sleeves slashed at the elbow revealing the soft red velvet undersleeves that reached to her wrists. She looks barely thirty, possibly younger, but the portrait is undated. Googling *Singer with a Clarsach*, brought it up instantly and it was relatively easy to find Cathleen Mann's biographical details.

The same age as Héloïse, Cathleen was born in Newcastle but her father, Harrington Mann, was a painter associated with the influential Glasgow Boys and her mother, Florence Sabine-Pasley, was a ceramicist. Cathleen trained in London at the Slade School of Art and then in Paris. She was married between 1926 and 1946 to Francis Douglas, the 11th Marquess of Queensberry, with whom she had two children. Her paintings are hung in the Royal Academy, the National Portrait Gallery and other galleries across Britain and she designed posters for the London Underground Group, advertising posters for Shell and costumes for films. All the evidence indicated a very talented, engaged and engaging woman.

So when did she and Héloïse encounter each other and why? In searching to link the two women, I was confronted by the limits of my internet skills, or perhaps, by the limits of the internet. It seemed impossible to find a more personal route into Cathleen's history, to a person, or to an archive that might indicate when and why and where she painted Héloïse. I wondered whether Hélène, so proud of her daughter, had commissioned the portrait although there are no other family portraits. Or might Cathleen and Héloïse simply have been friends? Perhaps their creative lives had crossed while Héloïse was at the Royal Academy and Cathleen at the Slade, and they kept in touch as their careers blossomed. I wondered whether Héloïse knew that Cathleen had committed suicide in 1959.

Thinking about those early years of Héloïse's life studying in London, I recalled 'Absence', which she had dedicated to M.C.S. Musing as to whether she might have wanted to obscure the name, to keep private the individual to whom she had dedicated her work, I shuffled the letters in my head. If she had transposed their order to place the surname at the beginning rather than at the end, then the surname would have begun with M. And the three letters would make C.S.M. Cathleen Sabine Mann. I was becoming fanciful.

The more I learned or felt that I might reasonably deduce about Héloïse, the more I was frustrated by how much I still didn't know. I knew that her life had been full of freedoms, creativity, and travel yet at the same time she seemed essentially a loner, quietly romantic and deeply spiritual. I knew next to nothing about her friendships. I wanted to understand who she turned to when she was sad or when she needed inspiration; to know whom she loved and who loved her. It was tempting to put Marie Dare in at least some of those roles but would that be fair? Or was her key relationship really just with her God?

As for assembling a linear chronology of Héloïse's life, that process had transformed all too quickly into an increasingly dense and knotted web. It had become compulsive and utterly absorbing, although all too often I just got lost in its interminable tangle, picking up, following and then discarding threads, staring into space, thinking.

CHAPTER THIRTEEN

THE SONG-TALES

D espite post war austerity and lack of opportunity, Héloïse picked up her spirits and with Marie Dare's collaboration, she set about devising a song-tale. They made a careful selection of music and developed arrangements and narrative for a performance called *Tir-nan-Og, a Folk Tale of the Western Isles* that drew heavily on the traditional *Tir-nan-Og* story from Celtic mythology about the Land of Eternal Youth. Presented in three parts, they mixed Kennedy-Fraser arrangements, some of Héloïse's compositions and cello music composed by Marie.

By June 1949, it was cast with two characters for a week's run at Bolton's Theatre in London, directed by Kay Gardner. An Irish actor called Allan MacClelland played 'The Islander' and Héloïse 'The Singer' with Marie on cello and Margery Davidson on harp. According to the publicity, the production revealed, 'how slender can be the thread on which a verbal heritage depends for its continuity; how easily that thread can be snapped or at times, left only within the frail hands of some old man or some tiny girl'. It certainly drew interest; the Dowager Queen Mary, mother of King George VI, attended a performance and asked that the company be presented to her. Describing it in *The Scotsman* on 9 June first as 'an experimental play as befits an experimental theatre', the critic then modified the description to state, 'Perhaps the term play is a misnomer – it is more an excuse for Madame Russell-Fergusson to let us hear the songs which have deservedly made her famous.'

A year later, Héloïse secured a ten day run for *Tir-nan-Og* at the Cygnet Theatre in Edinburgh. The International Festival had been set up in 1947 to counterbalance the palpable post war weariness and it offered an impressive programme of international orchestras, ballet and opera. But, like many Scots, Héloïse felt that it should also be affirming Scottish culture and offering something more home grown. Details of *Tir-nan-Og* were presented to a meeting of the Edinburgh Council of Women by Miss Jean Hunter Cowan who claimed the performance would fill a gap that had been all too evident in previous Festivals. Hunter Cowan, who was not only a sculptor and the founder in 1927 of the Women's Section of the Edinburgh Society of Musicians, but also the first Scottish woman to fly solo in 1911, sounded a formidable champion. *The Scotsman* announced on 29 April 1950, that 'Something specifically Scottish is to be presented in Edinburgh during the Festival by Miss Russell-Fergusson who, with the blessing of Edinburgh Education Committee, is to give twelve performances of Tir-Nan-Og, at the Cygnet Theatre'. The blessing, presumably, was some funding to stage the show.

Héloïse was supported on stage in Edinburgh mostly by Marie Dare but sometimes by the Scottish harpist, Sanchia Pielou and sometimes by the Canadian, Carla Emerson. An emerging Scottish actor named Andrew Faulds played the part of 'The Islander'. The memorabilia box disclosed a black and white photograph of Héloïse wrapped in a tartan shawl sitting on a cardboard shore, Faulds standing behind her, pointing soulfully into the distance. In another, she sat squarely in her Bardess's robe ready to play Harplet, a solemn expression on her face. On the reverse, she had written in pencil, 'not good'.

She was fifty-four and Faulds about half her age. He had served in the Royal Navy during the war and graduated from Glasgow University before joining the Royal Shakespeare Company. I wondered whether Héloïse had advertised the *Tir-nan-Og* role or whether they already knew each other. Faulds was born in 1923 to Scottish missionary parents in Tanganyika, the country that Héloïse had struggled to enter in 1933 until Harplet was designated 'a tool'. Perhaps the Faulds family had turned up at one of her concerts or had given her a bed for the night. Later elected as Labour MP for Smethwick, Faulds was an outspoken left-winger in the House of Commons while also pursuing a successful acting career, appearing in films that included Ken Russell's *Dante's Inferno*, *Mahler* and *The Music Lovers*. My mother had looked at the *Tir-nan-Og* photographs after Héloïse died and recognised Faulds with surprise. There was so much the family didn't know about her.

Promoting the event in July 1950, the *Edinburgh Evening News* reported that Héloïse:

> feels, as many Scots do, that insufficient use has been made in previous Festivals of the wealth of Scottish folklore and hopes by her presentation this year to show, in a non-aggressive, charming way, that Scotland has a heritage of her own – an aim well in keeping with her career, which she has undertaken for the love of her country's tradition.

Héloïse had stepped forward to champion Highland culture in a Festival that she found heavy with international and mainstream British cultural events. Yet, the phrase 'non-aggressive (and) charming' seemed to anticipate that readers of the *Edinburgh Evening News* might be chary of any depiction of Scottish 'heritage' that was too assertive or perhaps too political.

After all, this was the year in which four Scottish Nationalist students, driving an unassuming Ford Anglia, would steal the Scottish Stone of Destiny from under the Coronation Chair in Westminster Abbey on Christmas Day and take it to Arbroath. The previous year, Hugh MacDiarmid had railed against the entire Edinburgh Festival, more or less encouraging Scottish writers and cultural figures to boycott the event which, presumably, he saw as something of an imperialist plot. Like many a national festival it divided opinion.

Over fifty years later, similar sensitivities still prevailed. In 2014, it was reported that the Festival Director had declared that the programme would not include productions that directly addressed the Scottish independence referendum to be held later in the year. Of course, there was never the likelihood that it could be ignored. Referendum-related drama, debate, music and comedy were scattered liberally across the irreverent and often highly political Fringe events that have been squashing themselves into every imaginable Edinburgh venue almost since the Festival began.

In 1950, *Tir-nan-Og* was just such a Fringe event, staged far from the glamour of the Glyndebourne Opera that was performing in the Usher Hall and the orchestra conducted by Sir Thomas Beecham, wearing tails and a hard hat high up on the Castle Esplanade at the first grand fireworks display. *Tir-nan-Og* made a modest stand for Highland culture. Children's art decorated the vestibule of the Cygnet Theatre and the programme noted that 'by courtesy of Darling & Co., Princes Street, the portrait "Singer with a Clarsach" by Cathleen Mann will be on view at their premises during the Festival'.

The memorabilia box contained several newspaper clippings from the time. In two of them, the *Daily Record* on 29 June and the *People's Journal* of 26 August, I was startled to read Héloïse described as having written *Tir-nan-Og* when she had been 'working as an estate manager in Appin'. Jenny's first hand wartime recollections of Héloïse had been only of Madam Scrap, of her salvage activities, her book strewn room, Rose's Lime Juice, the typewriter. But perhaps Héloïse had been quietly trying to manage things at Ardtur before it was sold in 1943.

The Scottish reviews of *Tir-nan-Og* were not glowing. Andrew Faulds had made the most of what he had to work with, telling a story across three 'acts', although the *Glasgow Herald* noted that 'this is a misnomer as there is no action in the tale, which consists entirely of narration punctuated by songs.' 'And why the dim, religious light?'

asked *The Scotsman*. 'To the foreign visitor, looking for strangeness, all this may appeal. To the authentic Scot it only emphasises that idea of a Celtic twilight from which he would escape, and which never truly represented island life.' Kenneth MacLeod attended a preview. In a letter to a friend he complained about the lengthy narrative and Faulds' accent but noted that Héloïse 'sang well and did the little rhythmical things in quite a tricky way'.[33] The *Glasgow Herald* found the combination of an unseen cello and harp 'unusually effective' and *The Scotsman* concluded that Héloïse was at her best 'in the gay working songs of which she catches the lilt'. It noted also that 'a herding song … was reminiscent with its "tom-tom" accompaniment, of Africa'.

I had heard Héloïse drum a rhythmic tom-tom on 'Deer Herding Chant', one of the songs that Bill Dean-Myatt had sent me and which she had learned from Annie Johnston on Barra. It is a traditionally unaccompanied waulking song; unaccompanied, that is, apart from the rhythmic sound of the waulking or fulling process, the pounding of tweed on the wooden table by women as they sang. The *Scotsman* reviewer could have found her inspiration for that regular beat, played probably by hand on the sound box of the harp, a little closer to home.

Héloïse had long been attracted to the power of drumming. The Ob-Ugrian shamans' drumming that she had learned about in Finland and the drums that she had heard in Africa and in Bali were part of the inter-relationships she had witnessed between music, spirituality and daily life. The year after performing together in Edinburgh, she invited Carla Emerson to a performance of Pearl Primus and her Dancers in London. Carla told me she had been amazed to find the performance was accompanied solely by drumming. One of the first black modern dancers, Primus came from America with a style that was passionate and angry, declaring, 'Dance is the fist with which I fight the sickening ignorance of prejudice'. Her debut performance in New York had been

33 Glasgow University Library (GUL), MS Gen 1650/Box 62.

staged without any music at all, choreographed simply to the anti-lynching poem 'Strange Fruit', written by Abel Meeropol and sung later and most famously, by Billie Holiday.

I had been sustaining in my mind's eye a 1950s image of Héloïse based on that *Tir-nan-Og* photograph; a plump middle-aged woman rapt in her romance with an increasingly distant Hebridean cultural history. Yet her compulsion to see Pearl Primus at the first opportunity, to witness the passion of an angry, politicised contemporary dancer accompanied only by drumming, had to be fitted into that equation. Héloïse wasn't living romantically 'in the past' or, at least, not all of the time. I wonder how far she noticed the class driven inequalities and prejudices that were being exposed much closer to home.

1951, the year after her production of *Tir-nan-Og*, saw the inauguration of The Edinburgh People's Festival, a week of drama, music, poetry, filmstrips and lectures organised under the slogan 'By Working People for Working People'. The organising committee was made up of representatives from the Labour Party, the Communist Party, the TUC, the Miners' Union, arts organisations and activists, with a shared aim:

> To bring the Edinburgh festival closer to the people, to serve the cause
> of international understanding and goodwill and … make what is best
> in the cultural life of our country more accessible to working people and
> … secure fuller facilities for the development of the cultural activities of
> working people.[34]

Hamish 'Henderson, the legendary poet and folk revivalist, took responsibility for organising a Ceilidh at the Oddfellows' Hall. He wrote in the Festival programme:

> The main purpose of this Ceilidh will be to present Scottish folk song
> as it should be sung. The singers will all without exception be men and

---

34 *'Tis Sixty Years Since*, ed. by Eberhard Bort (Ochtertyre: Grace Note Publications, 2011), p. 37.

women who have learnt these splendid songs by word of mouth in their own childhood, and who give them in the traditional manner. This fact alone will make the People's Festival Ceilidh an absolutely unique thing in the cultural history of Edinburgh.[35]

Involving native Gaelic and Lowland singers, the Ceilidh was a resounding success and it has been regarded since as the start of the Scottish Folk Revival. Earlier that year, Henderson had supported the American folk song collector Alan Lomax as he toured Scotland and by 1952, the second People's Festival Ceilidh was deemed to be outstanding. By then, Hugh MacDiarmid had cast off his reservations and agreed to chair the People's Festival Committee and, at the Ceilidh, which happened to take place on MacDiarmid's sixtieth birthday, the entire audience rose to their feet while Calum Johnston, Annie's brother, played 'Blue Bonnets over the Border' in tribute to him. In expressing his thanks, MacDiarmid said:

> One thing might have struck you, I think in the programme tonight
> – that is, the extent to which all the items on the programme have
> been correlated to the lives of the common people, to the work of the
> common people, the daily darg of the common people. We are not
> going to be taken from that – we're not going to be persuaded by the
> advocates of snob art, that some mystical palaver is better than that
> which comes from the working life of our own people.[36]

The People's Festival was an overdue breath of fresh air. Its commitment to support and celebrate the creativity of 'the common people' represented a direct challenge, not only to the prevailing social order,

---

35 Hamish Henderson, 'The Edinburgh People's Festival, 1951–1954' in *'Tis Sixty Years Since*, ed. by Eberhard Bort (Ochtertyre: Grace Note Publications, 2011), p. 39.

36 *'Tis Sixty Years Since*, ed. by Eberhard Bort (Ochtertyre: Grace Note Publications, 2011), p. 42.

but to the arts establishment. It sought out and provided a platform for voices rarely heard outside their immediate neighbourhoods, for songs learned largely through the oral tradition of family and community. Such raw authenticity cut through the structure and gloss, the mystification that shrouded the recital room or the concert hall.

Where did that leave Héloïse? Would this new and enthusiastic championing of unheard voices mean that hers would be silenced? Although she had worked hard to insert 'something specifically Scottish' into what was on offer two years earlier, *Tir-nan-Og* would have been regarded probably by MacDiarmid and many champions of the People's Festival, as being too full of 'mystical palaver', too remote from the 'daily darg'. The wrong kind of Scottish.

Certainly, Héloïse's work reflected an enchantment with Celtic mythology and folk tales and she held what often seemed to be a romanticised view of daily life in the Hebrides. Perhaps there was no longer a place for romance within a political climate that demanded realism, which prioritised attention to injustices that had been ignored for too long. But I can't believe that she thought her work 'better' than that which came from people's working lives as MacDiarmid's speech inferred. Wherever she travelled, it was the authenticity of what she saw and heard that attracted her. Whether she replicated it accurately was another matter but it seemed unlikely that she would deliberately bowdlerise a song to please an audience. Was introducing a drumbeat to Annie's 'Deer Herding Song' an unacceptable piece of 'palaver'?

Taldir had remarked upon Héloïse's lack of pretension and from the outset, reviews had noted her straightforwardness of style. Her family had given her encouragement, financial support and the chance of a formal musical education. But she also carried the family baggage; her voice sounded 'posh', that catch-all of insults, invoking variously, arrogance, insensitivity, unfair privilege and the exploitation of others. Did that make her work 'snob art' or exclude her from being part of 'the People'? In the eyes of some, probably it did.

During the Scottish referendum campaign I swithered about my vote. Without doubt, the 'Yes' campaign had all the best tunes. Representing the SNP, the Green Party and a motley collection of left leaning groups and individuals, it swiftly colonised the moral high ground regarding social justice and environmental issues and enthused huge numbers of people who previously had little thought for politics or for voting. I felt at home with its values. Yet the 'Better Together' campaign reflected such an ill-judged and dour alliance between the Labour Party, the Conservatives and the Liberal Democrats that abandoning the rest of the UK to such a glum bunch seemed cruel. Both sides talked rather proprietorially of 'the Scottish people', inferring a homogenous group which made me instinctively back away. Such ready tribalism made me feel uneasy, corralled. I inclined to the edge of the debate, watching and listening, hoping for some insights that would help me decide how to cast my vote.

In 1952, MacDiarmid had been fulminating against the establishment as a whole, against a suffocating social order shot through with class distinctions and which on a daily basis, reinforced the marginalisation or the silencing of working class people. The literary world would soon be embracing the 'Angry Young Men' of the mid-1950s kicking up a storm about social justice, or injustice. Aspects of the rise of modern folk music reflected a similar political anger amongst many singers and musicians. Héloïse did not bring social or political anger to her work and although she felt her own unshakeable sense of connection to the Hebrides she had not lived the 'daily darg'.

It was rare for her to go into print but in 1950, she wrote to *The Scotsman* about a Gaelic manuscript of the late Frances Tolmie, concerned that such manuscripts should be 'acquired permanently for our country'. John Lorne Campbell, the folklore scholar based on the Isle of Canna, had written at length to *The Scotsman* a few months earlier with an impassioned plea on behalf of the short-lived

Folklore Institute of Scotland which he had founded in 1947, arguing for a professionalising of the process of gathering and cataloguing all aspects of traditional Highland culture. He offered a measured critique of Kennedy-Fraser's work and appeared to chastise the Scottish establishment for having assumed perhaps that the job of collecting traditional songs had been done:

> We may indeed be grateful to Mrs Kennedy Fraser for braving the hardships of travelling to the Islands in the old days and arousing public interest in our folk-songs; but the arrangements she published have no scientific value and the notion that she has exhausted the subject has done great harm.[37]

By 1951, it should probably have been clear to Héloïse that the appetite for her repertoire of Hebridean songs was diminishing, at least in Scotland. Reviewing a February concert that she gave in Edinburgh, just months before the first People's Festival, *The Scotsman* had described the songs as 'a nostalgic and sophisticated compromise [which were] irritating both to the specialist and to the general musician'. For many, that would have been hard to take. Yet the week after the performance and writing from the Station Hotel in Perth, she told Margie about the event with effusive enthusiasm. Marie Dare had accompanied her along with Sanchia Pielou, and the elderly Kenneth MacLeod, by then living in Edinburgh, had been in the audience:

> Dearest Marg, Thanks so much for your kind cable. It was sweet of you, when you are so far off, to have thought of my hour and this is to tell you about it. The days after a big recital like this are always sad for me. For weeks one has been living with the programme, loving and working, revelling, altering, touching it up, paring it down and then suddenly, it all slides down the greased slipway, and off – never to return and one feels absolutely lost and almost incomplete.

---

37 J.L. Campbell, 'Gaelic Folk-Songs: Work of Collectors', *The Scotsman*, 17 September 1949, p. 9.

However, now a week after, I know it was the best recital I ever gave and the audience was quite transformed. Oh, my dear, I had everything and I am so humbly grateful – Kenneth MacLeod was there and first round afterwards! He is 80 and this was his birthday present (tho' that was only between our 2 selves). They didn't want me to go, at the end and I had two encores – they poured round afterwards, all with shining faces and happy smiles. I was told and retold, 'you looked beautiful' – as if you weren't there – at times as if 'caught up' etc. etc. I only tell you as it is not vainglory – it was really the result of spiritual thinking and working.

Margie was perhaps the only person with whom Héloïse shared her state of reverie, the only person close enough and who shared her understanding of the Christian Science 'spiritual thinking and working' that sustained her confidence and resolve. Such faith might also have protected her from the criticism or perhaps it gave her tools for dealing with it for, undaunted, she had raced on to describe her collaboration with Marie on a new song-tale. This time, it would be supported by a series of slides and a narrator:

And now, mercifully, I've got 'Hailing the Highlander' to work for. The Pitlochry directors are boosting it wonderfully (owing to their friendly regard of 'Tir') ... I've now got a film: the pick of beautiful Highland slides; someone at Fort William frantically writing a 'script' on my plot; an actor in Embra panting to begin it, Marie measured for a 'stunner' (frock by Charles) also me for one and I'm on my way back from Pitlochry with my 'projectionist', a keen wee man from Edinburgh who has 4 shops but a mad hobby for films ...

Hailing the Highlander opened with Elgar's Cockaigne Overture and drew on Kennedy-Fraser arrangements with cello accompaniment composed by Marie. Under Héloïse's guidance, the script was developed by Edith MacGregor, a local historian. The tale described a romantic and necessarily brisk history of the Highlander that began with the arrival of the Phoenicians to trade with the Celts embodied by, 'a man of inborn dignity, of fearless eye and rightful pride' and it ended in the 1850s with the arrival in Waipu, New Zealand, of the Scottish community of migrants from Assynt who, famously, had been shepherded there via Nova Scotia by the indefatigable Reverend Norman MacLeod.

The actor 'panting to begin it' was Hal Fairless, President of the Makars Drama Group in Edinburgh. As narrator, he took the audience through a series of historical milestones illustrated with slides that included the standing stones at Callanish and Applecross, Deirdre's Farewell in Glen Etive, Bonnie Prince Charlie, Culloden and the Clearances. The 'keen wee man from Edinburgh', who projected the slides in synchrony with Fairless's narration, Héloïse's singing and Marie's accompaniment, was a John B. Stewart.

Running from 11 to 23 June 1951, *Hailing the Highlander* had to compete with a small storm of performances and events generated that year by the Festival of Britain. Advertisements for it in the *Oban Times* spanned several weeks and they became increasingly detailed, with urgent notification of the times and costs of buses to Pitlochry from Oban, reassuring readers of a good day out with a secure return journey. The *Perthshire Advertiser* reviewed an early performance. Broadly positive, it was cautious about potential audience numbers:

> Hebridean songs sung to harp and cello accompaniment in their proper setting were enthusiastically received by an appreciative but small audience, the latter being due to it being a public holiday in town. The type and quality of the entertainment deserve to attract good houses for the remainder of the 12-nights' run.

The song-tale was well-titled. The memorabilia box revealed a copy of the annotated script showing the Highlander to have been well and truly hailed. As the paean drew to a close, the narrator reflected not only on the tangled symbiosis between the wild, natural environment of the Hebrides and the qualities of the people, but on the inevitability and complexity of change:

But for the wanderer, hungry still for home, the mountains stand as old familiar friends and deer still roam the moors. The burns in spate, the homely reek of peat fires, the sweet fragrance of the wild flowers on the machair, the gentle strains of harping in lullaby and croon to soothe and please, or stir to gallant deeds – these remain. The people's steady kindliness and trust, their quiet courage, their pride in sons abroad who prosper and construct and in whose hearts a peaty hearth is Home. The welcome ever ready for the Stranger, the space and solitudes that make men wise.

The things that really matter? Who would know? The Gaelic tongue is still alive, the native speech of many of the folks. The houses may have changed – the people? Well, a little. Their ways and customs altered to the times. And the songs have changed in some ways too. Instead of using them just to go with the work or because they had been handed down so … simple Hebridean tunes have inspired symphonies – that is a great thing! And some can prefer the one style and some this other, for that is the way of it.

This final paragraph seemed to embody a plea regarding what had become a longstanding controversy about the collection and interpretation of Gaelic songs, perhaps even anticipating the 'snob art' and 'mystical palaver' remarks that would emerge shortly from MacDiarmid in Edinburgh. Héloïse was suggesting that there is, or there should be, a secure place without hierarchies for both the historically traditional and for the new; that individuals should be free to compose, to create, to express and to enjoy their preferences.

Perhaps, too, the heated debate about authenticity was getting to her. Despite her spiritual security blanket, she may have felt bewildered sometimes, marginalised, perhaps even hurt. She took no further song-tales to performance although the mystery of the 1960s tapes in the Mitchell Library remained to be resolved.

Hélène wrote in June 1951 from Southern Rhodesia to my mother. She praised Héloïse's work and was full of curiosity about *Hailing the*

Highlander. She wanted to know whether Donald had made a trip to Pitlochry with my five year old sister Ruth to see a performance. And she asked for a picture of her newly born second grand-daughter, her namesake, me.

CHAPTER FOURTEEN

WHAT'S IN A NAME?

In 2011, a new edition of Marjory Kennedy-Fraser's autobiography was published by the Islands Book Trust. Called *A Life of Song*, it included a detailed introduction by Dr Per Ahlander, Research Fellow at the University of Edinburgh, who offered a rich picture of Kennedy-Fraser as a strong, determined individual whose life merited some examination even without the Hebridean songs. In addressing the latter, he acknowledged her critics but argued also for a re-assessment of her work in 'the specific art song context ... of recitals by trained voices usually to piano accompaniment'.

Anne Lorne-Gillies, singer and well-known promoter of Gaelic in Scotland, was unconvinced. Reviewing the book for the Spring 2012 issue of the Scottish literary magazine *Northwords Now*, she echoed previous Kennedy-Fraser critics and asserted bluntly that Dr Ahlander's proposal was 'rather too facile for me'. Having performed art songs 'all [her] life', Lorne-Gillies claimed that Kennedy-Fraser's songs 'set [her] teeth on edge'. It seemed a very unequivocal response. In fact, Lorne-Gillies had described some of Kennedy-Fraser's melodies and arrangements as pleasant and even pretty a few years earlier, albeit tempered by the remark that she also found her to be an irritatingly unreliable source.[38] But her uncompromising view of Dr Ahlander's

---

38 Anne Lorne Gillies, *Songs of Gaelic Scotland* (Edinburgh: Birlinn, 2010), p. 204.

introduction was a reminder that Kennedy-Fraser's work could still inflame intense personal, cultural and professional sensitivities a hundred years after she had been performing.

In May 2014, I was alerted to a three day interdisciplinary conference at the University of Edinburgh entitled 'A Wide New Kingdom: The Celtic Revival in Scotland (1860–1930)', hosted by the Department of Celtic and Scottish Studies at Edinburgh University. The conference was inexpensive and as a layperson, I could dip freely into it. Dr Ahlander was there, along with academics from across the UK, Ireland, Germany and the USA. I scrutinised the programme for sessions that might bring most enlightenment.

Over the three days, a series of earnest faces addressed me from behind the lectern. They spoke of Alexander Carmichael, the nineteenth century folklorist from Lismore, about his elegant daughter Ella who apparently had caught the eye of Taldir Jaffrenou. I learned about the long standing symbolic significance of the harp and about the early work of An Comunn Gàidhealach to secure Gaelic teaching and establish summer schools. And of course, I learned a little more about that mischievous Mrs Marjory Kennedy-Fraser, who seemed to have been such a cat amongst the cultural pigeons. I longed for Héloïse to be beside me; chuckling, pondering, maybe nodding in agreement, posing a challenge or putting up her hand to ask a question.

There was an exhibition in Edinburgh's Talbot Rice Gallery of associated paintings, books and periodicals, supported by a music soundtrack. As I clamped on the headphones my attention was drawn to the thirteenth item, one of Héloïse's 1933 recordings, singing Kennedy-Fraser's arrangement of 'The Island Herd Maid', ''Sa Choill' Ud Thall'. I sat at the back of the gallery listening to her pure, sweet voice, the recording cleaned up and devoid of the crackling that had characterised the version I had heard on Bill Dean Myatt's CD. Was it 'authentic' in traditional cultural terms? I hadn't a clue. It was enough for me that it was, authentically, her. It was

Héloïse, my father's sister, aged thirty-seven, singing her heart out and playing the clarsach.

The conference was just what I needed. It offered confirmation that Héloïse's story was not only a family one but also that it nestled within a lively cultural context and an arena of contemporary debate. She had, and had still, a lasting resonance.

The music had been assembled by Dr Stuart Eydmann, an ethnomusicologist, whom I had met a few months earlier. Someone had sent me a flyer for a long gone seminar that Stuart had given at Edinburgh University, entitled, 'Héloïse Russell-Fergusson, clarsach reviver, collector, innovator, outsider or what …?' When eventually we met, he showed me the slides he had prepared about her. He had not focussed simply on her music, he was also curious about where she came from and what made her tick. He was interested, he said, in the influence of people whom he described as being 'on the edge' of cultural movements. His first slide was a meaty quotation from *The Prime of Miss Jean Brodie* in which Muriel Spark had established a context for her protagonist.

Spark's Edinburgh in the 1930s was full of robust and energetic middle class women, unlikely to marry because the war had taken so many men, yet with a reasonable degree of education and modest private means they were keenly exploring new ideas and new places. Such independent women, Spark suggested, were unlikely to join committees. Stuart felt this was particularly apt in describing Héloïse, for he knew that she had not followed the same trajectory as other clarsach players emerging at the time. She had not, for example, devoted herself to the work of the Clarsach Society; he wanted to know why.

His second slide prompted a double take. It showed the Diesel Engine Works built in 1913 at Barclay, Curle & Co.'s Clydeholm Shipyard at Whiteinch. Architecturally, the building had represented a significant leap forward in industrial design in Scotland for it had been modelled on the architect Peter Behren's 1909 modernist AEG turbine factory in Berlin. The Scottish company had sought out the original engineer, Karl Bernhard, to come to Glasgow to oversee the construction of its twin at Whiteinch. As the managing director of Barclay, Curle & Co. at the time, Héloïse's father William would have been a key player in the whole process.

Stuart had been a young architecture student in 1970s Glasgow and one of his first assignments had been to explore the building. Years later, pursuing a musicology career and investigating Héloïse's background, the name Russell-Fergusson led him to put two and two together. By including the picture of the building he was suggesting, albeit tentatively, that Héloïse had sprung from a family unafraid of grasping contemporary ideas.

I booked myself onto a Clyde Cruises 'Doon the Watter' boat trip to see the building for myself. Under a granite sky, the little tourist boat set off from its mooring by Glasgow's very contemporary Riverside Museum designed by Zaha Hadid, and headed downstream towards Dumbarton Rock, offering passengers a modest cup of tea and a scone on the way. Some had been wise enough to bring stronger supplies, and I could have done with a nip of something myself for it was a sobering journey. An intermittent commentary noted the sites and landmarks of Glasgow's shipbuilding history which, with the exception of the new aircraft carrier emerging from the BAE Systems yard at Govan, exposed only rotting or rusting dereliction. In Berlin, the Peter Behrens factory built by Karl Bernhard is used still, proudly, as a University building; I could not hold out such hope for his Scottish version.

As we approached the Diesel Engine Works I drew close to the loudspeaker waiting expectantly for a further piece of family history. The commentator directed our gaze to the riverbank at Whiteinch, but it was not to the modest building standing defiantly in place, its characteristic curved roof with the name of Barclay, Curle & Co. Ltd. still visible. Instead, he urged passengers to muse on the gigantic stacks of scrap metal piled uncomfortably beside it. These, he told us with a seeming and strange pride, were waiting to be shipped to China or to Spain.

I slumped over the cold railing, my anticipation evaporating in the chill air. Neither the architecturally unique building with its long history of service to ship building and engineering on the Clyde, nor even the gigantic rusting yellow crane that still stood beside it were worthy of mention. A pile of scrap was deemed more relevant, more engaging for a twenty-first century audience.

Then my brother-in-law, a train enthusiast, pointed up to the crane, one of the four remaining Titan cranes on the Clyde. He told me that it would have been used to load locomotives onto ships. I followed his eyes, trying to imagine the complexity of that task early in the twentieth century: the forest of people milling around, the foreman on the quay using a series of whistle blasts to direct the activity, the pulling and pushing, the turning and twisting, the sheer unimaginable weight and balance of an enormous engine, the smell of grease, the harsh raw tearing grasp of metallic cables and wet ropes; the grunts of effort, swearing, shouts of warning, the gasps of relief, of satisfaction when the job was done.

As the extraordinary Diesel Engine Works at Whiteinch was being planned and brought under construction in 1913, William was travelling between Glasgow and wherever Hélène and the children had settled themselves: Callander perhaps, or Port Appin or Taynuilt. He must have been excited. I wondered whether he invited Karl Bernhard home for dinner, whether he brought the plans home, unrolled them across the dining room table, instructing the children to hold down the corners and examine the fine drawing as he launched into the details of the building about to take shape. I recalled the fairy tale turret on Muckairn. William was not short of dreams, nor of the determination to bring them to life. Héloïse would have been influenced as much by his eclectic imagination as by her mother's hardy stoicism. Her parents were a remarkable pair.

Sitting in the Talbot Rice Gallery in Edinburgh, I pondered all that I had been learning at the conference, watching the visitors as they paused in front of John Duncan's rather dreary Celtic Revival paintings and peered into the display cases of books and periodicals. I puzzled over that word 'authentic'. Prompted partly by the debate about Kennedy-Fraser's musical arrangements, Héloïse's voice also gave me cause to reflect more deeply. I had been uncovering the story of a colourful, confident woman, albeit with a deep spiritual sensibility, a passionate performer, an inquisitive and systematic scholar. There was a mass of adjectives that seemed to fit the character, yet still I was struggling to pin down the essence of her.

There was something else. She used various stage names after returning in 1938 from East Asia, Australia and New Zealand: Bardess Scotia, Madame Scotia, Bardess of the Gorsedd; names that reflected her passion for Scotland and her sense of theatricality. I knew that from the 1920s she had occasionally dropped 'Fergusson' from her billing. But during the late 1940s she suddenly adopted a different first name. She discarded 'Héloïse' completely and insisted that family and friends call her Jane. It was deeply personal.

The memorabilia box held bitter evidence of rejection. Heavy lines of black ink obliterated the name Héloïse printed on the music that she had composed and published in 1917 and 1918. The programme for the 1931 recital at the Aeolian Hall in London where she had been joined by Kenneth MacLeod telling his stories, had the name Héloïse neatly snipped out with scissors on both the front and the reverse, leaving slim rectangular gaps before every 'Russell-Fergusson'. Given the esteem in which she held MacLeod, this was vandalism. She must have done it herself. What would have prompted anyone else to snip or scrawl?

I realised that it was not her authenticity as a musician that was bothering me. There was a query about her fundamental sense of self. I wanted to know why she had felt so strongly about her first name at this later stage in her life that she was moved not only to change it but to cut it out, quite literally. It pointed to a depth of feeling, of anger or frustration or of pain, a profound sense of rejection, whether by her or of her, that I had not found anywhere else. What drove her to such action? Had the person named Héloïse thought or said or done something so terrible that she had to be banished? Had something unspeakable happened to her?

I know a double-barrelled surname can draw unwelcome attention. An unusual first name, made far worse with accents over some letters, would compound the embarrassment. Into secondary school, exasperated teachers would call to me, 'stand up, speak out' and 'spell that', rousing sniggers amongst classmates. At times, I longed for a name that was less conspicuous than Hélène. As a young adult I silently accepted 'Len', a nickname I hated but friends found easier and I was too embarrassed to insist otherwise. It's possible that as a child Héloïse felt the same, but this vehement adult rejection of her name was inexplicable. And why did she choose Jane, not a traditionally Scottish or Gaelic name?

On professional correspondence, cheques and publicity material she stuck simply to Russell-Fergusson: *Tir-nan-Og* (1949), *Hailing the Highlander* (1951) and the four EPs released in the 1960s were written and arranged by Russell-Fergusson. I used Russell Fergusson as a pen name myself once, on an article in a professional paper, briefly curious as to whether readers would respond differently to an apparently male rather than female moniker. Had she been a writer, I might have contemplated a gender bending explanation, but Héloïse was a public performer, very comfortable in her Celtic robes.

I wrestled hopelessly with the question of why she had discarded Héloïse and turned eventually to query why she chose Jane as the alternative. It didn't take long to find one of her father's three older sisters, Jane Gemmill, who died in 1943 aged nearly ninety. At her funeral, Héloïse would have heard an impressive eulogy.

Jane Gemmill had been Vice-President of the British Women's Temperance Association in Scotland and her work with children, with refugees, as a member of the Women Citizens and Equal Suffrage Association and as convenor of the Visitors' Committee of the Infant Health Visitors' Association in Glasgow, led to her being awarded an MBE in 1925 at the age of seventy.

The *Glasgow Evening News* had recorded then that, 'although of the older generation, Mrs Gemmill has wide sympathy with the best of modern thought and such spirit and vigour in good works as younger women may well and often vainly long to emulate'. Several years later, a writer in the Temperance magazine *The White Ribbon and Wings*, described staying at Jane's house in Partick. Having returned home for supper after campaigning all day in foul weather, Jane, by then nearly ninety, had braced herself to go out again, announcing, 'my body loves ease, but my soul scorns it!'

If Héloïse had suffered some blow that rendered her first name unacceptable, her search for an inspiring alternative need have gone no further. Here was a doughty Ferguson, an upstanding, selfless woman descended from those weavers in Strachur who offered a fine model of resilience and compassion. Had Héloïse adopted Jane's name as a permanent reminder of this powerful character, trusting that she might guide and sustain her? It seemed possible. In the absence of other explanations, it had to do.

The disturbing mystery remained as to why she had discarded 'Héloïse' so vehemently in the first place but I mollified my frustration with the knowledge that she had at least found a solution. I recalled her triumph at deciding to name Harplet a 'tool' in order to enter Tanzania where the term 'musical instrument' would have prohibited entry. Whatever had so troubled her about the name Héloïse, she overcame it by renaming herself.

Her story was slowly revealing a woman who was far from straightforward. Like her mother, she felt an inherent connection to the outdoors and revelled in being alone in the natural world, whether playing clarsach on the shore at Ardtur or trekking in New Zealand amongst 'the hanging drippingness of wet mosses and ferns'. Taldir had described her as modest, hesitant to stand in the limelight off stage yet she was obviously assertive and successfully so, when circumstances demanded it. And she happily poked fun at herself. I imagined her engaging deeply in conversations that interested her but probably having little interest in small talk. I wondered about her political thinking.

Her paternal grandfather John Ferguson had been a Liberal, for several years the Provost of Partick and, according to his obituary, a benevolent and compassionate individual. As Convenor of the Committee that planned Glasgow's new Victoria Park he had been especially keen that miniature regattas be held on the new yachting pond so that 'the many model builders in the district had an opportunity to display their craft and exhibit any new departures'. His sudden death on 11 June 1887 due to the onset of gangrene after relatively minor surgery, prompted the postponement of the Park's opening.

Her maternal grandfather William Russell had sat briefly 'amongst the Radicals below the gangway' as a Liberal Member of Parliament in 1885. There is no evidence of her father William being involved in local or in national politics, nor any other member of the family, although my father served later as an Independent on the Stirling County Council. Because of their social class, I was inclined to pop the family into the broad bottomed, small 'c' Scottish conservative box. But I had been proved wrong on other assumptions.

The fledgling Scottish National Party was represented at the 1934 Gorsedd in Brittany but there are no formally recorded connections between Héloïse and the SNP. On that occasion, she had focussed her speech solely on the importance of global harmony, echoing Mildred Dilling's evocation of early peoples turning their bows into harps, and describing clarsach music as 'the key to international goodwill'. In 1939, again in Brittany, she had expressed a view that, 'the word nationalism represented a noble cultural expression that went beyond borders'. Her love of and loyalty towards Scotland were indisputable, but she expressed that sense of cultural identity through music; through her traditional repertoire and later, through her much more personal EPs.

I cannot place her confidently as an early champion of independence, yet it was clear that she had consistently encouraged others to explore, protect and promote Celtic culture and heritage from John Carmichael Watson's 1934 publication of *The Gaelic Songs of Mary MacLeod*, to her final gift in 1969 of tapes and narrative that she hoped would be shared, 'in their completeness', by the Mitchell Library. She was moved by the struggles and achievements within Scottish history and leaned unsurprisingly towards its romantic interpretation. There was certainly more than a hint of romance in her descriptions of Malcolm, the humble, hardy Scot in New Zealand and I was a little startled to read a 1937 press cutting from Singapore, where she had addressed the Rotarians and described Hebrideans as people who:

> Sing naturally and express themselves in every movement, and the fact that they sing at their work shows what a simple crowd of happy people they are. Life is very hard for them on these islands where there is never any silence. There are certainly periods of the year when they work very hard but in the other periods they do not do very much except sing.[39]

The paper reported also that Madame Scotia had spoken of the great famine in Scotland which resulted in scores of Hebrideans leaving their native islands for the open world, taking with them, 'a strength, courage, hardiness, a great integrity of outlook and a great honesty of purpose'. She had remarked also that, 'The songs of the people just sprang out of their hearts spontaneously and that is why these songs spin into the hearts of those that hear them.'

---

39 *The Singapore Mercantile & Free Press*, 25 February 1937.

Albeit loving the image of a song 'spinning into my heart', I was discomfited by her language, by a tendency to generalise and stereotype and by the fact that although she had acknowledged famine she had not, reportedly, mentioned the Highland Clearances. Yet, the language was not unusual for the period. The adjective 'simple' was not necessarily a pejorative and inferred, more likely from what I've learned of Héloïse, that she found the Hebrideans that she met to be straightforward or at worst, unsophisticated; characteristics which she admired. Her depiction of them as relentlessly happy, working hard between hours of musical relaxation was more difficult to understand. I pondered her actual experience; what she had done during her visits to the Hebrides. She had observed waulking, stirred crotal dye, had learned how to catch spouties on the shore, saw wild geese being brought in for salting. All peppered with lots of walking, talking and listening, especially to songs.

Of course, as remains the case for most women across the world and as Kennedy-Fraser had noted in her dedication in *Songs of the Hebrides*, women's work is never done. Not only Héloïse, but Annie Johnston's brother Calum had observed this fact somewhat romantically during an interview with Alan Lomax in 1951 when asked about his mother. He had replied:

> She was a very hard working woman; never idle at all. Well, at that time she worked on the croft of course, and she milked the cows and attended to them in everything. And in the evenings she carded and spun and made cloth. There wasn't an idle moment in all their lives. They were all the same, the women at the time; working all the time. Of course, working that kind of work they treated it as a recreation. They didn't consider it as work. It was a pleasure to them. They took pleasure in their work, especially the work of the cloth, the carding and spinning and all that. They had a pride in it and they took pleasure in it.[40]

---

40 Margaret Bennett, 'The Singer behind the Song and the Man behind the Microphone' in *'Tis Sixty Years Since*, ed. by Eberhard Bort (Ochtertyre: Grace Note Publications, 2011), p. 66.

Kenneth MacLeod had seemed happy enough to spend time with Héloïse and she had described picnicking 'often' with Annie, sitting on the hillside watching the kettle boil. People, it seemed, had extended her a warm welcome. Perhaps it was their courtesy that led Héloïse to conclude that they had all the time in the world to sing and to talk about music. I concluded that if she took up too much of some people's time, it's likely that she met others who enjoyed her company and conversations. Her failing, if failing there was, was that of a woman unfamiliar with the myriad nature of domestic duties; she didn't take into account the chores being set aside because she had little idea of what they were.

Yet for all the warmth with which Héloïse was greeted, I heard later that Kenneth MacLeod had watched her ferry leave Gigha with relief. I wondered whether he had found her enthusiasm overwhelming. Kennedy-Fraser had acknowledged MacLeod's influence on her work and described him as 'the dreamer'.[41] In 1924, T. Ratcliffe Barnett dedicated his book *The Road to Rannoch and the Summer Isles* to Kenneth MacLeod, describing him as, 'Bard of the Isles: Gleaner of Gaelic Legendry: and High Priest of the great Mysteries'. Héloïse, in the notes that lay in the Mitchell Library, described him simply as 'elfin' and as muddling up songs and their origins while making her a cup of tea. Romantic she may have been, but when she was concentrating on work, I suspect she was dogged, persistent and a stickler for accuracy. For a dreamer, a High Priest or even an elf, that could have been very wearing.

Her insistent questing for the origins and details of music wherever she went in the world reflected a deep desire to get it right. *The Russell-Fergusson Collection of Harps* offers meticulous detail about the instruments and music that she had heard or learned about wherever

41 Marjory Kennedy-Fraser, *A Life of Song* (Kershader: Islands Book Trust, 2011), p. 149.

she travelled. It seemed that she could be emotionally rapt by the music that she was hearing yet had the curiosity and the capacity to simultaneously stand back, to analyse exactly how and why it was constructed as it was; that she was driven always by a desire to learn about its social and cultural context. And she respected the origins and authenticity of what she was hearing, even if the music might later be re-arranged or developed differently. At least, that was the inference of the final words of *Hailing the Highlander*, in which she had asserted 'some can prefer the one style and some this other, for that is the way of it'.

Madame Scotia, Bardess of the Gorsedd or Bardess Scotia were ideal names for conveying a compelling and mystical link to the Celtic world. Combined with her musical style and her clothing, they reflected her theatricality and her fascination with early history, ramping up the romantic appeal of her performances. But it was not all about marketing. The rough embroidery of Celtic symbols on Harplet's cloth bag, echoed in the early drawings on the programmes when she played with Mildred in Glasgow, her dedication to exploring the history of the harp and, perhaps most importantly, her final experimental EPs, led me to believe that her inner sense of self was entangled inextricably with the whole soundscape, the natural rhythms, the *feel* of the west coast and of the Hebridean islands of Scotland.

Of course, none of that explains why she rejected her first name. As for her surname, invented by her parents, it lacked romance but had its own passing intrigue. My father attended Clan Ferguson events occasionally and would sport a little badge displaying the clan crest. It showed a bee on a thistle with the Ferguson motto, '*dulcius ex asperis*', which translates roughly as 'sweeter after difficulties'. One Russell crest, visible on cutlery appropriated from a much grander family of Russells, was a goat, possibly with a thistle in its mouth but bearing the slightly more cheery motto, '*che sara sara*' [sic]; 'what will be will be'. Thus, William and Hélène had blended two mottos, urging their family to take chances, to experiment, poke the hornets' nest or at least the thistle, with a mixture of optimism and pragmatism, trusting that in the end, all would work out as it should.

Perhaps the real significance of the Russell-Fergusson name was simply that it was unique. It helped Stuart Eydmann make sense of two disparate aspects of research over thirty years apart. It has made internet searches easier. My sister and I carried the name for a while before casually abandoning it, surrendering to the conventions of marriage. Only I had children: two girls, each carrying a grandmother's surname to ensure some matrilineal continuity. So, within the span of three generations, the Russell-Fergussons will have been and gone.

CHAPTER FIFTEEN

NEW FRIENDS, NEW MUSIC

Héloïse, now Jane, left Garden Cottage in 1952, moving into lodgings at Corranmore, a house which stood behind the esplanade in Oban overlooking the sea. Annie and Janet Vass lived there as well, a mother and daughter perhaps, or two sisters. A Donald Vass was the Clerk of Works at the time but no one could tell me who the women were. In 1955, Jane left Corranmore to take up residence next door in the Alexandra Hotel. It would remain, intermittently, her home in Argyll until her death.

Having reached this stage in her story, it seems right to call her Jane. Not only does it feel more respectful of her decision but I was meeting people who remembered and talked about her only as Jane, people whose parents had been her friends and supporters. The musicians amongst them congregated often at An Cala on Seil Island, the home with large and glorious gardens bisected by a stream and overlooking the sea where Iris Blakeney lived with her family. Iris played violin and piano and painted water colours inspired by the sea and the natural world. She offered a generous open house, welcoming fellow creative spirits.

As Jane clambered out of her car clutching sheaves of music, they would be joined by Mrs Foreman, affectionately called 'B', just off the ferry from Luing and carrying her cello. Iris's daughters, Melody and Joy, watched while Jane arranged herself at the piano, their mother tucked her violin under her chin and 'B' rested her cello between her knees. The three musicians exchanged glances and nodded in time. They were glad to have found each other. The daughters soaked up the warmth, basked in the music. During the long summer holidays some of their friends had clarsach lessons with Jane at the Alexandra Hotel.

Shuna Duncan, whose parents had advised Jane about those final tapes sent to the Mitchell Library, was one of them. As Jane played a snatch of music one afternoon, Shuna cast her eyes around the hotel room and noticed with a start of surprise that the wallpaper was attached with drawing pins. It seemed that Jane had taken quiet exception to the hotel décor and had come up with a simple solution; attaching paper more to her liking while she was in residence, she would roll it up on her departure to keep in the car till next time. When I suggested to Joy Blakeney that Jane was rather eccentric, she contradicted me roundly. 'No, no, she wasn't eccentric,' she said, 'she was extremely artistic and very practical. But not eccentric at all.'

Alongside this enriched social life in Argyll Jane held on to her connections in London, still staying at the Curzon Club for weeks at a time. She may have visited the Ferguson cousins although there are no records of that. Certainly, she made new friends. One was Carla Emerson from Newfoundland who had played at some of the performances of *Tir-nan-Og* in Edinburgh in 1950 and whom Jane invited to see Pearl Primus and her Dancers. It was on Carla's urging that Jane later sent a copy of the Tolmie collection and four volumes of *Songs of the Hebrides* to the Royal Conservatory in Toronto. Sadly, although the volumes were received in 1956, they are no longer to be found in the collections there.

—————

In April 1952, Hélène died in Southern Rhodesia, aged eighty-one. For around twenty years, with the support of Crichton and 'G' (as everyone in the family called Margaret Glendinning), as well as a handful of farm workers, she had overseen the growing of wattle for bark and timber, tended orchards of apples and plums and cultivated soft fruit and flowers for market. Ten pedigree Aberdeen Angus cows were amongst the mixed stock listed on the faded inventory that I unearthed, alongside a 1938 Dodge sedan and a Thurlow brick making machine, about which Hélène had enthused in a letter to my mother written the year before she died, 'I have got a brick making machine so we have all been trying our hand at that. In goes earth and cement – pull down a handle and up pops the brick very easy and hard compressed.'

Margie and Denise, the latter now married, were with her when she died, along with her dear friend 'G'. Crichton, according to family anecdote, had died some years earlier following a bar brawl in Johannesburg. Margaret Glendinning wrote to my mother, full of grief and confirming the importance of Hélène's Christian Science beliefs:

My dear Mrs Donald, What a beautiful letter of understanding and sympathy and I thank you for it. I miss my dear friend and employer at every turn and this place is just an empty shell without her mind and energetic presence. I often wonder if more could have been done for her but though we could see her strength was failing we did not realize the seriousness of her illness. We now know what a brave effort she made to carry on as usual. She had such a horror of illness and being thought ill and, often, often said, 'Remember G, no hospital, drugs or nurses for me, [they must] never come though I may be unconscious. Remember that.'

Even though so far away, Jane had drawn deeply on her mother's spiritual resilience. Hélène's death must have left a gaping hole in her cache of personal support, underlining her distance from the rest of the family. Her sisters showed no sign of returning to Scotland and as for Donald, Jane's relationship with him was negligible. Anyway, he wasn't around. Not long after his mother died, my father took our family to Harbour Island in the Bahamas. Ruth was enrolled at a local school and we believe he toyed with the idea of moving there permanently and of sending us eventually to boarding school in the USA. We stayed possibly six months, maybe more. I don't know why we returned.

A month after her mother's death, Jane performed again in Pitlochry, providing musical accompaniment for the first staged production of Walter Scott's play, *The Doom of Devorgoil*. It was rare to find her in a performance not masterminded by herself. The *Manchester Guardian* of 26 May slated the play and felt that it wasn't worth staging although it did note that 'the person who came through the evening most impressively was Miss Russell-Fergusson who had arranged the songs and accompanied them on her clarsach'.

Perhaps it was Hélène's death that had prompted Jane to leave Garden Cottage and to sever finally, after all the comings and goings, the last family link with Ardtur. For a couple of years there is scant evidence of her taking part in any other performances or activity. Perhaps she stepped back from the creative flurry of the song-tales to come to terms with her grief. It affects everyone differently of course. When my mother died aged ninety-seven, it took at least a year, closer to two, for me to feel even half myself again. Since my father's death she had devoted herself entirely to the well-being of others, tenderly overseeing the slow demise of both her parents, of their long-term lodger Don, of her older brother John and of her sister-in-law Margie. I missed her terribly. At the back of a drawer I kept a pair of her soft pale blue gloves. Sometimes I would pull one on and slip my other bare hand feebly into its grasp, trying desperately to find comfort, to conjure her touch. It was a time of great reflection, sudden unstoppable tears, random interests, unexpected behaviours and of a profound need for stillness.

I imagined Jane reading in her room at Corranmore, perhaps playing a little music, eating a solitary meal, pulling on her coat to stride north along the shore road past Dunollie Castle to Ganavan Sands to hear the rhythm of the waves breaking on the shore. Perhaps she leaned on the railings to watch the black guillemots fussing around their nests in the sea wall below the esplanade, raising her eyes to the clouds gathering over Kerrera. In 1955, aged four, I had my appendix taken out in hospital in Glasgow. Mum took me to Ganavan Sands to convalesce. I have no recollection of the trip but the phrase Ganavan Sands has long remained a comforting, satisfying sound, rolling around in my head like a nursery rhyme, *Ganavan, Ganavan, Ganavan Sands*. I wonder whether we booked into the Alexandra Hotel and if Jane ever sat on the beach with us. Perhaps that would have intruded on Jane's privacy. It was never discussed.

Of course, Jane may not have been there. Her collection in the Mitchell Library revealed that by the mid-1950s, she was busying herself often in Europe. In 1954 she was in Neuchatel in Switzerland at the Musée d'Ethnographie, examining the collection of Gaston Bardout. She brought back an associated soft bound booklet and had marked in pencil the section where Bardout acknowledged that his wife had contributed as much to the work as he had. She visited the Völkerkunde in Munich that year too, and wrote later that she had seen:

A large crate still unpacked, full of native instruments of many types which I understand had recently come from the Belgian Congo where they had been collected on an Expedition. In 1956 I asked Herr Neuner for some photos of the ivory and skin instruments and he kindly forwarded these. Information regarding them is unfortunately rather sparse. A visit to this museum may well repay future students seeking information.

In the summer of 1955, she headed to Viggiano in southern Italy, a town long known for its travelling musicians and which the harpist Victor Salvi's family had left in 1909 heading for America. Salvi was back harp making in Italy by 1955, but much further north in Genoa. Jane was in Viggiano looking for early harp music and 'for peasant harpers said to play there'. She brought back a photograph of a traditional Hook Harp which is now in Volume D of her collection in the Mitchell Library and which she wrote was 'one of the last to be found'.

Elsewhere, there is a photograph of Olav Snortheim of Lillehammer playing the Langleik. She had written on the reverse, 'he is one of the best living exponents of Norwegian folk music … I heard him perform on the Langleik during an international folk festival in Oslo in 1955 and he subsequently brought the other instruments (the Buck's Horn, Seljeflyte and Mummharpe) to play to me.'

She complemented this research with practical interventions to secure the preservation of small harps in Scotland. Apart from Harplet, which on her death went to Glasgow Museums Resource Centre at Nitshill, she donated two others to Scottish museums. One is in the Highland Folk Museum in Kingussie. Called Am Fasgadh (The Shelter), the museum was set up in the 1930s by Isabel Frances Grant, who was influenced by the open air museum movement in Sweden and Norway and who wanted to establish a Scottish equivalent 'to shelter homely ancient things from destruction'. The museum's catalogue recorded: 'A Harp by Glen. Clarsach. Agate in Brass setting, different woods. Presented by Miss Russell-Fergusson, Coran more, Oban.' The notes state that it had been brought to Morley's in London from where Jane had bought it as a 'good specimen of its type'.

The West Highland Museum in Fort William houses the second small harp. This Poltalloch harp was named after the baronial mansion that belonged to the chief of the Malcolm clan. Some persistence led me to Robin Malcolm, the current hereditary clan chief living in Duntrune Castle. Did he remember the harp? No, he didn't. But he remembered Jane. He had been aged around nine or ten, home at Poltalloch from boarding school for Christmas. That particular year, sometime in the early 1950s, the entertainment included a production of Puss in Boots staged by the children. Robin had been very excited. He had been watching the evening unfold when Jane emerged from behind a heavy curtain, cutting a very theatrical figure in her Celtic finery and holding Harplet. He had never seen anything like it. Had his father and Jane been friends? He thought acquaintances, perhaps. His father and step-mother had called her 'Highland Hilda'. They found her rather eccentric.

When the contents of Poltalloch were auctioned in the late 1950s, Jane made a successful bid for the harp and in 1959 offered it to the West Highland Museum. In June 1968, the curator received another letter from her. Paying a chance visit to the museum, Jane had found the harp 'looking rather sorry for itself' and offered to visit Fort William to re-string it herself. There was no record of whether the museum followed up the suggestion.

The final resting place of the Dolmetsch harp remained a mystery. She had referred to it in Volume C, *British Isles*, of *The Russell-Fergusson Collection of Harps*, but there was no photograph of her playing it, nor any indication as to where it had ended up.

I left my desk in June 2014 and headed for Oban to look for more information and to find people who remembered Jane. Helpfully, the *Oban Times* had already published a photograph of her portrait alongside a request from me for information. Peter MacLeod had replied. His late wife, Jean, had been the receptionist at the Alexandra Hotel between 1955 and 1963 and had talked about Jane with some admiration. Jean and Jane had a quiet agreement that Jean would keep Jane's mail for her to collect, for Jane was adamant that she did not want it displayed on the residents' mail rack. Perhaps she found the rack too public, too likely to identify her correspondents, too compromising of her privacy or perhaps just too precarious, for she was not always there.

Around 1964, she wrote to Margie from Oban, saying, 'the Postmaster here (a Lewisman) says I can make the following my address, not having a permanent one, and this, in itself, has lightened the load'. The address is simply 'Miss Russell-Fergusson, Clarsach Recordings, Oban, Scotland'. Possibly, she set it up as a business address anticipating correspondence about her forthcoming EPs, but her evident relief suggested that receiving mail might not always have been straightforward. She would have missed Jean's support.

It was a swelteringly hot day when I sat in the *Oban Times* office leafing through back copies of the paper. I looked particularly at 1927 for reports of William's death and then at 1951, where I found the increasingly elaborate advertisements enticing people to take the bus to Pitlochry to see *Hailing the Highlander*. Surprisingly, Jane had a letter to the paper published in 1950 in which she sought confirmation that an ancient galley carved into rock on Beinn Churalain above Loch Creran was still visible and not overgrown. It was easy to get sidetracked. Every issue had regular 'Notes' from Glasgow and Edinburgh detailing activities of their Gaelic speaking communities and reports from local clarsach groups and An Comunn Gàidhealach, all of which appeared to be thriving. The reading was fascinating but I wanted to find people who knew Jane or at least knew of her. At the same time, I was hesitant. Anyone who remembered her would be at least my age or older, and my interest might inadvertently stir up all sorts of memories including those that might be tender.

I think it was Peter MacLeod who suggested I contact Nancy Black. I drove up the hairpin bends from the *Oban Times* office to the top of Pulpit Hill, walked up to the viewing point and hesitantly called Nancy's number. Looking over the water sparkling in the summer sunshine, I listened to Nancy talking about her late sister, Isobel. Isobel had worked with Jane, providing the secretarial and organisational skills that underpinned the systematic compiling and cataloguing of *The Russell-Fergusson Collection of Harps*. Although she had spoken little to Nancy about her work, it seems that between 1955 and 1965, Isobel and Jane had between them assembled the nineteen volumes that were lodged in the Mitchell Library. After Isobel's death, Nancy found a letter from Jane expressing profound gratitude to her sister and she sent me a copy of it:

Dear Isobel, Well, the deed is DONE! At last. I saw Mr Black last week
when I took down all the catalogues, indexes etc. etc. and formally
handed over the Collection. I found that Mr B had already bound
the small Yellows so he has now only one large book to complete and
another one for the script – 19 in all. This brings to you my very deep
appreciation of all you have so painstakingly done for so long, to help
the work to materialize. It really became fun! And I shall never forget
how you turned out on Saturdays too at one point, to help. ... It may
be that you will still receive anxious phone calls from me ... I have
embarked on something else and might need you to the rescue!
Yours very sincerely, Russell Fergusson.

Jane's letter was headed not with a hotel address but the name of a house,
Dunheanish. Nancy told me that it stood up the hill in Oban towards
McCaig's Tower and that Jane had rented a room there, although
for how long she didn't know. Had the Alexandra Hotel become too
expensive, I wondered? Perhaps it was the tourist season and rates had
increased. Nancy felt that Jane wouldn't have been very comfortable
'doing for herself', creating in my mind a picture of the now elderly
Jane struggling with a gas ring or rinsing her smalls in a bathroom sink.
It seemed more poignant to have heard this memory from Nancy as I
sat high above the town, a long stone's throw from Dunheanish itself,
watching the ferry cut its merry way towards the Western Isles. Jane
must have sat up here sometimes, relishing the view.

Late in the 1950s, Margie returned from Southern Rhodesia to
Britain to be treated for bowel cancer. She had witnessed her mother's
silent suffering and perhaps as a consequence had become less committed
to the Christian Science tenet that disdained medical treatment. After
the operation, she lived in rooms overlooking the sea in Bexhill-on-Sea
on the south coast of England, swimming every day from the pebbly
beach, stoically determined to make a full recovery. Later, she moved to
the small first floor flat in Helensburgh where I visited her often and,
perhaps through nostalgia for her years as a land girl in East Anglia,

she also bought a tiny cottage in Suffolk where she spent each summer. She made a good recovery, calling the stoma bag 'Susie'. When she came to Sallochy, she would quietly remind my mother, 'Susie hates onions and tomato skins', such a mysterious remark to my young ears.

As she recovered, Margie had been determined to find something purposeful to occupy her time. Although her vision was unimpaired, she acquired a small machine and taught herself Braille. Every morning without fail, she spent three hours meticulously transcribing books that she would parcel up and send to the Institute for the Blind. She told me with exasperation that the organisation kept urging her to transcribe 'improving books' as she called them, but she remained impervious. 'I think there are plenty of blind people who like what I like,' she said, and continued to visit the library to borrow and translate the next Mills and Boon romance. As a family, we saw much more of her than we ever saw of Jane. Of course, wrapped up in my teenaged self, I asked her few questions although I don't know how much she would have shared anyway. Mum often said that Margie preferred to keep people in separate boxes and that Jane had been the same. As sisters, they were affectionate and supportive of each other but to the wider world they remained very private.

So it was up to the people that I met in Argyll to give me a flavour of Jane's life in the late 1950s and the 1960s. They told me that she played the clarsach and the piano, traditional Scottish and classical music. She sang. She loved the Righteous Brothers' 'Unchained Melody' released in 1965. She was sociable, funny and would speak with anyone and everyone about anything. She was a welcome visitor, included at family meals and celebrations. She still went to the Oban Ball and watched the youngsters dance. They remembered her warmth and imagination, her quirkiness. As for her music, Shuna Duncan recalled Jane, by then in her mid-sixties, remarking that she was not daunted or sad despite having lost the pure bell-like quality of her young voice. Instead, Shuna wrote, Jane had insisted that she was happy to sing 'as she had become, like an old crone sitting by the fire ... continuing to tell the tales, mysteries and traditions in the time honoured way ... so they would be passed on to survive'.

One blustery afternoon, Shuna had scrambled with her parents and Jane along the shore below their house on Seil Island, clutching a heavy reel-to-reel tape recorder. Her father Hugh had been convinced they could record the waves crashing against the rocks to use with one of Jane's songs. Try as they might, they couldn't get the sound they wanted. Eventually, salt splashed and windswept, they plodded back up through the field to the house and sloshed water around in the washing up bowl while Jane plucked the strings of the clarsach and sang in the kitchen. In 1964, before Shuna left Argyll to start married life in South America, Jane presented her with a tape recorder. Shuna told me, 'It meant so much in so many ways, not just for the voices and sounds I would take with me, but the association of the other tape recorder onto which my parents, Jane and I, put some of her songs and all the fun and laughter that those times produced.'

Melody Blakeney and Libby Shaw, whose mother Grace Gibson had been a close friend of Jane's, met me in the Tesco café in Oban, where the clatter of crockery and scraping of metal chairs was overlaid with noisy staff announcements and special offers. We bent towards each other conspiratorially, trying to make ourselves heard. Jane had given Libby clarsach lessons in the Alexandra Hotel room with the pinned up wallpaper. Mel recalled walking along the Oban esplanade, seeing Jane's distinctive outline in the distance, leaning pensively on the railings and looking out to sea, the characteristic white plait encircling her head. 'You could talk to her,' they told me, recollecting Jane's presence in their teenage years. 'She was so easy to get on with. She was interested in everybody.'

They were both mystified by one elusive wisp of memory. Jane had given them a hand drawn map and instructions to find something and report back to her. It was an adventure. Clutching the map, the teenagers had spent the day clambering up and around the hillside above Loch Creran, looking for what? A ruin? A burial ground? Did they report back to Jane? Their memories were a tangled mixture of sensations, of having a powerful sense of purpose, pushing through the bracken up the hillside, the piece of paper whipping in the wind, clouds gusting across the wide skies above them as they searched and searched. But their memories had not stored the outcome; neither what they found nor when they next spoke with Jane. The adventure was all. We laughed ruefully with the frustration of it. Suddenly, Mel rose to leave. She must get back to the lambing. She gathered her bags and we embraced briefly, brought together this once by old memories.

I remembered the letter Jane had written to the *Oban Times* in 1950 about the ancient galley carved into rock on Beinn Churalain. Had this been nagging at her over ten years later, when she sent the teenagers off with the map? Was she seeking reassurance that such relics were being preserved and that they could still intrigue new generations and remind them of their history?

As I sat in Libby's house high above Loch Awe, she brought out her mother Grace's diaries dated from 1958 to 1966. They held tantalising slivers of Grace's friendship with Jane; lunch dates, occasional concerts, even a Yardley cosmetics demonstration that they went to together. In a phone conversation, Joy Blakeney had remembered Jane's white plait. I was curious. By the 1960s my mother, like many older women, inhabited the quietly conventional world of a weekly 'shampoo and set'. Why not Jane? 'She wouldn't be bothered with hairdressers,' claimed Joy, 'she would have wanted to keep life simple.'

Certainly, Jane had been interested in her stage appearance, in how her clothes and her poise reflected and enhanced her music and the stories that she told. Her style, including that encircling plait adopted as part of her Celtic romance, was an important part of her professional persona. During the 1960s, clarsach players assembled annually at Dunollie Castle, in the Regent Hotel or other locations near Oban for a clarsach summer school. Someone offered a vivid boyhood recollection of Jane sitting with another elderly player in the Station Hotel, their legs splayed nonchalantly around their clarsachs, revealing occasional glimpses of voluminous bloomers.

Despite the Yardley demonstration, I think that Jane was generally as uninterested in how she looked as she was in possessions. When she died, some heavy furniture came out of storage where it had languished since Ardtur was sold in 1943. Her will, if she left one, was not retained by her lawyer nor is it within the public records, presumably because she had no property. She had donated harps to three museums in Scotland. To the Mitchell Library she had donated her portrait and probably what she felt was her most important contribution; the nineteen volume *Russell-Fergusson Collection of Harps* and the associated archive boxes of notes and music from the Hebrides. Her car, an old Ford Anglia, must have gone to a scrapyard.

The car was strangely memorable. When she bought it, she had asked the apprentice at the Oban garage to remove all the Ford insignia. I wonder what this request reflected. Ford Anglias were extremely popular at the time and, with their reverse rear windows, extraordinarily distinctive, so it would not have brought her anonymity. Indeed, the former editor of the *Oban Times*, with an acute memory and a journalist's eye for detail, told me not only that the car was light blue, but that its registration number was SB 18. Some Appin residents remembered that too; the car had been as notable as she was. Habitually nomadic, I wonder whether sometimes she might even have slept in it. Certainly, she had used it as a recording studio and as a garden. Yet, its unreliability was well-known. It broke down regularly and there were rusty holes in the floor. 'Hope you've got strong legs!' Shuna's parents had called after Jane as the car lurched down the winding track from Ardencaple on the miles back towards Oban. Twenty years after the war had ended, I can understand why she might still be remembered as Madam Scrap.

She wrote to Margie in 1966 about getting the car shipshape for the spring with new shoes on its 'front feet' and towards the end of that year, she described skidding in the snow in Glen Falloch, 'whenever I got a bit slushed up, a kindly lorry came past and I travelled in its huge cleared tracks'. In 1969, and with no reference to her illness, she wrote to my mother saying, 'I'm afraid I won't be in Glasgow or anywhere just now, partly owing to the car (I never know when the self-starter will collapse), it happened the other day some miles out of Oban – and becomes too big a worry.'

CHAPTER SIXTEEN

CELTIC CONNECTIONS

As the 1960s progressed, the task of assembling *The Russell-Fergusson Collection of Harps* came to an end. Jane noted in the foreword that the work had been undertaken at the suggestion of the late Mr A.B. Paterson, former City Librarian in Glasgow, and she thanked the librarians and staff of the Mitchell Library for their encouragement and 'the many Curators and Collectors, Authors, Publishers and Photographers at home and abroad for their help and information'. She went on:

> [The Compiler] appreciates particularly the mounts obtained from Dr Hans Hickmann, at the time Curator of the Musée de Caire, Egypt, Dr Henry G. Farmer of the Oriental Library, Glasgow University, Herr Neuner of the Stadtmusikinstrumenten Sammlung, Munich; Major D.A. Campbell (Regimental Badges) of Argyll, Scotland; and to the British Museum for the facilities granted by them. Thanks are due also to Miss Isobel Black for her typing and invaluable assistance in preparing the Catalogues.

As that project drew to its conclusion and prompted perhaps by the breadth and depth of her research, she started to experiment more boldly with her voice and with her clarsach. Disengaging from her singular loyalty to the traditions of the Hebrides she began to explore the instrument's potential more freely, drawing on its sounds to express the intensity of her connection to the natural world and invoking the depths of her spiritual longing and belief. She set up a small company named Clarsach Recordings and between 1964 and 1968 she recorded four EPs at the Craighall Studios in Edinburgh.

The first EP, *Ceol Clarsaich*, was released in 1964. To Margie, she described its purpose, its 'Reason', as bringing peace and contentment. Its actual release seems to have been quite chaotic although, typically, Jane believed that things could have been so much worse had it not been for a kind of divine intervention. In conspiratorial tones, she described to Margie what had happened:

> I am so glad you like my little Pet. He came as such a surprise … and took all my time and thoughts and care and love. Now he is launched and I'm immersed in advertising, reviews, comps, etc … Involving how much? When? Where?, and laying them all out, and every tiny detail of the way and each step is shown me in its marvellous order. It is quite wonderful. Like you, I hope he will bring peace and contentment to listeners, for that is the Reason –

> … And, between you and me only, there is to be a second edition about Jan 15th as, besides the fire, another such howler was made that on my going to collect the 2000, with taxi at the door and retailers all waiting, they found one flaw – and then the whole issue!! And only one was found for me to take. They sat up the whole night playing every one and found just enough to satisfy my commitments. Besides the flaw, they had missed out a piece. And I should have arrived innocently at my hotel with the whole consignment, unknowing. … Such protection leaves one humble in the extreme – NOT A WORD.

> With love to you and many thanks, my dear – Yours, J.

I wondered uneasily what she thought would happen if her secret was spilled: a dilution of God's love, of God's protection?

Two years later, *Highland Harper* was released, followed the same year by the third EP, *An Treisamh*. Anticipating its release, she wrote again to Margie:

Dear Marg, Thanks so much for your letter which I found on my return from Embra last night. Glad 'Spring River' cheers you! It is designed to make people happy! And now I'm in 7th heaven as I've just completed The Welkin for CRO 3 and have to make the decision whether to publish it. It was a sweltering day but Harplet behaved very well and the thing got on, on the 2nd take which was marvellous! This is quite the most lovely little piece I've heard. The voice was fresh and I was inspired by a letter from Evelyn Rothwell. It will intrigue musicians as I've gone Modern suddenly with a change of style. Peter (who records) noticed it too – as I was rather bewilderingly wondering what had happened! We both reached the same words at the same moment, "infinite possibilities" so it's all frightfully exciting artistically!

It's a wonderful thought of yours to offer your help but all is under control – has to be for all the rules and regs. which are sometimes rather tiresome. My big problem is 'marketing' and getting it known and heard in the right quarters and this is almost ceaseless effort. However, Marks & Sp started as a barrow boy, I believe, so one must press on. Afraid this is all about me – sorry. Welkin has been with me for nearly a year – waiting for some place where I could work it out. Can hardly realize it is at last accomplished. Love to you all, Jane.

PS Last week I had an order on Monday from a Frenchman in Central Africa, Lake Tchad and on Tues, one from Champaign, Illinois, also a man – so it's really quite exciting. Enclose some leaflets.

Both 'The Welkin' and her voice had taken her by surprise but was she really so startled? 'The Welkin' is certainly more dramatic and sombrely complex than 'Spring River' but she sang without words on both tracks. But what would I know? Initially, I thought that 'The Welkin', albeit with unusual spelling, was to do with gathering whelks on the seashore. After all, it sounded a little like 'waulking' and I recalled her description of gathering spouties, or razor clams, on a North Uist beach. Then I learned that 'the welkin' is an archaic term that describes the vault of heaven, the firmament, the celestial sphere.

No wonder she was so proud of it. 'The Welkin' was her celebration of the spiritual universe.

Reading the sleeve notes, she described the first EP, *Ceol Clarsaich*, as being in Hebridean Idiom; the second, *Highland Harper*, as including tone poems; the third, *An Treisamh* comprising sound spells for harp and voice and the sleeve of the fourth EP, called *Seascape* alluded to mermaid's singing and rhythmic reiteration. Each of the EPs had three tracks. They were far removed from the Kennedy-Fraser repertoire. Each track dispensed with verses, with words, with the telling of a story. Instead, they offered simple and unrestrained expressions of her attachment to the rhythms of the sea and to the natural world. 'The Welkin' she described as 'bringing portent of nebulous space, through which the voice wanders freely in an unending theme'. And it does. Perhaps she didn't know where 'the voice' had come from but it seemed, in these four records, to reveal the release of her deepest personal experiences and feelings.

No longer was she performing to meet the expectations of the Kennedy-Fraser fans, of the Clarsach Society, of community or concert hall audiences or even the expectations of the homesick and romantic Scottish diaspora. She was expressing her spiritual passion for and relationship with the water, the sky and her natural surroundings. She drew on gamelan sounds and on the mbira and she used her voice to express something closer to what Beryl de Zoete had described when watching the Kejak Monkey Dance in Bali as, 'less words than power giving sounds; reiterated bird-like cries, lonely wailing voices, hoarse ejaculations …'

On *Seascape*, a track called 'Ostinato' offered persistent, trancelike repetitions composed, the sleeve notes said, to invoke an old tramp steamer chugging through a starlit sea, its rhythmic beat invoking some distant drumming. On *An Treisamh*, she chose the Scots word *jabble*, reflecting agitation and turbulence of water for another track of deep insistent rhythm. Such sounds had been with her since childhood;

the swirling water of the river Leny in Callander; the hypnotic tidal race that is the Falls of Lora at the mouth of Loch Etive between Ardtur and Muckairn. On the sleeve note, she described 'Jabble' *as* 'the exhilaration of steering through a *jabble*, those agitated waters of a tide-race with its contrasting eddies. A Hebridean Witch meets a Nile boatman's chant!'

Was 'Jabble' then, a metaphor for intercultural understanding, a triumphant mixing up of music, a celebration of human commonality? At some point, undocumented but for that undated *Sphinx* review lodged in the Mitchell Library, she had performed in Egypt. She had explored the ancient carvings of harps, compiled a volume dedicated entirely to ancient Egyptian music and had quoted from Ptahhotep, the fifth century vizier whose words had so moved her. It seemed that she might also have sailed with a boatman on the Nile.

Trying to describe the music on the EPs to my contemporaries was difficult. Had Jane been twenty years old in 1966 and living in Greenwich Village, youthful determination might have secured her music a better hearing. Instead, she was seventy and living in an Oban hotel with questionable wallpaper. For the general audience at that time, the clarsach was still fairly remote and seen largely in traditional settings, the Clarsach Society focussing on encouraging players to learn pieces for competition at the Mòd. Jane's more conventional contemporaries were baffled by the music and, I was told, some recalled playing the EPs for a laugh.

The arrival of mains electricity in the early 1960s had brought television to Sallochy, albeit one fuzzy channel, the BBC. The only Scottish music I can recall seeing was the White Heather Club, which to me seemed a rather stuffy, stilted interpretation of Scottishness where executing accurate dance steps in stiff clothes seemed more important than enjoying the music. I don't recall seeing any clarsachs on the programme but then, I wasn't looking for them. I was listening to Irish rebel songs, to Bob Dylan and to Bert Jansch, sneaking into pubs where there was a burgeoning of more politicised live folk music. Jane was not on my radar. We had yet to meet.

Locally, her friends remained loyal, offering her practical help as well as encouragement. Iris Blakeney painted water colour illustrations for two of the record sleeves and Hugh Duncan was happy to experiment with his recording equipment to help her achieve the best sound quality. Early in 1966, Grace Gibson and Jane went to a concert featuring the pianist Iris Loveridge and the oboist Evelyn Rothwell, a long standing friend of Jane's who was married to John Barbirolli. Conversation that evening may have prompted the letter from Evelyn which so inspired and encouraged Jane as she recorded 'The Welkin'.

When touring in the 1930s, Jane had used her energy and persuasive skills very effectively, moving fluidly between conventional and unconventional circles, readily picking up bookings and concentrating almost entirely on live performance. Her few recordings at the time seem incidental. By the 1960s, the recording world had become a major industry which worked in ways with which she was completely unfamiliar. Not only was she ill-equipped and her music distinctly *avant garde* but it was a decade devoted to the celebration of youth. Jane was hampered as much by the cloak of invisibility that wraps ever tighter around women as they age, as by her ignorance of record companies or of modern distribution systems.

Her first publicity leaflet stated quaintly that *Ceol Clarsaich* was available in Harrods, London, in The Bookshop, 57 George Street, Edinburgh, in two Glasgow music shops and in Highland retailers. In the winter of 1965 she had an article published in *Gairm*,[42] a quarterly Gaelic literary magazine, in which she focused largely on the musical significance of the clarsach in the Highlands and described her record *Ceol Clarsaich* as an example. I came across a number of polite letters from music shops that acknowledged receipt of a parcel of EPs but none

---

42 *Gairm*, No. 53, Winter 1965, pp. 81–82.

that confirmed further orders. Her letters mentioned occasional buyers, sometimes from overseas but, by and large, the recordings seem to have disappeared without trace. Nevertheless, she doggedly assembled extracts from some positive reviews onto her publicity material. Emelie Hook of the *Connoisseur* magazine wrote in January 1966 of *Ceol Clarsaich* that 'this recording deserves to be widely heard'. The following year, W.A. Chislett wrote in *The Gramophone* of *An Treisamh* that he would, 'recommend this little disc urgently … particularly to those who appreciate say, Holst or Bantock in their most mystical moods'.

Wemyess Craigie, writing in *Scotland's Magazine* in November 1966 had noted 'a hauntingly beautiful record … a heart tugging disc that is so deliciously different …' and followed that in 1968 writing in response to the release of *Seascape*: 'a big welcome for the latest release by Clarsach Recordings, the fourth in a wonderfully original series. "Seascape", the ocean in a mood of sheer enchantment. "Ostinato" is a bold attempt, completely effective, at something quite new for harp and voice'.

The leaflets also noted, 'As broadcast on BBC's Home and Overseas Programmes' and, 'As broadcast on BBC Television and Overseas Programmes', but I could find no traces of these in the BBC archives.

I found a few contemporary individuals who had discovered that later work. In New Zealand, Deirdre Newall, the mainstay of a psychedelic folk band called Tiny Pieces of Eight cited Miss Russell-Fergusson as one of her influences, having found the four EPs in *Too Tone*, a second hand music shop in Dunedin. She wrote:

> When I first heard Miss R-F … my jaw hit the floor to be honest. I have heard a lot of music in my time (thirty years of being a musician), but the ethereal beauty, delicate subtle rendering of instrumentation, the voice, the tunes themselves are spellbinding. They inspire me constantly as a songwriter, musician and as a singer. I write music with a lot of space in it, and I find Miss R-F does the same …[43]

---

43 Deirdre Newall, personal communication, 6 June 2017.

The proprietor of the shop had picked them up in Mossgiel, a hamlet outside Dunedin, amongst an old classical collection that had belonged to a Lions or a Rotary Club. Jane might have sent them to friends she had made during her New Zealand trip in 1937; possibly the men at that Rotary Club lunch or their wives. I fired a few exploratory messages across the internet to Scottish organisations in South Island but no replies pinged back.

Closer to home, Simon Chadwick, a specialist in the ancient harp music of Scotland and Ireland, responded to an inquisitive email from me saying, 'I think she [Jane] was one of the most original and creative Scottish harpists of the 20th century and I really admire her music.' He generously sent me a CD of all four of her EPs alongside the flyer for Stuart Eydmann's seminar. Meeting Stuart led me then to discover other groups and individuals interested in the Celtic Revival period and also in Jane's later music.

In late 2014, I watched a television programme about Celtic Connections, the well-established folk, roots and world music festival that brings welcome warmth to Glasgow each January. Its artistic director Donald Shaw enthused about the diversity of musicians from across the world who come together and collaborate so readily. Jane would have loved Celtic Connections, that chance to meet musical strangers, to explore similarities and differences. I pictured her on stage with Harplet, mbira player or drummer at her side, probably also a cellist. By chance, I saw Donald on another programme, performing in Brittany with his band Capercaillie and only then realised, belatedly, that he was the son of Libby Shaw who had sat with me in the Tesco café in Oban, the same Libby who had clarsach lessons with Jane in the Alexandra Hotel, who had trekked with Mel Blakeney across the windswept hillside above Loch Creran, clutching Jane's map. Libby, whose mother Grace Gibson had noted so many lunches with Jane in her diary.

By late 1968 and aged seventy-two, Jane must have been deeply disappointed by the public indifference to her recordings. Margie had encouraged and supported her as had her Argyll friends, but these are the records at which my father had rolled his eyes and Clarsach Society members had sniggered. We probably had the EPs at home but I have no memory of them being played. Then I remembered the still unheard tapes in the Mitchell Library. Would they contain more experimental music or something traditional? Returning to the Mitchell, I copied down the titles written on the four grey envelopes that were still sitting quietly in the archive box.

Jane had not put all her eggs in the experimental music basket, for the tapes offered twenty-three titles that she had called, collectively, *Hebridean Song and Story – The Young Piper Series*. A large coloured photograph also lay in the archive box. It showed a boy aged about twelve, standing barefoot on the seashore with his trouser cuffs rolled, playing a chanter. On the reverse, a date stamp recorded 'Colour Laboratory, 1964' but nothing else. Perhaps she had planned that the photograph would illustrate this new work. The youth must have been somebody's son, somebody's brother. I negotiated with the librarian to take a photo of the photo and emailed it round my few contacts in Oban, hoping that someone would recognise him. Nobody did. I sent it to the *Oban Times* which printed it with an appeal to find anyone who recognised him. Again, we drew a blank.

Hearing what was on the tapes in the Mitchell Library was proving to be much more difficult than anticipated. Although the conservationist had confirmed the tapes were in reasonable condition, the library collections as a whole were being reorganised so there had been no progress. In early July 2014, I returned to the library with Stuart Eydmann to discuss the practicalities of getting the tapes digitally recorded. He had not seen *The Russell-Fergusson Collection of Harps* before. When he opened the volume entitled 'Harp Players', I heard his sudden intake of breath. 'The trip is worth it just for this,' he said. I felt ridiculously proud.

On the librarian's trolley was an archive box that I hadn't seen before. Lifting the lid, I found twenty-five tightly packed boards, around

A4 size, each numbered and showing a page of closely typed narrative, marked sometimes with pencil or coloured references and entitled, 'Presenting Song and Story from the Hebrides of Long Ago'. Without doubt, this was 'the narrative' that she had asked Mr C.W. Black to ensure would not be divorced from the tapes. In the margins of each board were song titles, instructions for performance and on several boards, pencilled names of individuals some with place names beside them, often under the heading 'characters'. It was a series of scripts in which Jane named people who had worked with her. I copied them down. They seemed to represent the cast of a performance. I began to wonder whether their voices might be on the tapes although in her letter, Jane had said that she had not delegated 'any of the original songs' to another singer.

Stuart and I sat in the café with the librarian adding this new find to the urgency of getting the tapes copied and heard. He outlined the expertise in digitally copying old material that existed at Edinburgh's School of Celtic and Scottish Studies, assuring her that a copy would be made for the Mitchell Library as well as for myself and inserting delicately that, as long as the process was not protracted, the School would rarely charge family members for copies of recordings that it would be adding to its collection. The Mitchell librarian was animated and enthusiastic. She seemed to 'get' Jane's story, its significance, the import of the resources locked in the library. But again, we would have to wait. Glasgow's entire cultural facilities were engrossed in preparing for thousands of visitors to the Commonwealth Games to be held later that month. Fair enough.

I circulated the names on the storyboards and discovered that most of them, remembered affectionately and often as members of the Oban Gaelic Choir, were now deceased. Summertime overtook us, medals were won at the Commonwealth Games, I welcomed a new grandchild and then was floored by pneumonia. It was mid-November before Stuart and I met again with the librarian. To our dismay, the loan process had become more convoluted. I had assumed the library owned the tapes, which it did, but in the absence of a will, Ruth and I still held the copyright, broadly speaking, to what was recorded on them. Broadly speaking that is, because until we heard the tapes no one could be sure what other factors might need to be taken into account. The loan process seemed fraught with anxieties about who would own what once the tapes were copied. We couldn't be sure what we would hear, but that was part of the problem. We were mired in a catch-22 situation.

Eventually, it was agreed that while the library's legal people were finalising the loan agreement that would allow the tapes to leave the building to be digitised, they would also prepare a document for us to sign about the copyright. It should be straightforward, something which for me was important as the search had become more urgent. I had had a bronchoscopy following too many bouts of pneumonia and the consultant had referred me for further tests to look, she had said gently, for 'mild' lung cancer. Looking at websites, I learned that lung cancer was rarely mild. I needed to get my skates on. Jane had been assiduous in her preparations for death, in her gifts to museums and the library, in leaving a legacy of music and ideas. The least I could do was finish her story.

In a spirit of optimism, Stuart submitted a proposal that he and I make a joint presentation entitled 'Héloïse Russell-Fergusson: the basement tapes' at the Musica Scotica conference in Glasgow at the end of April 2015. I was feeling extraordinarily tired, sleeping a lot during the day and with little energy to do much more than brush my teeth, but I thought of Jane sitting doggedly in her car with the tape recorders, ignoring her exhaustion and discomfort. I got off my sofa and returned to the storyboards. The librarian had agreed that they would be scanned and lodged with the digitised tapes in keeping with Jane's wishes but I hoped that by transcribing them myself, I would gain more insight into her thinking.

I puffed along the street from St George's Underground Station to the Mitchell Library wrapped in copious layers of clothing. Fumbling through the contents of the archive box I realised that there was another tape, without attribution but which held, according to the notes, recordings of the Lord's Prayer and the 23rd Psalm in Scottish Gaelic, Irish Gaelic, Welsh, Breton, Cornish and Manx. Putting it to one side, I focussed on the boards.

Each offered a story fragment set in an imaginary community on South Uist, around the mid-nineteenth century. It was seen largely through the eyes of children and reflected Jane's experience: gathering spouties at low tide, crossing the great ford to Benbecula, hearing songs and tales from an old woman. There were interludes of magic and lots of music; some attributed to Kennedy-Fraser or Annie Johnston but much more to Kenneth MacLeod, with a series of almost indecipherable abbreviated references which appeared to relate to the envelope of loose papers from her visits to Gigha that lay in the archive. Each board was headed with a running time, noted in minutes and seconds. Named individuals played the pipes, interjected, sang or played the fiddle. It was a structured and already cast series of vignettes.

I had sent a copy of the Young Piper photo and a list of the names on the storyboard to Peter MacLeod in Oban. He didn't recognise the boy but he put me in touch with a friend called John MacFarlane, who recognised some of the names. Another contact recognised the name of a man living on the island of Luing, an accomplished singer and former gold medallist at the Mòd. She told him of my search and that his name had cropped up. He thought long and hard, finally retrieving a distant memory of sitting in a car waiting for the Cuan Ferry at the tiny crossing to Luing from Seil Island. A woman with a tape recorder had sat beside him as he sang although he could not recall her name. It could only have been Jane. I turned to Jane's 1969 letter to Mr Black. 'Much of the work was done in my car,' she had written. I had assumed this referred only to herself. Now I recognised that others had sat there, clearing their throats, watching while she set up her tape recorder, preparing themselves to sing.

Peter's friend John in Taynuilt was eloquent on the subject of Gaelic. His grandfather had been something of a bard; a collector of folk songs and stories who had moved to Glasgow during what John called the Highland Renaissance. His mother had enrolled in 1919 on Glasgow University's Celtic course and she had taught Gaelic in Oban and in Tobermory before the family moved back to Taynuilt. One of Jane's storyboards noted 'Mrs MacFarlane, Taynuilt – Blackbird's Call'. John emailed me after our phone conversation to confirm:

> My mother's involvement was no doubt a little poem she used to recite in which the Gaelic imitated the song of a blackbird. It is probably written down somewhere but the only bit I can remember is '*Òl e òl e a h-uile dìd a h-uile dìd*' - 'drink it drink it every drop every drop'. The Gaels were very good at interpreting birdsong and there are other examples …

Working in Gaelic broadcasting and an active member of the local Gaelic Choir, John was well placed to give me advice about Jane's singing. She probably had little chance to use Gaelic other than on stage, and I wanted to learn how she would sound to a native speaker. Moreover, there was that Kennedy-Fraser repertoire. Would that make her singing less worthwhile?

I met John at Libby's house where the fire crackled quietly in the grate and her dog Nuala lay snoozing. Sitting upright like an anxious parent at a child's audition, I watched while John listened intently to recordings of Jane singing in the 1930s and 1940s. When the music ended, he paused a moment and then commended the musical qualities of her voice. Despite some mispronunciations and inattentiveness to certain word endings, she had made a good effort with her Gaelic, he said. With just a touch of '*blas na Beurla*', an English accent, he had heard a serious non-native trying to get it right. Then, with disarming local loyalty he added that she was a little less proficient than the non-natives in the current Taynuilt Gaelic Choir.

Nevertheless, I felt reassured. Her Gaelic had passed muster in terms of effort. So what about the potentially contentious Kennedy-Fraser repertoire? John laughed aloud. He recalled his mother who had been, more or less, Jane's contemporary. She wouldn't have worried about the Kennedy-Fraser arguments, he said. She would have been happy that Jane was singing and celebrating Gaelic songs. His mother, like John himself and like Jane, would have felt there was room for everyone. With no little humour, he went on to describe differences in Gaelic pronunciation between islands and in different parts of Scotland, the rivalries and teasing that exist between Gaelic speakers in different places. I drove home happily, listening to Jane singing. Well done, I whispered.

I hoped John would be free to pass opinion later on the storyboards as well as on the unheard tapes, for whatever the content, without appraisal by a Gaelic speaker, the Mitchell Library would be in danger of missing meanings entirely, of not understanding what they represented. Confusingly, I had no precise idea of when Jane sent them to the library. One storyboard was mounted on a piece of card dated 1963 and the photograph of the 'Young Piper' was dated 1964. Yet it wasn't until 1969 that Jane had sent the final tapes to Mr Black. By then, the Young Piper would have been a young man. Perhaps the tapes and the storyboards were part of a project recorded well before 1969, possibly at a performance.

At Stuart's suggestion, I contacted Kenna Campbell, a renowned Gaelic singer and teacher who agreed to meet me in the Mitchell Library to look at the bundle of loose leaved papers, assembled during Jane's visit to Kenneth MacLeod. With the archive laid out before us, I glanced at Kenna as she pored over Jane's scraps of writing and the careful notations in the songbook, humming quietly now and again. With her help, I realised that there was a clear progression within what had seemed haphazard materials. From that bundle of scrawled notes, Jane had sifted for the song book around fifty finished and carefully numbered songs; most attributed to MacLeod, but a few to other sources. She had tallied them with numbered references on the storyboards, incorporating them systematically into the vignettes and noting down the names of the singers.

Would we really hear all these people on the tapes? I wondered what had stopped her from finishing the project earlier. It seemed to depend heavily on the participation of others, particularly members of the Oban Gaelic Choir. Perhaps she had put the Young Piper series aside once she had started recording her EPs in 1964. Her letters to Margie gave no hint of this parallel project and spoke only of the new recordings. On Christmas Day 1966, she had written:

> My dear, I was unable to wait until today to open that Gay Green parcel, and the Gay Happy card along with the pretty bulb container gave me a lot of pleasure! Thank you so much for your kind thought. As for the other, I feel it is <u>more than generous</u> and accept it with gratitude. It will make up for the moment for monies owing me and will probably go to further advertising or the new leaflet. I am awaiting 2 more reviews before drafting the latter – the 'Record Retailer' on Dec 31st and the 'Gramophone' on Jan 1st, when CRO3 (with my darling Welkin) is to be reviewed. I can hardly wait. I hope you had a happy day today and expect you went to the family. The roads are horrible here but friends very kind about 'lifting' one.

> Again, I've been given the key to an empty house and expect to spend every spare minute there with Harplet. It is <u>quite, quite Marvellous</u> the way things work out. How is the Braille getting on? And I wonder what you are at now? When weather improves later I must lunch in Helensburgh to find out. Love to you, dear, and again many thanks to you, Jane.

I was intrigued and a bit concerned by the empty house. With her now familiar underlining and capital letters Jane had attributed the gift of the key to divine intervention, but I craved details. I recalled early 1960s winters at Sallochy, where we had depended on the unreliable generator for light and on the Raeburn, an open fire and a couple of paraffin stoves to keep us warm and dry.

Yet I could understand Jane's thrill, relief even, to have private space in which to be alone with Harplet: to be utterly herself, to do what she wanted; to make a lot of noise or enjoy complete silence, to stay up all night or to doze in the afternoon. In the hotel there would have been always bustle and noise, the comings and goings of other people, the clatter of feet and background conversations in rooms and corridors, guests calling to each other, inflexible mealtimes, the intrusion of staff who wanted access to her room. I took comfort that she had been given a key 'again'. This was not a new challenge. She had been there or, if not there, somewhere similar, before. Probably she had long perfected the skills of making anywhere a comfortable home. And her letter confirmed that there were friends around and a social life.

But given that it was written on Christmas Day I felt frustrated by her omissions. She didn't tell Margie who had given her the key nor where the house was located. Even to her sister, she let slip no personal markers. Perhaps she and Harplet remained in that empty house while Christmas went on elsewhere. Someone suggested that the Alexandra Hotel may have closed for the Christmas period, politely consigning Jane and her rolls of wallpaper to the old blue car. Maybe she had found it hard to afford to stay there. Certainly, she was hugely grateful for 'the other', for Margie's gift.

We all lived less than a hundred miles from Oban. Margie had a spare room in her Helensburgh flat. And we could have made room for her at Sallochy. But after such a long and solitary lifetime coupled with the ongoing impetus of her work, it may have been impossible for Jane to think of staying cheek by jowl with family even for a short time. I wonder whether it had ever been discussed.

CHAPTER SEVENTEEN

A LIFE LEARNING

In late April 2015, Stuart and I presented the paper at the Musica Scotica conference in Glasgow. Entitled 'Héloïse Russell-Fergusson: the basement tapes', we talked about Jane as Héloïse. Stuart had assembled samples of her music from the 1930s, 1940s and 1960s and against a backdrop of illustrative slides, we described her life and her music. But we had to admit that we had no basement tapes. They lay still in the Mitchell Library.

Happily, although still succumbing to unexplained pneumonias, the clouds in my lung had thinned sufficiently to reveal no evidence of cancer. Just as well, I thought rather grumpily, for Ruth and I had still not received any paperwork about the copyright. The catch-22 situation had become Kafkaesque. The council lawyer had left before Christmas, either resigned or laid off, who knew? Before the new lawyer had a chance to grapple with the task, she was assigned to work on the impending 2015 general election. The muddied world of local bureaucracy began to feel like a quagmire. I wished I'd slipped the innocuous grey envelopes into my pocket when I first saw them. They had lain ignored for forty-five years. No one would have missed them.

The conference was small and specialist, full of esoteric contributions that flew over my head but some very interesting individuals. Fiona Donaldson, writing about the history of the Reid Orchestra in Edinburgh, revealed unique personal knowledge of Marie Dare who had not only taught her cello at school but had also given her home tuition.

'Hugely talented,' Fiona said, describing Marie, whom she remembered dressed in a twinset and sensible skirt, personable and humorous yet very private. Before the war, Marie had been principal cellist with the Reid Orchestra but had switched afterwards to play double bass, as well as teaching at the Royal Academy of Music in Glasgow.

In a paper entitled 'The Hebrides or Fingal's Cave' which explored Mendelssohn's overture, Benedict Taylor from Edinburgh University talked about eco-musicology. Was this what I had been grappling with when trying to describe Jane's 1960s EPs; the way that her music seemed to have emerged so viscerally and late in life and drawn directly from the tangled reaches of her connection to the natural world? In 'The Lochan', 'Drifting Wrack', 'Sea Rain', 'Jabble', 'The Sound', 'Seascape', 'Spring River', and 'Dance of the Drops' she offered transparent titles invoking liquid movement, returning always to the insistent waves and rhythms that had swirled and pounded throughout her life, comforting and inspiring her.

The music seemed to express that blurred immersive interface between her inner self and the natural world, a profound, intense space in which she seemed to dissolve, to experience a sense of rapture. She didn't just describe 'The Lochan', she *was* the lochan. I imagined one of those small moorland lochs, set deep within the heather high up on South Uist or above Loch Creran, its bronzed water dense with the swelling buds of water lilies, surrounded by waves of cotton-grass and bog asphodel rippling in the breeze; the scent of bog myrtle and the sound of skylarks in the air and her voice, still clear as she was approaching seventy, soaring intermittently above it all. I knew what it was to be a blue-grey pebble scoured smooth, brushed by the bellies of passing trout heading for the mouth of the burn, nestled gently under the lap-lap of the loch. I could imagine being a lochan.

Of course, I couldn't explain all that to the faces at the conference. I had learned gradually about Jane's spirituality, her other-worldishness, that underlying predisposition to keep at a distance from the mainstream and with which I felt entirely in tune. Yet there was also that very determined and pragmatic side to her. From the audience, Dr Per Ahlander reminded participants that Kenneth MacLeod had been relieved to see Jane's ferry steaming away from Gigha. A year or so earlier, I might have felt defensive on her behalf but by then I knew better. Per was right. During his extensive research on MacLeod he had uncovered a letter MacLeod wrote to Cathie Johnston in January 1933 which said:

> At last I have a few minutes to spare. A harpist/singer (Miss Heloise Russell-Fergusson) has been staying at the hotel (on Gigha) and has been coming here every day for lessons in Gaelic etc. Luckily she left this morning. Although I am quite glad to help such people, it takes up far too much of my time.[44]

When pursuing her research, Jane would have been an exacting visitor, expecting details and clarity regarding sources, words, historical facts and, given her intervening experience, probably all the more so since her first visit to him in the 1920s. MacLeod would have been worn out.

Overall, there seemed to be a sympathetic understanding that Jane had been too late to be embraced by the early Celtic Revival, and too early for the instrumental folk music revival in the 1960s that saw a rehabilitation of the clarsach; the latter all the more poignant since, at least tangentially through Gildas, she had influenced the development of the Breton Alan Stivell, one of its most renowned modern champions. Both inevitable and remarkable then, that she had so determinedly ploughed her own furrow.

Meanwhile, the loan agreement for the tapes had ground to a halt. Some impasse emerged between the Mitchell Library in Glasgow and the School of Celtic and Scottish Studies in Edinburgh. I resisted the temptation to see this as indicative of ancient city rivalries. After

---

44 GUL, MS Gen 1650/Box 62.

a prolonged silence, the Mitchell decided to look for a company to undertake the digitisation. I recalled Jane's 1969 letter to Mr C.W. Black. She had started confidently, enthusing in detail about making the tapes and describing precisely what they comprised. But then, as she broached the subject of loan arrangements, her tone had become cluttered with conditionals, saying, 'I wonder, if I could suggest … that if borrowed …'

She had visited and worked with museums and libraries across the world, discussing artefacts, photographs and documents, yet she seemed extraordinarily hesitant when making this final donation. Perhaps it was down to modesty, a hesitation to acknowledge that anyone would ever *want* to listen to her work. Or maybe, in 1969, she feared that reels of tape presented the Mitchell with an unfamiliar challenge. Despite her long working relationship with Mr Black, she seemed to doubt the library's readiness or capacity to loan them, feared that they might become separated from the storyboards, inaccessible, ensnared in bureaucracy, trapped in an archive box. Maybe she could see into the future.

I had liked the gentle enthusiasm of the librarian and the ready friendliness of the lawyer when we met. These women didn't want to deny Jane a hearing but I could sense the weight of anxiety that seemed to lie across their shoulders, the responsibility to ensure that Jane's tapes were not only cared for but that they, the Mitchell Library, Glasgow Life, Glasgow City Council, were all properly protected. For the life of me, I couldn't understand what these bureaucracies, perceived as the threat; who or what they were to be protected *from*. But I recalled the British Library's reluctance to give me a photocopy of 'Absence' until I had the notional approval of the Music Publishers' Association and I remembered tortuous training sessions on copyright when I worked in the public sector. I knew too, that the copyright industry was huge and developing as fast as the complex new technologies with which it interacted, perhaps most especially in relation to music and film. But I couldn't help feeling that a mighty sledgehammer fit for Barclay Curle's shipyard was being repeatedly honed to crack this sweet little nut.

We would wait. Paradoxically, the absence of 'the basement tapes' from the Musica Scotica conference stimulated a small flurry of interest in Jane. One person suggested that all her music should be re-released, another offered to play some of her sheet music for me. I began to wonder how her music would be received in the twenty-first century. It could certainly reach wider audiences with more eclectic tastes and it might resonate more readily than in the 1960s. Stuart was in the process of re-establishing the website that he and a friend, sadly deceased, had first set up in 2006. Called rareTunes.org, it offered a carefully curated audio archive of Scottish recordings that ranged from near studio quality to noisy house sessions, from digital media to old bits of tape, vinyl and obscure 78s. He was keen to devote space to Jane's story and to her music. I wondered whether he would be able to include some of the music from those last tapes. As for me, I would need to match her resilience and be patient.

The delay gave me pause to reflect on what, if anything, I had learned during this long process. The research had been gripping, not just because it demanded some satisfying sleuthing, but quite literally it wouldn't let me go. I would switch on the bedside light to scrawl late night notes before nearly dropping off to sleep and then another phrase or question would swim into my head and I would have to sit up again. I felt mildly irritated if social engagements intruded on quiet days of working with her story. Knocked about by ill-health, by my struggles to find answers or locate people who knew her, by the mind-numbing bureaucracy of the library, by the disdain of an early reader who said the story would get nowhere without a steamy romance, there was never a chance that I would give up. I just kept digging deeper, listening to her voice, to her music, struggling to work out who she was. I had always thought myself a rather shallow character; readily intrigued by new ideas and then too quickly bored, flitting to something different. Jane revealed my own surprising capacity for doggedness.

The process of writing also drove home the importance of listening; I had neglected so many chances to learn, not just while she was alive but in the years that followed. Nevertheless, I felt that I had been able to walk through snatches of time with her, sometimes in step and picking up clues, sometimes lagging behind, lost in my own thoughts, struggling with contemporary connections. She was so full of contrasts: that unswerving, serious determination matched by mischief and experiment; the deep spirituality and creativity that existed so comfortably beside pragmatism and practicality. I could see that she might have been demanding company, irritatingly other-worldish or focussed single-mindedly on her own priorities. Yet she had been popular with the 1960s Argyll teenagers, an open-minded listener and a good friend too, valued amongst their parents.

Jane was not an academic but she was a deep thinker, at least about music, and she had impressed some significant academics, musicologists and collectors of her day; James Carmichael Watson in Edinburgh, the Jaffrenous in Brittany, Dolmetsch in Haslemere, Andersson and Väisänen in Finland, probably Walter Spies and Beryl de Zoete in Bali, Hans Hickmann in Egypt and who knows how many others. In Dilling, Korchinska, Emerson and Pielou, an impressive range of harpists had been drawn to work with her. Not forgetting the loyal and very talented cellist, Marie Dare.

Although I am a hoarder compared to her minimalist life style, I especially like her disdain for 'stuff'; her rejection of the trappings of the material world, the relentless acquisitiveness that can restrict us, where the 'having' of things is valued more than the 'doing' of things, valued more than simply relishing 'being' in the magic of the world. And I recognise her profound relationship with the natural world, for that is where I too feel most deeply and comfortably rooted, most at ease and free from judgement. I understand her preference for being alone and know there is something intensely joyous about the solitary life.

I had experienced marriage for a while and later relaxed happily on the warm shoulders of occasional partners but such relationships usually fell apart, almost always because I would begin to feel uncomfortably hemmed in. Maybe I had inherited a trait: being sociable enough but with a predilection to do my own thing for hours on end, preferably unobserved and without need of validation, free from any requirement to interact or to explain myself, preferring to trade the comforts and compromise of companionship for the challenge of my own imagination. Was it nature or nurture that made me feel so akin to her? Or a dollop of both?

Perhaps we were both a little paranoid, suspicious that just when human company seemed comforting and benign it might suddenly and without warning, turn on us. Or maybe that bit was just me. Such defensiveness may have started at primary school, and been reinforced that Easter holiday when I turned seventeen and my father announced without warning that since we children were grown up, he was leaving home.

A few years later, in my mid-twenties, I had a near-miss one sunny afternoon when a crazy youth with a mask over his face and aiming an air rifle knocked on our back door. My boyfriend opened it and burst out laughing, believing a friend was playing a joke. It wasn't a joke. The gunman, as we came to call him, ran away but was apprehended a few days later, charged and convicted of 'assault with intent to ravish'.

It emerged that I had cut an irresistible figure leaving the house earlier to get a pint of milk as he had stood nearby, unobserved. It was the mid-1970s and we made light of the event, boasting to friends that the police had not detected the cannabis plants in the house and, after all, no one had been hurt. But the experience made me jumpy and self-conscious. It was a reminder that it was still not safe to be myself;

a penalty, a punishment, could emerge at any time. Around ten years later, I had another scary encounter involving that homely word, domestic, abuse; although not, it should be added, at the hands of my children's father. Overall, personal solitude seemed a safer choice. I wondered whether Jane ever had such a scare.

Her comfortable, benign world had been turned upside down by the horrors of war for years at a time, not once but twice, and the psychological impact on her generation was profound. Solitary living became the norm for many women in a country stripped of so many men. It was not really a matter of choice. I couldn't know whether something else, some personal threat or attack, lay behind her consistent preference for solitude, but if it had, she did not hide from life as a consequence. Yet, when I observed casually to a psychologist friend that Jane seemed to stride through her professional and social worlds with such unrelenting curiosity and good humour, she had responded by asking rather darkly, 'What had happened to her? Why was she protecting herself?'

These questions threw me. Certainly, Jane's background had nurtured that relaxed self-possession, the 'sunny' disposition, her lack of qualms about approaching strangers or broaching new ideas to possibly sceptical audiences. Yet Shuna Duncan had told me that one of the plants in Jane's car, grown from a grapefruit pip brought back from Southern Rhodesia, had seemed incredibly important to her. It had represented, Shuna felt, a kind of mythical union with the family that Jane had not been able to achieve. Yet Hélène had written proudly of Jane and there was plenty of evidence that she was close to Margie, at least in those later years. There was, of course, the unknowable gulf between Jane and my father, the little brother with whom she had played on the magical island in the river Leny. I have no idea why they hardly spoke to each other. Was that what lay behind the black scribblings and the cuttings out, the new plain name? I had been told of the palpable passion in her 1916 composition, 'Absence';

however the dedicated initials M.C.S. on the music and later, the J.S.B. engraved on the kettle, remain unsolved mysteries.

The independent and sometimes unconventional lives of both her parents may have instilled an unconscious feminism within Jane. That confident capturing of traditional male roles was most evident when she played to troops, performed at boys' schools or addressed Rotary Clubs. She anticipated the stereotyped attitudes of men around her and was gleeful in challenging them or proving them wrong. It never seemed to occur to her that she couldn't explore something new, whether it was flying over a glacier or staging a song-tale. Such confidence was derived, partly at least, from the unconscious sense of entitlement brought by her social class, yet she had underlined the section in Gaston Bardout's book where he acknowledged the significance of his wife's contributions. She knew when she was breaking new ground as a woman and she liked that.

There was also that more obscure, deeper part of her; the magical, liminal space evinced by the music in her EPs, that place where she seemed so free. I envy her capacity to plumb her creative depths, her compulsion not only to explore and develop what she found there but to expose it with such raw intensity. I have always preferred the company of creative individuals; have felt most at ease around their passions, their imagination and unpredictability, their unselfconscious courage. Whatever might have lain in her shadows, Jane remained compulsively creative to the very end. She would not have known how to be otherwise. To her, creativity was life.

———————

Throughout the period of research and writing, the Scottish referendum campaign dominated the news, social media and conversation with friends. It brought to the fore my questions about whether and where I fitted in contemporary Scotland. I had worked in the public sector, teaching initially and then focussed specifically on promoting equality in schools and colleges. I spoke regularly in public, took stances on issues I believed in, raised a family. My holidays were spent mostly pottering around outside, often near the sea on the frayed west coast from Argyll up to Sutherland. Years flew by. Was I still that awkward child inside, squirming with my strange name and rather posh voice, feeling resented and rejected?

My internal sense of Scottishness was hardwired. Yet I was accustomed to friendly shopkeepers treating me like a tourist, to new acquaintances saying, 'you don't *sound* Scottish', provoking a feeling that I had to justify myself. I would mutter about my dad being 'a posh Scot', or of having an English mother, voicing the labels before someone else did; or try and fail miserably to send myself up, by alluding to the comedian Tony Hancock's 1961 Blood Donor skit in which a Dr MacGregor, challenged by Hancock for not sounding Scottish, retorted, 'We're not all Rob Roys, you know.'

Even in middle-age, I found an anti-English cartoon on my desk on the first morning in a new job. A joke, of course. A colleague expressed his envy to me, claiming that my voice must open doors, make life easy. Perhaps he didn't realise that his unspoken message cast doubt on whether I actually deserved my job in the first place. As for opening doors, I realised that the cumulative experience of embarrassment and self-justification had led me to internalise a kind of self-loathing. To use the old saw attributed to Groucho Marx, I didn't care to belong to any club that would have me as a member, any club in which people sounded like me. Bluntly, I was prejudiced.

Researching Jane's story helped to expose that prejudice and pull me up short. She and other women in her family, Hélène, Margie, her aunt Jane Gemmill and Elise, my own beloved mother, took stock of the world in which they found themselves and, none of them perfect, engaged with it purposefully in their own ways. Jane noticed the universal interweaving of people's spirituality and creativity within their day to day lives; she actively sought patterns while she also respected and celebrated the unique. It wasn't a million miles from my own much more mundane life, committed to recognising, respecting and valuing diversity amongst the individuals and lifestyles within Scotland's communities. And beyond the world of work, we both could lose ourselves in the pooling and swirl of water, in the sound of birdsong, in the feel of moss against our skin. In truth, it doesn't matter if someone takes offence at my voice, envies or teases me. We are all part of the whole, of something so much bigger than we can ever imagine.

The referendum campaigns rang with contradictory calls asserting the best kind of Scottishness, yet I knew that from Melrose to Mangersta, Lanark to Lerwick there were as many ways to be Scottish as there were Scots.

The night before the referendum, I was still worryingly ambivalent. In the morning, I left the house early, heading for the polling station to get it over with. As sunlight filled the street, I felt relieved when the conviction to vote Yes flooded through me. Building an independent Scotland would be an exciting and creative project, one to which I might contribute. I quickened my pace and smiled at the campaigners outside the community centre before picking up my voting slip. 'Should Scotland be an independent country?' it asked. I took up the pencil and put my cross, without hesitation, in the box marked No.

It was the 'should' that got me. I knew that would sound incomprehensible to my Yes voting friends and I could anticipate their counter arguments, but when faced with the question, I had felt suddenly thrawn, contrary, overwhelmed by a sense of defiance: why *should* Scotland retreat in the face of what appeared to be intractable difficulties.

I knew radical change for the better had happened before. No, I didn't know how it could be achieved, but I didn't yet feel ready to throw in the towel. And yes, I knew I should 'check my privilege'.

With little debt, a teacher's pension and some fine family table linen to my name, I was shielded from the bitter hardship and uncertainties that were overwhelming many people's lives in Scotland. But I knew that similar levels of poverty and despair prevailed in other parts of the UK. I wasn't ready to choose whom to care about most.

Still lost in Jane's story, I wondered how she would have voted. Her passion for the Hebrides seemed to be all about championing a way of life that she felt to be under threat and in *Hailing the Highlander*, she had acknowledged and welcomed diversity and change, saying, 'some can prefer the one style and some this other, for that is the way of it.' I couldn't be sure. She might have fronted gigs for the Yes campaign; she might have insisted that the world needed fewer borders and have resolutely voted No.

In 1969, absorbed in her recordings in Oban, Jane cannot have been oblivious to the extraordinary and tumultuous time she was living in. Neil Armstrong had walked on the moon and John Lennon had released 'Give Peace a Chance' while details were emerging of the My Lai massacre in Vietnam and of the famine ravaging the population of Biafra. Students were rebelling against war and against injustice in the United States and in Europe. Polaris submarines armed with nuclear missiles cruised quietly into their berths on the Clyde while the BBC launched a new comedy programme called 'Monty Python's Flying Circus'. Defiant optimism was see-sawing with rage and with fear. In the last months of that year, Jane acknowledged that her capacity to keep up with the changing world was spent. Not long after we met in Crianlarich, Mum invited her to address a local women's organisation about her life and work but in late August, she had replied that:

> I feel most honoured. But really, I have not been talking for some time now in public so must regretfully decline, much as I should have liked to go. Somehow, with the world in its present state, one has been retiring more and more to contemplate and I feel that my contribution to the

countering of the general chaos is best expressed through my little discs. Keep in touch dear, and let me know how things go and thanks to you for thinking of me. Love to all, from Jane.

Three months later, on 27 December 1969, she wrote to thank Mum for a Christmas present and to wish us all a Happy New Year. That week, a young Oban GP encountered her in the foyer of the Alexandra Hotel. Jane was not registered with the medical practice but he knew her as part of the community and as a pleasant if rather eccentric local lady who was suspicious of medical people. Perhaps she stumbled in the foyer or, running a high temperature, had been rather incoherent and had to sit down suddenly. Or perhaps her general appearance told him how very ill she was. Quite remarkably, she allowed him to examine her. Listening to her laboured breathing and discovering the evidence of her breast cancer, the doctor urged at once that she be admitted to hospital to be made more comfortable. When she refused, he pressed her to let the District Nurse visit the hotel to apply some dressings. Again, she refused.

Possibly, when she failed to appear at supper later that week, for who knows whether she was a creature of habit, someone went upstairs to tap on her door. The hotel staff must surely have noticed her decline although, as Miss G. had written to Mum in 1952, acknowledging the impact of Hélène's Christian Science beliefs before she died, 'though we could see her strength was failing we did not realise the seriousness of her illness. We now know what a brave effort she made to carry on as usual.'

Jane died at one o'clock in the morning on the 2 January 1970, aged seventy-three. The death certificate, signed by the GP, Dr Frew, stated the place of death as Oban's West Highland Hospital where the local mortuary was located. Her death was registered by William Leggat Smith, her solicitor from Glasgow. In the section on the death certificate that noted 'Usual Residence if different from Place of Death', was written the Park Hotel, Oban, not the Alexandra Hotel. The solicitor was a meticulous man so an error seemed unlikely. Perhaps she had decanted temporarily again that Christmas, too ill to take up any offer of an empty house.

A song called 'Bad Moon Rising' had topped the British charts for three weeks that September. Sung by Creedence Clearwater Revival, it was a jaunty tune at odds with its dystopian lyrics, 'Hope you got your things together, hope you're quite prepared to die.' It seemed unlikely that Jane was aware of it. Yet, that very month, sitting in the old car with the plant pots on the dashboard she had been doing precisely what it urged. Looking out across the waves, her pale blue raincoat buttoned against the chill and her white hair coiled in its soft plait, she was already aware of the cancer if not the impending pneumonia as she raised the chanter to her lips. She was prepared to die but she wasn't going to give up living until the very last moment.

Reprise (Afterword)

I listened to 'the tapes' eventually. Not, as I had half expected, in the Mitchell Library itself nor in a studio full of technical equipment where they had been digitised, but sitting at my desk watching thrushes busy in the garden under trees heavy with May blossom.

Sensibly, the library had set up a small listening committee comprising Kenna Campbell and another Gaelic singer called Iseabail MacLeod, Stuart Eydmann and myself. We were sent the sound files for *The Young Piper Series* to listen to in our own time before pooling thoughts on the content, the quality and possible edits that might improve their clarity.

I was glad to be alone and immensely pleased that I had transcribed the storyboards. Immediately, it all made sense. Following Jane's annotated narrative while listening to the files, I was witnessing her final song tale. She had pulled together the essence of what she loved about the Hebrides, interspersing her short vignettes with songs, mostly sung by herself but including other singers and musicians. In lively expressive tones she was story-telling as if to children, describing fragments of experience that I recognised from her earlier writing but set into the lives of youngsters a hundred years before; a little boy crossing the ford to North Uist, for example, who had heard, 'the sound of the large wagonette wheels as they bowled round. Sometimes gritty, at other times crunching, and on the sand softly yielding, whilst in the water they had another sound altogether.'

In a voice that was clearly struggling, she sang almost all of the female characters, conjuring as best she could a young girl or an old crone.

As I began to comprehend the complexity of the task she had set herself, I pictured her alone in the car at Ganavan Sands, shuffling her papers covered with notes, pausing to cough, to rewind the tape, trying doggedly to regulate her breathing, to concentrate on achieving the very best she could. Occasionally, perhaps, when she made a mistake or when the task was at its most frustrating, she lifted her eyes for a while, seeking peace and reassurance in the rhythmic movement of the waves as they reached out towards her across the shore.

It was not the systematic recording of a group in a theatre or community hall. The tapes were full of clicks and pauses and it was very clear that she had pasted in the musical contributions herself, sometimes four or five brief insertions within an eight minute vignette and there were twenty-three of those altogether. She had recorded seagulls and splashing water, the latter recorded perhaps on that playful day with the Duncans below Ardencaple. It was painstaking, meticulous work which at times must have been fraught with frustration. Her letter to Mr Black had warned of erasing material by mistake, noting that, frequently, she had done that herself. Despite the help of the Duncans and the contributions of several singers, it was an utterly unique, one-woman creation. It must have taken her ages.

I wondered what modern listeners would make of it. There are now many recorded first-hand accounts of early Hebridean life, the best available through *Tobar an Dualchais – the Kist o' Riches*, a website laden with Scottish folklore, music and poetry collected from the 1930s onwards. Listeners accustomed to such authenticity would note the weaknesses of Jane's singing voice, would almost certainly be sidetracked by her accent that so clearly signified 'an outsider'. Might she be dismissed once again, ridiculed? Had I been right in my persistence to have the tapes heard? She had asked Mr Black to ensure that the music and narrative remained 'in their completeness' but was there a contemporary value in preserving the tapes and the storyboards?

Struggling to answer that question, I turned it round. Was there value in *not* preserving them, in *not* listening to them? The answer came swiftly. To ignore the tapes would be to ignore the complexity, to deny the diversity, the truth of cultural experience. It would cheat history. Jane had been there, with her determination and insatiable curiosity, her posh voice and formal musical background, her romance and her optimism, leaving a small and tender footprint on the Hebridean storyscape. It should not be washed away.

Towards the end of assembling her story, I visited Port Appin to talk to the local historical society about Jane's life. Afterwards, a member of the audience approached me. She said that towards the end of the war, her grandmother had bought Jane's clarsach to give to her as a present. She had enjoyed playing for many years although most recently, her fingers had seized up a little and she felt that she could play no longer. I was sceptical. Surely, I had traced all of Jane's harps?

Then she told me that the clarsach bore an inscription. I felt a sudden and unexpected flush of emotion as I realised this might be the Dolmetsch harp. Two weeks later, we met for a much longer conversation about our family histories and about harps. I learned that she had been taught to play by Edith Taylor at Rahoy who had a very similar small harp. And we made a transaction.

That clarsach, with the handwritten inscription, 'This clarsach, the first of its kind, was made in Haslemere in July 1932 for Heloise Russell-Fergusson by Arnold Dolmetsch' now resides quietly in my work room. It is made of cherry wood. I have learned to tune it and, hesitantly, to pick out the simplest of songs. Mostly, I stroke its soft golden curves. I feel that it has come home.

Acknowledgements

I extend huge thanks to Stuart Carmichael, Jenny MacLeod, Iain McNicol, Ian Ross, Alec and Johnny MacCorquodale, Ronnie Laing, Ian Weir, Tina the Taxi Driver and others in Port Appin, to Libby and Paddy Shaw, Andrew Russell, John MacFarlane, Peter MacLeod, Mel and Joy Blakeney, Shuna Mulholland, Nancy Black, Archie Mackenzie, Alex and Sean Honeyman, Tor Justad, Moira Anderson, Lena Karlsson, Malin Gazelius, Tets Halbertsma, Felicity Campbell, Christine MacKay, Carla Furlong Emerson, Kathryn Adamson, Jürgen Steiner, Dr Glenn Colton, Professor Mike Roche, Evelyn Lennie, Helen Carfrae, Robin Malcolm, Alice Douglas and David Queensberry, all of whom helped me in very practical ways and/or shared so honestly their personal memories of Héloïse and of the Russell-Fergusson family.

I am immensely grateful to Dr Stuart Eydmann for his sustained support and for providing so many insights into the significance of Heloise's contribution to harp music both in Scotland and in Brittany, to Simon Chadwick for his kindness, for giving me a copy of all of Heloise's 1960s music and instructing me on using the Dolmetsch harp, to Dr Per Ahlander for generously sharing his research, to Kenna Campbell and Iseabail Macleod for their insights in making sense of the archive and to Jane Freshwater, Bill Dean-Myatt, Deirdre Newall, Anne and Fanch Postic, Dr David McGuinness, Sally Garden, Katy Wylie and Julian and Daisy Darwell-Stone, all of whom have helped me understand aspects of Héloïse's musical achievements.

This story would have been significantly thinner without the knowledge and understanding of Patricia Grant, Susan Taylor and other staff at the Mitchell Library in Glasgow and of the archivists and curators at Glasgow Museums Resource Centre, The Highland Folk Museum, The West Highland Museum, Argyll & Bute Archives and Stirling Archives. The Scottish Book Trust boosted my confidence when it shortlisted this book for their New Writers Award in 2016 and I thank also Sophy Dale, Jenni Brown and Sue Bard for their critically friendly eyes. Alayne Barton at The Islands Book Trust was particularly skilled and patient in nursing a rookie through the process of bringing the book to fruition.

But my thanks are due most especially to my beloved family and to the close friends who displayed such forbearance during the years of writing when I had only one topic of conversation. I set out to uncover Héloïse's story as best I could and I take full responsibility for any errors or misinterpretations. If there is more detail to come, I look forward to learning about it.